Selling Olga

Also by Louisa Waugh

HEARING BIRDS FLY: A NOMADIC YEAR IN MONGOLIA

Selling Olga

STORIES OF HUMAN TRAFFICKING
AND RESISTANCE

Louisa Waugh

Weidenfeld & Nicolson
LONDON

First published in Great Britain in 2006
by Weidenfeld & Nicolson

1 3 5 7 9 10 8 6 4 2

A CIP catalogue record for this book
is available from the British Library.

ISBN-13 978 0 297 85070 0
ISBN-10 0 297 85070 9

Typeset at The Spartan Press Ltd
Lymington, Hants

Printed in Great Britain by
Clays Ltd, St Ives plc

Weidenfeld & Nicolson

The Orion Publishing Group Ltd
Orion House
5 Upper Saint Martin's Lane
London WC2H 9EA

The Orion publishing group's policy is to use papers that are
natural, renewable and recyclable products and made
from wood grown in sustainable forests. The logging and
manufacturing processes are expected to conform to the
environmental regulations of the country of origin.

www.orionbooks.co.uk

For Olga, Anna, Bright, Annette, Lan and Mr He

Contents

Introduction   1

Chapter 1
Instructions for Trafficking   11

Chapter 2
Selling Olga   18

Chapter 3
The Last Resort   26

Chapter 4
Anna Would Go Back   36

Chapter 5
When the Peacekeepers Arrive   42

Chapter 6
'Well, They Sell Footballers, Don't They?'   52

Chapter 7
The Short Life of Olena Popik   62

Chapter 8
The Useful Women of Albania   69

Chapter 9
Burrell   84

Chapter 10
Article 18   94

Chapter 11
On the Streets With Franco 104

Chapter 12
God's Work 111

Chapter 13
Whose Side Are You On? 126

Chapter 14
What Is Not Said 144

Chapter 15
The Downfall of Luan Plakici 154

Chapter 16
How to Catch Traffickers 168

Chapter 17
Mr He, Lan and Keung 186

Chapter 18
UNMIKISTAN 204

Chapter 19
The Impunity of Peace 223

Epilogue 232

Sources 245

Acknowledgements 247

Index 249

Truth is often grey and deceit is full of splendour   HASIDIC RABBI REBBE MEDAHEM MENDL OF KOTSKER

There is a crack in everything . . . that's how the light gets in   LEONARD COHEN

Introduction

Kosovo, April 2003

The town of Obilic lies smack in between Power Station A and Power Station B. Both stations spew up towers of bitter black smog that curse the air and threaten to erase the sun even at noon. Ringing the outskirts of Obilic are empty ruins: houses destroyed during the war. They stand ravaged and bare-boned, reduced to piles of bricks and collapsing timber frames. There are no windows or doors, and I can see straight through them to an orchard of dead trees behind.

It is late afternoon. The muddy streets, which froze hard and slippery last night, have melted into furrows of thick, dull paste. The driver brakes and his minibus gasps to a halt outside a kiosk that's been painted a violent yellow. As I pay him and clamber down into the rutted road, I see a neat stack of buckets and spades on display in front of the kiosk; all decorated in cheerful matching colours and motifs. It seems provocative, almost cruel, to remind people that there's no ocean or sand for hundreds of kilometres in any direction.

I turn the corner and use the indent of tyre tracks to avoid the worst of the mud as I make my way back towards Maggie's house.

When I told her I was coming to Kosovo, Maggie invited me to stay with her family. Her mother, Vera, smiles at me affectionately, offers me food as soon as I walk in the door, and then asks Maggie where I've been. Vera bakes huge trays of spicy chicken and rice in the evenings, and brews tiny cups of potent Turkish coffee all morning. Maggie's father also smiles, but he's far more reticent, at least with me; he looks frail and goes to bed very early, as though he is constantly recovering from having made it through another day.

By the time the Serbians had capitulated and NATO suspended its bombing campaign, on 10 June 1999, Obilic had been battered by shells, fire and bullets. Four years on, there are still mounds of rubble in the streets, whilst, indoors, the electricity supply is erratic and the hot-water tap usually runs cold. The kitchen range is the only heater I have seen in the house. Maggie, her sister and I sleep on couches in the freezing living room.

Maggie's full name is Magbule Kelmendi. She is a police officer but used to be an actress; that was one of the first things she told me when I met her in London at the beginning of December last year.

We were both at a training course about human trafficking in the Balkans. She was speaking, and I was there to listen, invited by one of the organisers who had thought I would find it useful for my research.

Maggie was presenting a paper on the policing of trafficking in Kosovo. After she had finished speaking and answering questions, there was a coffee break. I sat on my own, scribbling notes and indulging in a bit of delegate-watching, and she came straight over and sat next to me. She was striking. Pale-skinned, with shoulder-length onyx-black hair that glinted when her red streaks caught a beam of direct light.

'So you are a writer?' she said.

We had all done our introductions on the first day: the statically awkward moment of each explaining to the others what we did for a living and why we were attending the training course. I kept my introduction brief: just said I was a writer researching a book about trafficking in Europe. Some delegates said even less than that. They were prohibited from talking directly about their work.

I told Maggie I'd just started my research and wanted to find out more about the Balkans, which were constantly cited as the trafficking gateway into Western Europe. I deliberately tried to make it sound straightforward, rather than admitting that I was struggling to know how to begin a book like this. I said I was thinking of visiting the Balkans at some point, to do some research for myself.

She nodded slowly. 'So, you should visit Kosovo.'

'What is it like there now, after the war?'

'It is very different now. Our capital, Pristina, used to be a wonderful city! I was an actress at the National Theatre, and that was a good time for me for a few years. But our cultural life was completely destroyed by the war, so now everything has changed, and I am a police officer instead of an actress.'

'Do you like your work?'

'Yes, I do. But the trafficking is a very serious problem. Women are brought in and out of Kosovo all the time, even though the United Nations is everywhere with their troops and policemen. I have some contacts, so you can come to Kosovo and stay with me.'

*

One of the first papers we had been given at the course was the agreed international definition of trafficking, adopted by the UN in 2000.

(a) Trafficking in persons shall mean the recruitment, transportation, transfer, harbouring, or receipt of persons, by means of the threat or use of force or other forms of coercion, of abduction, of fraud, of deception, of the abuse of power or of a position of vulnerability or the giving or receiving of payments or benefits to achieve the consent of a person having control over another person, for the purpose of exploitation.

Exploitation shall include, at a minimum, the exploitation of the prostitution of others or other forms of sexual exploitation, forced labour or services, slavery or practices similar to slavery, servitude or the removal of organs.

The consent of a victim of trafficking in persons to the intended exploitation set forth in subparagraph (a) shall be irrelevant where any of the means set forth in subparagraph (a) have been used.

(b) The recruitment, transportation, transfer, harbouring or receipt of a child for the purposes of exploitation shall be considered "trafficking in persons" even if this does not involve any of the means set forth in subparagraph (a) of this article.

(c) Child shall mean any person under eighteen years of age.[1]

By the end of the course, we had read through papers covering everything from links between globalisation and migration to interviews with men who visited prostitutes and case studies of women trafficked from the Balkans to the UK. The conference did not set out to trace the history of human trafficking but to identify and explore its current context. We discussed how the combination of chronic poverty in 'countries of origin' combined with increasing demands for cheap, low-skilled labour in 'countries of destination' fuels migration. However, trade liberalisation, aka globalisation, has not been matched by liberal migration policies in these affluent destination countries. In the face of restrictive immigration laws and ever tighter border controls, more and more migrants are being pushed into 'irregular migration channels'. They turn to facilitators, who can arrange documents and insertion into wealthy countries. But facilitators have their price, and whilst many of them are smugglers who dump migrants at their agreed destination and

1. 'Protocol to Prevent, Suppress and Punish Trafficking in Persons, Especially Women and Children: Supplementing the United Nations Convention Against Transnational Organised Crime', 2000. This is often called the Palermo Agreement, as it was adopted by the UN in Palermo, Sicily, in November 2000.

leave them to get on with it, others are traffickers who literally buy, sell and coerce migrants for profit. Women who are trafficked into commercial sex work are a huge and very lucrative component of this brutal trade.

Later that week we discussed regional demand for trafficked women. One of the papers that stood out for me was entitled 'Demand for Trafficked Women by Peacekeepers in the Balkans', which described women being trafficked into the Balkans as soon as UN peacekeepers arrived en masse. Citing evidence of peacekeepers frequenting bars where women were being forced to sell sex, the paper also criticised police raids of bars where it was suspected trafficked women were being held. It described bar owners being frequently tipped off in advance of raids, and local and international UN police being regular brothel clients. Madeleine Rees, a senior human rights lawyer working for the UN, was quoted claiming that bar raids did not tackle trafficking at source: 'You don't deal with trafficking by closing night bars. We've driven it underground and now it's much more difficult to trace.'

During the rest of the course, and for weeks afterwards, I thought about going to the Balkans. Despite having met Maggie, I was nervous of travelling there alone, for several reasons. Partly it was because of the long, bloody conflicts that had erupted across the region, and partly because of its reputation for organised crime, but mostly because I didn't understand enough about either to be able to separate real from imagined personal danger.

I didn't understand enough about trafficking either, which was the whole point of going to Kosovo. I did know the experience of being trafficked had ruined many women's lives, and that, despite lurid newspaper exposés about Eastern European 'sex slaves', and assurances from the UK and other governments that they were doing their best to combat the problem in their own countries, the trade was escalating across Europe.

Reports of legal and illegal migrants being forced to work in other UK industries were also emerging, and I wanted to try to unravel the links between the two. Most of all, I wanted to hear about trafficking from the people directly affected by it.

If I was going to write a book about people being trafficked across Europe, then the Balkans seemed my logical starting point. I called Anti-Slavery International, who forwarded the names and telephone numbers of several local Kosovan organisations, but the only personal contact I had was Maggie. Three months after the course I called her at home.

She answered on a clear, distant-sounding landline from Obilic. She said she was fine. She'd been having a few problems at work, but really everything was OK.

'So are you coming to Kosovo?' she asked.

'Yes, I am. Would it be OK to stay with you? Are you sure it won't be a problem?' There are certain national traits you never quite manage to shed, no matter how hard you try. She had already invited me to stay about four times.

'Just fly to Pristina, and I will collect you at the airport. I have already said you are welcome to stay in my home.'

Pristina is hedonistic, chaotic and edgy. The entire city has been scarred by the war and is as ugly as the contents of a skip. Most people seem to live in dirty white tenements that are fifteen storeys high, with windows the size of air vents. The streets have no trees, and there doesn't seem to be a park or public garden anywhere. The average local salary is €3 a day.

Street life flows along the main Mother Theresa Boulevard like blood through an artery. There are new-looking bars, restaurants, nightclubs, Internet and open-air cafés on both sides. Maggie tells me some of these places are suspected to be brothels where trafficked women are held. From the outside, they all look very similar to each other.

Just off Mother Theresa Boulevard is the UNMIK (United Nations Mission in Kosovo) compound, and opposite the UN compound is the resident expat pub, the Kukri. Maggie insists we come here almost every evening. She wants to change her job within the police force, so she needs to schmooze amongst the foreigners who run Kosovo between them, and this is the easiest place to find them. We get a taxi from Obilic.

On my third evening in Pristina, Maggie and I share a table in the Kukri with a few American CIVPOL (UN civilian police) officers she knows from work. One of them, Carl, tells me his two-year mission is just finishing. I ask him what it's been like living and working here.

'Interesting,' he says, turning his beer clockwise slowly without taking his hand off the glass. 'When I first got offered this post, I had to go check a map, 'cos I didn't even know where Kosovo was! Still feel like I don't know much about this place. I've been mostly confined to Pristina, except for a few weekends' R & R in Macedonia.'

'What exactly do you do?' I ask him.

'Uphold law, order and national security, ma'am! There's 5,000 of us CIVPOL officers on mission here; we have contingents from every country I ever heard of!'

The man sitting next to Carl, who looks Latino, laughs bitterly into his pint. 'This place sucks,' he says. 'If we weren't here, these goddamn people would still be killing each other, yet they hate us. The second my mission is over, I'm gone. And what about you? – why are you here?' The Latino glares at me.

'Erm, just a short break from home,' I say lamely. I don't want to tell him anything.

'Maggie a friend of yours?'

'Yes, she is.'

He smirks at me, lights a cigarette and loses interest.

I've offered this explanation of being on holiday in a city with no tourism to a few people, none of whom have looked particularly convinced. Visiting Kosovo to research trafficking is perfectly legal, but I'm reluctant to explain why I am here, because this place is crawling with troops and police officers, and I don't know who to tell, and who not to. In addition to the CIVPOL officers, NATO has 30,000 KFOR (Kosovo Force) peacekeepers stationed here. More than anything, Kosovo feels like a huge military barracks.

Trafficking is a chronic problem here. The first publicised cases of women being brought over the border and confined in bars and nightclubs began to emerge at the beginning of 2000, just months after the war had finished, and the international community arrived en masse to take over. The UN Mission in Kosovo responded by setting up the Trafficking and Prostitution Investigation Unit (TPIU). One of Maggie's contacts is Brian Wilson, deputy of TPIU. I call him and arrange to meet him at his office in the UN compound.

Brian Wilson is a stocky, fair-haired Englishman. He shakes my hand and gestures for me to sit in the black swivel chair opposite his.

I ask him how he came to be working in Pristina.

'I used to work for the MoD in London. The UN offered me this job because of my work background and firearms expertise.' He flashes me a smile. 'We're all armed in this unit.'

Everyone in Kosovo seems to be armed, except for me. Maggie carries a gun at work, and the nightclub we went to last night had a large sign next to the entrance: 'No weapons'.

Brian tells me the TPIU was set up in October 2000 to identify trafficking victims and prosecute traffickers. The unit gathers information on foreign women, mainly Eastern Europeans, working in Kosovo, to assess whether they are likely to have been trafficked. Kosovo currently has no visa regulations, so a lot of their work involves keeping track of women coming over the borders to work in bars and nightclubs.

'As a precaution, we publish a monthly list of premises that are "off limits" to all UN and international personnel because women may be held there against their will.'

'How many places are off limits?'

'Two hundred and ten,' he tells me matter-of-factly.

I am silently staggered by this number. In a territory of just under two million people (not including the international community) that seems like an awful lot of suspect bars and nightclubs.

'If we suspect a premise,' Brian continues, 'then the Organised Crime Bureau gather further intelligence, and we organise the raid.'

'What happens during a raid?'

'We usually raid at night, and always without warning. We work with a special police unit, who enter first to secure the premises. Some of these clubs are fortresses, with electronic gates and CCTV cameras every-where. If you're not careful, they can see you coming and will have the place empty before you've parked the cars. There are also bars in flashpoints, like north Mitrovica. When we raid a bar somewhere like that, I want my men in and out within fifteen minutes max. If we need back-up, we call in Team 6: they're the "entry and extraction" operation specialists.'

'What is entry and extraction?' I don't know what to make of these tactics or this language. It sounds like the TPIU have declared war on trafficking.

'Team 6 are ex-SAS. They can enter any premises and immediately extract people from inside. We separate the men and women, check their documents and escort suspects to the police station for questioning. Most women want to go straight back home . . .'

He pauses and I interject. 'But there has been some criticism of these raids from within the UN itself, hasn't there?' I can feel the atmo-sphere in the room beginning to cool even as I speak, but I carry on, because this is what I really want to know. 'Human rights lawyers say women are terrified by the raids, and often too frightened afterwards to tell police what has really happened to them. They also say bar owners can just bribe police officers to tip them off about the raids in advance, and the women can just be moved out of the bars in time, or locked up in private apartments . . .' I am trying to sound more confident than I feel right now, because Brian Wilson is staring at me coldly, disdainfully.

'My officers do not tip off anyone.' His voice is categorical. 'I trust my team, and besides, they don't usually know where we're going until we set off in the cars.'

He is obviously offended, but I wade on, because I genuinely don't understand how this particular war can be won with these tactics. 'Do you think these raids have made any real impact? You've been raiding bars for two and a half years now, and trafficking is still a huge problem here, isn't it? Aren't the pimps just opening new bars as fast as they are being shut down?'

There is a terse silence between us.

'We are making progress,' he says. He hands me a thick sheath of papers. 'This will give you some idea. Now, is there anything else?'

'Well, yes, I do have another question. What about KFOR troops? Are they ever found in these off-limits bars?'

'We have a "gentleman's agreement" with KFOR that their troops will not go to any of the off-limits premises,' he says, 'so the issue doesn't really arise.'

I thank Brian Wilson for his time and leave the UN compound feeling more perplexed than when I first arrived. I stand at the compound barrier, at a sudden loss, realising how little I actually understand about trafficking.

Maggie and I spend most evenings in town together, and I meet a friendly US CIVPOL officer. He in turn introduces me to a posse of other officers, one of whom, an English policeman, jokes about having me detained at the airport when I want to leave Kosovo. I bump into this man several times over the next week or so, and every time I see him he cracks the same damn joke, until I ask him whether he is threatening me.

'Maybe,' he says, smiling.

I don't actually believe I will be detained at the airport, but I've never been inside an environment like this, where people openly make barbed jokes about the power they wield. It seems to me that the UNMIK runs Kosovo like a police state. The official language is English, and information is controlled by the UN and international organisations, whilst the local population seem uninvolved in the running of their own lives. I feel no room to manoeuvre. I know I am not meeting the right people, but I don't even know who the right people are.

However, I do have the contact numbers from Anti-Slavery International. I make several calls and end up speaking to a woman called Igballe Rogova, director of the Kosova Women's Network. I arrange to meet her in a local bar.

'We told them. Back in 1999 we gathered all the international donors together, and we told them there was going to be a trafficking crisis in Kosovo.'

Igballe is a straight-talking political activist who has witnessed trafficking evolving here over the last four years. We spend the evening together, drinking beer, eating dinner and then drinking more beer.

'It was bloody obvious what was going to happen here,' she tells me.

'Look at the regional pattern: look at what happened in Bosnia after the war. But the donors, the troops and the UN did not listen to us, so trafficking started almost as soon as the conflict was over. I saw carloads of women being driven over the border, straight down from Serbia. There were no proper border controls: it was an open season for trafficking. And as for the KFOR, I remember one general from Norway telling me to my face, "Madam, boys will be boys. You had better educate your girls." The peacekeepers created this market in the first place, and now they are attempting to mop it up.'

Igo tells me bluntly that I have no chance of interviewing any women who have been trafficked into Kosovo. 'No way. Access to trafficked women is controlled by organisations like the IOM [International Organisation for Migration[2]]. Once the women have been taken out of the bars and nightclubs, they are handed straight over to the internationals.'

It is unexpectedly easy to arrange an appointment with the IOM, or at least their press officer, a Spanish woman called Tomara. She is polite and professional, and doesn't give away very much at first. She agrees with Igballe that I will not be able to interview any of the women that the IOM are currently 'assisting'. Nevertheless, when I ask her about the issue of foreigners visiting brothels, she nods slowly.

'We estimate that 30 per cent of the clients of trafficked women here in Kosovo are foreigners. The remaining 70 per cent are local.'

This is a revelation in itself. 'Where did you get that information?' I ask her, surprised at her candour.

'From the trafficked women we have interviewed, and our own research.' She also hands me a thick sheath of papers. 'This has all our statistics in it.'

I ask her where the women who are trafficked into Kosovo come from.

'Moldova,' she replies immediately. 'Poorest country in south-eastern Europe, and the main sending country in the whole region. We have a mission there too.'

'So that's the starting point,' I say, meaning it should probably have been my starting point, because it might help me to understand how trafficking is evolving in the Balkans.

Tomara's expression shifts slightly. I think she's weighing up whether I am worth helping. We break eye contact. I take in the shelves of case reports stacked high and wide across her office and wonder if she will

---

2. The International Organisation for Migration (IOM) was set up in 1951, and describes itself as 'The principal intergovernmental organisation in the field of migration.' It works in more than a hundred countries, providing advice, services and humanitarian assistance to governments and migrants, including victims of trafficking.

consider breaking rank. She opens a tray of index cards and slowly rifles through them.

'OK. Give me your email address, and I will call my contact at the mission in Moldova and see what he can do for you. I make no promises,' she tells me almost severely. But she is smiling now. 'He might be able to arrange for you to interview a woman we are assisting.'

Kosovo, I think on my way out of her office, is either the middle or the end of the story, and I need to retrace the route back to the beginning, to where many of these women originally come from before they end up being confined here. Moldova is one of the beginnings.

Chapter 1

Instructions for Trafficking

Chisinau, Moldova

Doru and I are having lunch at the Green Hills Café in the old diplomatic quarter of the city. The food is excellent and so is the local Chisinau beer. Most of the tables have been moved outside on to the patio because it's a warm, sunny afternoon. When I glance around, we are surrounded by chic-looking customers in dark glasses, and there are shiny four-wheel drives parked all down the street.

'This is not at all what I expected,' I say to Doru, hoping even as I say it that he won't be offended. 'I thought this was the poorest country in Europe! I don't know what to make of all this conspicuous wealth on display.'

Doru makes a sound halfway between a laugh and a sneeze. He is slender and bespectacled, and has feathery dark hair receding towards his crown. 'You thought everyone here was poor?' he retorts. It's obviously a rhetorical question because he doesn't wait for an answer. 'Most of the people sitting in this café are businessmen. They don't live like other people in Moldova. You have to understand straightaway that we have two economies here: one is official, and the other isn't. Many of the people who work for the official economy can't afford to eat in a place like this. I am not saying that all these people are Mafia, but crime is very well organised in my country.'

Doru is Tomara's IOM contact in Moldova. As we eat our chicken stroganoff he tells me about his country. Moldova made a peaceful separation from the Soviet Union twelve years ago in December 1991, and since then has been ruled by an ex-Communist government that never quite gets voted out of office. The initial nationalist elation faltered alongside the struggling economy, and the decline has been especially relentless in the last few years. There are no domestic industries left to speak of, and the average local income has dropped to MDL10 (Moldovan lei) a day, the equivalent of 80p. People are leaving in droves.

'We think that between six hundred thousand and a million Moldovans have left to work abroad in the last ten years, most of them illegally. That leaves maybe three and a half million. But as there has not been a government census since the end of the 1980s, no one knows for sure how many people still live here.'

He tells me that over this last decade, human trafficking, mostly of women and children, has become one of Moldova's biggest national industries.

'How does it actually operate here?' I ask him, as we finish eating.

'I will show you.'

We pay the bill and stroll slowly down the sunny street. At a small kiosk Doru buys a newspaper called *Makler*, and we stand there together while he translates some of the small classified ads for me.

Mirage Travel Agency: Au Pairs in Germany.

Nightclub work abroad. Travel expenses paid.
Assistance given with visas, etc. Travel is accompanied.

Visa: Schengen.

Nursing assistants wanted in Italy.
Excellent pay & conditions. Contract and visa provided.

Visa: England, Ireland.

'Some of these adverts are genuine,' he says. 'Some are companies looking for au pairs, nurses and dancers to work abroad. Other companies advertise for girls "bez kompleksov" – "without complexes" – which is slang for saying that they are offering work abroad as a prostitute.'

He says the emphasis has changed recently from bar and dancing work. Now adverts are frequently being placed by private bureaus offering to arrange work visas, especially the sought-after Schengen visa, which allows the holder to travel throughout most of the European Union, although not the UK.

On first contact, potential clients are often told all they have to do is pay a fee in advance, and then everything will be arranged for them. Some bureaus are legitimate businesses, with the right contacts at home and abroad, and can secure genuine work contracts. Others are run by fly-by-nights who perpetrate the simplest of scams: people who answer their ads are offered work in Romania for a flat fee, and a large group of unsuspecting migrants is assembled. They pay up, are transported over the border into Romania and calmly abandoned to wait for their new employer, who will apparently be arriving 'very soon'. Cities like Timisoara, Bucharest and Sofia have become notorious dumping grounds for duped migrants, who then either scrabble around to find work or struggle back to Moldova with less money than they started with. Amidst these pages of opportunities, scams and risks are adverts placed by traffickers.

'They work in different ways, the traffickers here,' says Doru, as we walk back towards his office. 'Some of them operate alone; others work in small groups, which are often part of a larger network, with links to Romania and Serbia.'

According to a report recently published by his IOM colleagues, well-connected solo traffickers are considered the most ruthless and elusive of all:

> Solitary traffickers, also called brokers, are the most dangerous type of traffickers. Many of them are foreign citizens and do not have permanent residency in Moldova. One day they can be in Chisinau, the next in Turkey, and they can have false passports and names and are very difficult to identify and apprehend. They usually rent apartments for a single use and never get back there again.[1]

Brokers are paid by networks or wealthy individuals to find and transport batches of people to order; they flit through cities like spectres, have multiple identities and business partners. They are the freelancers of the trafficking industry.

Other traffickers are employed just to do the initial recruiting. Based in one location, like Chisinau, their job is to find people who want to work abroad and then pass them on to other traffickers who arrange transport and auctions. Sometimes these recruiters are women who were trafficked into sex work themselves and have negotiated their way out by agreeing to recruit other young women. They are often good recruiters because they have already been brutalised, and hardened, themselves.

Recruiters are entrepreneurs: they have their ears to the ground because they are usually local. Their *modi operandi* are creative, and very flexible. In Chisinau they often use one of the many empty city-centre offices or apartments to establish a bogus business. It goes something like this: the recruiter rents premises under a false name, pays the rent up front and immediately has furniture installed and the landline reconnected. As soon as the office is ready, he notifies his network outside the city that he is now ready for business. They will then place their order, using all the technology available to any modern industry. As soon as the order has arrived, the recruiter will put an advert in the press. *Makler* is a good paper to use, because it comes out three times a week, and every

---

1. 'Trafficking of Women for Sexual Exploitation', IOM Moldova, 2002.

issue has half a dozen pages of small ads. Everyone in Chisinau seems to read it.

The recruiter includes the landline number in the advert because it seems more genuine than a mobile-phone number, and the rates are cheaper, which also encourages women to call. When a woman responds to the advert, he gives out very little information and arranges to meet her immediately, so he can have a look at her first.

'What about the police?' I ask Doru. 'What are they doing about all this?'

He shakes his head. 'The police were extremely busy with trafficking long before our government set up the "Moral Police Squad" last year. This Moral Squad is eighteen officers, who share three vehicles between them, and they do not have much chance. They earn $30 a month and often have to wait for overdue wages. A trafficker can just offer them $10, which is more than they receive for one week of work. What would you do?'

In the IOM office later that afternoon Doru's colleague Liuba explains that she regularly reads through the *Makler* adverts to see how the emphases change, and sometimes calls a few of the numbers herself to find out if they are genuine.

'I can tell the fraudsters almost straightaway, because I try to keep them talking and they put the phone down as soon as they realise I'm not going to turn up for an interview!' She laughs out loud at her own defiance.

Liuba is in her late twenties, self-possessed and extremely beautiful. She has worked at the IOM office since its inception in 2001 and says she enjoys her work as a counter-trafficking officer.

'It is a constant challenge,' she says calmly, checking her lipstick in her compact mirror as she sits at her desk. 'The trafficking industry is now very well established here. All we can do is alert women to the dangers they face if they leave without documents or agree to go with a stranger who says he has arranged work for them. We go into the villages and schools to distribute information. But so do the traffickers.' She snaps the compact shut.

Liuba works alongside a rotund woman with long, black hair called Natalia, who runs the IOM shelter somewhere in the suburbs. Part of Natalia's job is to drive to the airport to collect women who have just arrived from a foreign brothel or jail, which in some cases is one and the same.

'There are some days when I drive up there two or three times in order to escort women to our shelter,' she tells me in her quiet, low voice. 'They need medical and psychological care, and most of them have nowhere else to go. They were poor even before they left, and they come home with nothing. Their families often don't welcome them back. One of the worst things a migrant from a poor country like ours can do is to return without money. They are supposed to come home rich.'

I spend a couple of hours sitting around talking with Doru, Liuba and Natalia. There is a good atmosphere in the office, and when I finally finished scribbling notes, they ask me to join them for dinner at a local restaurant, where they are going to celebrate a friend's birthday. It's a generous offer, and I'm happy to accept: partly because the one time of day I really don't like being alone is dinnertime, but also because I just like being around them. Then there is a slight pause in the conversation before Doru asks me 'what time I would like my trafficking victim to arrive for her interview tomorrow'. He's just being honest, but the connotation still makes me inwardly cringe.

Olga arrives at the office just before half ten. We all move into a small private meeting room together and introduce ourselves. Olga is accompanied by her psychologist, Liliana Gorceag, and I am accompanied by a translator called Natasha.

I have just signed a confidentiality waiver, agreeing not to publish anything that will personally identify my interviewee. Very few traffickers have ever been convicted in Moldova, and government officials have been directly implicated in trafficking crimes, which puts women who speak out even more at risk.

The first thing I ask Natasha to ask Olga is whether she wants me to change her name when I write up the interview. To my surprise, Olga shakes her head.

'Nyet. It's OK.' She shrugs. 'There are so many other girls called Olga in this city, who will ever know it's me?'

Natasha and I sit opposite Olga and Liliana. Olga looks tired and sits wearily, but insists that she is prepared to answer my questions and it's OK for us to talk. Her hair has been dyed blonde, but obviously a while ago because brown roots are seeping out from the centre parting. On a healthier-looking woman, her face would be described as plump, but in her case it looks slightly swollen and faintly discoloured. Her eyes are so pale blue they look almost transparent.

'I grew up here,' she tells me. 'On the outskirts of Chisinau. My mother worked all the time when I was a child, cleaning shops and offices early in the mornings. My father was a drinker and he was violent when he drank. He would beat both of us then, my mother and I. In the end it was me who suggested that she leave him and get a divorce. And eventually she did. But not till I was twelve. Then I didn't have to call the police any more.'

Moldova shares the Soviet scourge of chronic alcoholism, induced by boring, relentless poverty and the despair that things have still not got better.

Liliana, the psychologist, comments that many women pay a terrible price for the malaise their men endure. 'The drinking is severe,' she says calmly, 'and the physical and sexual violence has become so common, especially within families, that it is considered almost normal in our society. Children grow up being beaten at home and seeing their mother beaten by their father. It has taken its toll on our national psyche.'

Olga left school when she was fourteen. She transferred to a vocational training college, where she spent the next three years as an apprentice commercial-building painter. But she couldn't find any work in her trade, so instead she took a job at a Moldovan TV factory.

'I was testing components for three years, until I had my son, Kolya.' She shakes her head again and continues in the same flat voice. 'I was living with the father of my child. He was OK at first, but then he turned to drink too, and I worried I was going to repeat my mother's mistakes, so I left him. I went back to the factory and stayed there for the next five years, but the break-up of the Soviet Union had a bad effect on all our jobs. The factory gradually started to downsize, and I had to find other work. The only job I could get was in the Chisinau Central Market, on one of the food stalls.'

Olga worked at the unheated covered market from eight in the morning until ten at night for MDL5, the equivalent of 35p a day. If she was sick or needed to take time off for her young son, she wasn't paid, but she stayed there for two years because she had no choice.

'After two years and all that work, all I had to show were heavy debts. I was even going to lose my apartment,' she says.

She had never even thought of working abroad, but she and an old school friend called Stella found an advert in *Makler* that tempted them with its promise of money and travel. Olga remembers the exact wording: 'Girls and women under thirty-five. Well-paid jobs abroad.' There was a local phone number. Olga rang, and two days later she and Stella met a well-dressed young man from Chisinau, who swiftly made them an offer.

'We met him in a café, and then he took us to an office in the centre. He told us we would be caring for elderly people in Italy, and that we would earn $1,000 a month each. The temptation was too much. I had spent the whole of the last winter working in a freezing market! I told him the truth, that we did not have the money to get to Italy, and that neither of us had a passport, only an ID card, but he said it was no problem at all. We could just pay him back for everything in monthly instalments, out of our salaries.'

Olga willingly gave the man, who said his name was Simeon, her home phone number, and he said he would call a few days later to agree the departure date.

Olga and Stella were in no doubt they had made the right choice in spontaneously deciding to go and work in Italy, although neither of them had ever been abroad before. Simeon was a Moldovan from their own city, and they had both liked him. They had often heard that Italy needed young women like them to care for and clean up after elderly and infirm patients. Neither of them had heard anything about trafficking.

'I met him at the end of June 2000, and by the middle of July I had been sold to a bar in Kosovo,' she says quietly. 'And I really thought I was going to Italy.'

Chapter 2

Selling Olga

Recruiters act swiftly. They hire women to work abroad and then get them out of town as soon as possible. These days the stakes in Moldova are slightly higher: leaflets warning women about trafficking are widely distributed all over the country, inserted into villages, schools, cafés and bars. There is a national hotline number that women can call for information and advice, and where worried parents can report their daughters missing. There are even huge billboards on the road leading to the airport emblazoned with the words 'You are not a commodity.' The accompanying illustration is of a woman squirming in a man's fist. But when Olga and her friend Stella were taken out of Chisinau in 2000, there were no such public awareness campaigns in Moldova. There wasn't even a law against trafficking.[1]

Olga and Stella left Chisinau less than a week after Olga had first spoken to Simeon. At the designated meeting place in a Chisinau suburb, they met half a dozen other young Moldovan women who were also going to be taking care of elderly Italians in Milan. The women were all escorted into a minibus by a Moldovan called Lydia. The driver was a man who said he was from Serbia. Simeon, the recruiter, was nowhere to be seen. The Serb drove west to the Romanian border, a journey of less than two hours. As they approached the border, Lydia handed Olga a passport.

'I had never seen it before,' she says.

'It wasn't yours?' I ask, just to be sure.

'No.'

'Did it have your name or your photo in it?'

She looks straight at me for a moment and then down at the table, obviously embarrassed. '*Nyet*,' she replies. 'No. It wasn't me. It didn't even really look very much like me. That bothered me, but I didn't know what to do. And when the border guard saw Stella's passport, he just

---

1. Moldova passed domestic legislation against trafficking in human beings in July 2001.

laughed out loud. But that woman Lydia gave him some money, and we went through into Romania.'

The party drove west towards the city of Timisoara, resting in a village en route. For the next few days they were shunted from house to house in obscure villages away from the main roads. They stayed one night in each place and became quickly disorientated. Olga and the other Moldovan women could easily understand anything that was being discussed in front of them in Romanian, as the Moldovan language is a dialect of Romanian,[2] but the only thing Lydia and the Serb ever seemed to say, at least to them, was that they would all be arriving in Italy 'soon'.

Olga suddenly looks exhausted, and the room falls silent.

A few moments later she raises her head. 'I had just left my own city for the first time, and I really didn't know what to expect.' She shrugs; it's a small gesture of resignation that her body seems to express whenever she speaks. 'It had all seemed OK at first, but from that moment when the guard laughed at Stella's passport, I knew something was not right. The signs were all around us, and I thought about running away even then. But there was nowhere to go.'

A few nights later Olga and the others were rowed across the Danube river and into Serbia and Montenegro in a boat that leaked so badly the women were urged to throw their belongings over the side so it didn't capsize. Olga scrambled up the bank on the other side, soaked and shivering. She talks me through her subsequent journey south, via another bewildering twilit labyrinth of villages, where there was always someone waiting for them whenever they arrived. Some of their hosts were pleasant, even kind people, though others were abrupt and intimidating. Sometimes the Moldovan women were locked together in a room at night; sometimes the door was left open, and they were allowed to wander around the dark fenced yard and smoke outside. At one house the man in charge that night insisted on watching them even in the toilet; at another they were all given decent food and fresh clothes and allowed to shower in private. The only constants on this journey were their continual movement and the daily mantra from Lydia and the Serb, who came most of the way with them, that they were all still en route to Italy.

'I was trying to still believe them,' she says. 'We all were. No one tried to escape. We just did what they told us to do.'

After another lengthy journey in another different car, Olga, Stella and the others spent a night walking through a pitch-black forest, following behind a guide as closely as possible. The guide had already warned the

2. Moldova was part of Romania until 1924, when the Soviets created a partition and renamed the land the Moldovan Soviet Socialist Republic.

women to trace his footsteps as best they could. He said this border was heavily mined and if they deviated from the path, which he knew, they would have their feet blown off. There was someone waiting for them at the other side of the forest, like there was always someone waiting for them wherever they arrived.

'Don't worry,' this new man told the exhausted women, 'now you are in Kosovo and you are going to good jobs. Everything will be fine.'

For some reason, despite the dark and the people and the hushed, fearful chaos, Olga clearly remembers that the cars waiting for them had no number plates.

I clearly remember Kosovo, with its troops and its atmosphere of tension that felt as though it could be reignited all too easily. Beyond Pristina, the roads are patrolled by KFOR troops, who plough through the countryside in their armoured vehicles and tanks.

The road from Pristina towards the southern border with Albania passes through the town of Prizren; it is a beautiful town with the old town centre built around a mosque. It was also spared much of the bombing and is now a popular local tourist destination. Prizren has a myriad of cafés, bars, small restaurants and hotels, many of them tucked away in its narrow labyrinthine cobbled streets. Some of these places are brothels, where women are auctioned, confined and forced to have sex with whoever pays for them.

Two or three kilometres from Prizren is the village of Lubizhde, where you used to be able to visit a bar called the Palm Tree, though it's been closed down now. Olga, Stella and the other Moldovan women travelling with them were all brought to the Palm Tree the day that they entered Kosovo.

'When we got to the bar, they explained what we had to do,' she tells me, her face devoid of expression. 'They said that we each owed DM2,500 [around £1,000] for our travel expenses, and that when we had paid this back we could leave. But later on that night two of the Moldovan girls who had come to Kosovo with us were sold to local Kosovo men.'

The two women were sold for DM2,000[3] each. Olga knows how much was paid for them because the sale was openly conducted at one of the bar tables.

She says very little else about her time at the Palm Tree, except that she later learned many Moldovan women were sold there, and that while she

3. In 2000 Kosovo was using the German Deutschmark (DM) as currency. Now they use the euro.

was at the bar she had to do what the bar owner said, 'or I would be beaten in the bathroom and then taken back into the bar'.

Olga was beaten, and not only by the owner of the bar. She left the Palm Tree three weeks later with her arm in a sling. Her wrist had been badly sprained by a man who had hired her for half an hour for DM50, the equivalent of about £20. Olga was taken from the Palm Tree to a bar called the Sylvia somewhere near the centre of Prizren and sold to the owner. Her friend Stella was kept at the Palm Tree. Lydia and the Serb had vanished at the edge of the forest.

The Sylvia was a new bar; it was long and narrow, with a clutter of tables and a small raised stage at the back, where Olga and two other Moldovan women danced at night. The three of them slept together in the large basement when they had finished work. Their routine was quickly established for them, and as far as I can tell, it never varied. During the day they cleaned the bar and the bathrooms, and cooked food for the bar owner and his friends. They had to be ready for work by four in the afternoon, and the bar closed at three in the morning. Around 10 p.m., after dancing to entice customers inside the Sylvia, they were each rented out by a single client for the night. Olga saw KFOR tanks through the bar windows and says that foreign men in uniform also came to the bar.

'I think they were German and Swiss, because of these small flags they have on their uniforms. They gave the Sylvia man presents because they wanted to have us, but he refused. He said that he didn't want his bar closed down. The men who took us were Kosovan and Albanians.'

I underline the words 'German' and 'Swiss' in my notebook as KFOR's 'gentleman's agreement' comes to my mind.

The men who took Olga and the other two women away at night to have sex with them usually took them to local hotels, but occasionally to their homes, and brought them back to the Sylvia early the next morning, because of the post-war dusk-to-dawn curfew. After sleeping in the basement of the bar, Olga and the other two had a late breakfast and began cleaning the bar again. And so it went on.

For many trafficked women, Kosovo is the equivalent of a truck stop. They are sold to local pimps, but after a few months usually resold and moved south, either to Albania or Macedonia, and then on to Italy or Greece. The turnover is high because women are constantly passing through like freight. Olga was kept in Prizren much longer than most of them.

'I was at the Sylvia for more than two years,' she says. 'I don't know why he kept me there so long, though I could have been somewhere worse. That man, the Sylvia owner, he was better than the one at the

Palm Tree, who didn't care who we went with. But the Sylvia man only allowed men he knew to take us. We were registered with the police as waitresses or something, and eventually he started to pay us an allowance, when he had got back what he had paid for us.'

I've never heard of a trafficked woman being paid before. But it makes a certain brutal sense to pay her an allowance and register her with the local police as an employee. If she suddenly starts being paid, albeit not very much money, for the sex that she is forced to have every night, then her situation has not changed but her perception of it may be altered. And if he registers her as an employee, the bar or café owner is unlikely to be prosecuted for pimping.

Liliana tells me some bar owners eventually allow a woman to send money home to her family, and even occasionally to call them to reassure them that everything is fine. And so the relationship between the woman and her pimp becomes murky and distorted and, for the pimp at least, easier to manipulate.

The Sylvia man started paying Olga a percentage of the money that she persuaded men to spend at his bar. She spent a lot of this money on food, because she was always hungry.

'He didn't feed us much. He often just gave us bread to eat and tea to drink, so we had to buy food from his bar with the same money that he paid us. It was expensive. He always charged us full price, and I also began to spend money on cigarettes, and alcohol too. I drank to forget their ugly faces.'

Olga never mentions the actual name of her pimp. She calls him only the 'Sylvia man' or the 'bar owner', and maybe it's because of that, and because of what he does to her, that he actually starts to feel more like a malevolent physical presence than a human being.

I am looking straight at Olga and suddenly wonder what she must have looked and sounded like before she was trafficked. She was probably quite beautiful. Now she sits opposite me, pale and hunched, fidgeting with her glasses case on the table in front of her, with the glasses still inside.

The men who rented Olga for the night sometimes gave her tips afterwards, and this money she saved to send home to her young son, Kolya. She had been confined at the Sylvia for about a year and had saved almost a thousand Deutschmarks when the bar owner sat her down and told her that he was thinking of selling her on.

'He was very honest with me. He told me he had been offered good money for me, and he said that if I was going to stay with him, then I had to find a way to pay him, so he didn't lose out. It was just business for him. Once I had earned for him what they would have paid for me, then I would be free to go.'

He told Olga her options: she could either give him all her savings and effectively sell herself back to him or she could take the risk of being sold to another bar.

'He warned me . . .' – her eyes skim the room – '. . . he said that the two men who wanted to buy me would take me to Pec or to Ferizye. Pec is a terrible place, up in the mountains. The other girls told me that if you cause trouble there, you are just shot like an animal and your body dumped outside. And Ferizye is even worse. From there they took you to Macedonia, and we were all terrified of ending up in Macedonia.'

It is the first time she has used words like 'terrified' or 'terrible'. Until now she has been telling her story in vague, euphemistic language, and all in this flat voice that doesn't tremble or falter but just delivers her lines for her.

'How did you feel about what the bar owner said?' I ask her quietly.

Olga's reaction is instantaneous. She sits up, not upright but up, glances at me and then at Liliana, her face suddenly bright with rage.

'I was ready to kill him!' she shouts at me across the table. 'Can you imagine? There is my own son starving in Moldova and I had to pay *him* all my money! I wanted to get my hands on an axe or a branch to show him what I thought of his offer!'

'Yes! I bet you were!', '*Pravda!*', 'How dare he, the bastard!' All four of us are suddenly shouting, gesturing and laughing out loud together, like four women anywhere sharing an outrage between them. The painful tension in the room ruptures. Liliana pats Olga's arm affectionately; Natasha and I grin at each other as we all gradually quieten.

It feels bizarre to laugh at this, but it is a tremendous relief for all of us. It is as though between us we have finally jeered at this bar-owning pimp with no name.

Olga sits back in her chair, stretches and exhales, and for a moment her face looks almost serene. Then she takes us all by surprise by suddenly recalling a local Kosovan who used to come to the Sylvia quite regularly just to chat her up.

'Another drunk,' she says, slowly shaking her head. 'I never had much luck with men.'

Olga handed every penny that she had earned back to the bar owner and continued working at his bar. She had started to drink quite heavily, and it was only the presence of the other women in the bar that helped her survive. They all helped each other get through that bleak time. The other two Moldovans had told Olga that they were actually fairly lucky, the three of them, because at least their owner allowed them to be friendly with each other. There were many other places in Prizren where the women were deliberately taught not to trust each other and encouraged, or paid, to inform on one another.

Liliana, the psychologist, who has been quiet for a long time apart from our collective outburst, touches Olga's shoulder and then adds a few words of her own: 'The bar owner teaches them they can only trust him, and so they gradually become completely dependent on him and easy to control. They are physically confined and have little contact with anyone from the outside, because they usually work at night and sleep during the day. After a while this bar and this work is all that they know.'

Olga nods. 'He never let us out of the bar.'

'What? Never?' I feel my forehead puckering into a frown.

'No. The only time I went outside the bar was when one of those men took me out with him.'

But in spite of everything – confinement, sexual abuse, hunger and heavy drinking – Olga had not quite submitted to the bar owner. With the help of another woman who had also been trafficked, she formulated a plan of escape. The woman was called Nadia and she was also Moldovan. Nadia was confined in a bar called the Shpati, which was near the police station. Olga was occasionally dropped off at the Shpati by one of the men who rented her, presumably for convenience. The Sylvia man would collect her afterwards and bring her back to his own bar.

The next time that Olga was dropped off at the Shpati, Nadia hid her in a wardrobe, and when the Sylvia man came for her, she calmly lied to him, saying that Olga was still working, and he left.

Olga walked out of the Shpati and into the local police station, where she spoke to an officer from the local Kosovo Police Service (KPS). She was immediately taken into protective custody, interviewed in the presence of an international police officer and asked if she wanted to go back home. She said she did. The KPS drove her to Pristina, where she was picked up by the IOM and escorted to an interim security facility for trafficked women and girls.

As far as she knows, the man from the Sylvia was never questioned by the police, and when I ask her whether she thinks there might be a trial about her case, her only reply is a stream of bitter complaint about the local KPS.

'Kosovo police are traffickers and rapists. They took jewellery from us to sell for money, and I saw for myself when one officer burnt a woman's ID in front of her.'

Olga says nothing about being asked to testify at a trial, though she does tell us she has heard a rumour about the owners of the Palm Tree being prosecuted, and she thinks the bar itself has been closed down.

Olga flew back to Chisinau three months ago and is now being housed and supported by the IOM.

And that is the end of her story. Except that it doesn't feel complete. I sit at the table, puzzled, because some vital link is missing. I don't understand how or why Olga could just get up and leave after such a long time. I believe everything she has told me, but I can't quite grasp this final rapid-fire sequence of events. After almost two years she simply walked out of her prison and into the local police station to ask for help. I cannot imagine why she would have taken this final risk after everything she had already endured.

I sit thinking this through for a few minutes, and then I ask her.

'I had to leave the Sylvia,' she replies. She shrugs her shoulders again. 'I was almost blind. If I had stayed any longer, I would have completely lost my sight.'

'Were you beaten?'

'Yes,' she says. 'They beat me in my head and in my eyes.'

Olga has undergone eye surgery twice in the Ukrainian capital, Kiev. She is now waiting for a third operation to try to repair her detached retinas. She has almost no vision in one eye and 30 per cent capacity in the other. She is registered Category 1 disabled and therefore entitled to a Moldovan pension worth about ten dollars a month. She will never fully regain her eyesight, and at the moment lives in the IOM refuge with her son, Kolya. She hopes to eventually rent a flat nearer the city centre if she can find work. Liliana says she hopes that Olga will be offered a job at the Moldovan Institute for the Blind.

It is a quiet goodbye between the four of us. Liliana links arms with Olga and gently leads her from the room. Natasha and I don't say much to each other for a little while. It is only as I am gathering up my bits and pieces that I recall the other question I meant to ask Olga: the final detail of her story that she has left unsaid. She never mentioned what happened to her friend Stella.

Chapter 3

The Last Resort

The apartment I am renting is in the diplomatic quarter of Chisinau, ten minutes' walk from the Green Hills Café. It is spacious and very quiet, but whatever the weather is doing outside, the interior always feels overcast. The sun never quite manages to penetrate the heavy metal bars on the windows, or pierce the veils of lace curtain that hang from ceiling to floor in the silent living room. Whoever originally furnished this place was seriously into drapery, gilded ornaments and personal security. In addition to the barred windows, there is an inner front door, a spyhole for the outer front door, two mortise locks and an entryphone. The combination of all these safeguards makes me feel physically secure but emotionally jittery, as it implies there are people who definitely need to be kept at bay in this city.

I am spending another week here. Doru is trying to find another trafficked woman for me to interview. As many of the women at the IOM shelter do not, quite understandably, want anything to do with journalists or researchers, he says this interview is going to take at least a few days to arrange. He's rushed off his feet at the moment, especially as a film crew have just arrived from Scandinavia to shoot footage of trafficked women. Moldova has no industries or infrastructure to speak of, but offers a rich seam of personal tragedy and suffering, which now has journalists and researchers like me literally forming a queue. I am going to have to wait my turn.

I spend these next few days talking to counter-trafficking officers from the resident international aid agencies, of which there are plenty, and a few local organisations; gleaning as much information about the state of this troubled country as I can from anyone who has a spare hour or lunchtime to talk with me.

A lot of the information I hear is either anecdotal or based on educated guesswork. Moldova is a country saturated with estimates, stories and rumour; it has a national deficit of hard facts. Some of these stories seem almost comically exaggerated to me – like the one my translator, Natasha, has told me about four long-haired Moldovan students who apparently formed a 1960s rock band, managed to get themselves invited to play in Liverpool five years ago and haven't been seen since. Yet these tales do occasionally cross-reference: different people mention the same scenario or village, and I check up as best I can by asking around and scouring aid-agency reports.

Certain villages have, for instance, become renowned for specific trades. Minjir, which lies 60 kilometres south of Chisinau, is now infamous for the number of its men who have resorted to selling one of their kidneys in order to provide for their families. Many of them have been unable to work ever since, because their operations were botched. Others are in constant severe pain that will never be compensated by the dubious doctors who removed their organs in private Turkish, Bulgarian or United Arab Emirate clinics. One Minjir villager, Gheorghi Ungureanu, recently told BBC journalist Bethany Bell about being promised work in a factory in Israel but ending up being transported to Turkey instead. He was escorted to a hospital and given a form with a dotted line, so he could sign away one of his kidneys for $3,000 on the spot, which he did.[1]

The village of Kotesti in north-western Moldova has become notorious for the number of local young women who have gone missing and never returned, leaving a community of older people and young children stranded. Most of the young men had already left Kotesti, and many of the other rural Moldovan communities too. Young men are usually the first wave of migrants to leave, hopeful they can establish themselves somewhere more affluent, send money and then relay information back home to their families. Whole sections of a community often attempt to migrate to the same region of the same destination country and re-establish themselves in diaspora.

The Moldovans I speak to mostly want to reach Italy, which has a labour agreement allowing an annual quota of them to enter as permitted guest workers. They talk about Italy as though it's a promised land; several people assure me Italy even offers resident permits to Moldovans who enter the country without documents, as long as they can prove they've been working for an Italian company. I don't comment, because although I don't believe this for a moment, I don't know anything about the fine print of Italy's migrant labour laws. The Moldovan Embassy in Italy estimates there are eighty thousand Moldovans living there: the Italian authorities put the total nearer 300,000.

The Moldovans I meet say they want to work as hard as they can in Italy for several years and then come home, move to Beverley Hills and

1. Bethany Bell, BBC News, 21 May 2003.

build a fine house. Beverley Hills is the local nickname for the Chisinau suburb where the nouveaux riches live, in turreted mansions with terraced gardens, electric gates and private security. I'm also assured several times that the Beverley Hills residents are all members of the Moldovan Mafia, or migrants who made lucrative business deals abroad and have now come home to roost.

If they cannot reach Italy, ordinary Moldovans are confined to CIS (Commonwealth of Independent States) countries, Romania or migrating without documents. Hundreds of thousands of them have left the country illegally, and it is the local UNICEF office that tells me about the resulting orphanages, and the kids at risk. There are fourteen thousand or more children languishing in decrepit state-run orphanages. They've been abandoned by parents who couldn't afford to keep them or have left the country to work without them.

Traffickers are rumoured to constantly trawl these orphanages, and local schools, seeking out boys and girls they can tempt, persuade or abduct into begging or prostitution.

For some young Moldovan females, prostitution provides an income they badly need. 'Go past the Green Hill Café at dusk and have a look,' someone suggests. So I wander down from my apartment just as the light is fading and loiter opposite the Green Hills as it fills up with foreign-looking men, and Moldovan women dressed in low-cut tops and tight trousers. I watch, slightly uneasy and totally fascinated, as the men buy the women drinks, talk with them intently, and they begin to leave the café in couples.

I don't like drinking in bars alone, so I spend most of my evenings in the overcast apartment, lying on the long couch, reading or watching TV. I drink local wine, smoke and refuse to think about women or children being trafficked, or what happened to Olga. If my mind wavers towards disturbing recollections, I drain my glass and turn the TV volume up.

Natalia, Doru's colleague who works at the IOM refuge, calls me at the apartment one morning and invites me to join her for lunch. I say I'd be delighted, and she arrives by car a couple of hours later.

The driver drops us at a dark-green door in a quiet city-centre side street. Inside is an elegant Russian restaurant with stuffed animal heads mounted on its walls and tables laid with linen and heavy silver cutlery. The waiter speaks so quietly he almost whispers, and bows his head when he takes our order. We both eat gamey rabbit soup, followed by plates of Russian salad, delicate wild mushrooms that are served cold in oil, black bread and a bottle of chilled white wine. We are the only people dining.

I tell Natalia about the anecdotes and stories I've been hearing these last few days. She listens, smiles and changes the subject. I take her cue and we move on to more neutral topics. We talk about our families and where we have travelled for work, the places we like best and where both of us want to go next. We get stuck into the mushrooms and wine and stories of our own lives.

'We hear rumours of trafficking all the time,' she says suddenly, halfway through our meal.

I don't reply, waiting to see if this is a delayed response to my earlier comments or just a passing remark. I don't want to push her.

The sun is brilliant outside, but the restaurant is cool, and the air inside so still her voice seems to echo round the corners as she continues. 'I often don't know what to believe, because there are so many versions of the same story flying around. But I did hear about a plane being stopped on the runway a few months ago here in Chisinau. The staff on the plane were suspicious of this Turkish man who was travelling with six young Moldovan women. They were all apparently going to Turkey with him. The airport manager rang the national hotline, because these days they understand a little more about trafficking, and a man from the Interior Ministry was sent to the airport to investigate. He went straight on to the plane, and while the Turkish man was taken away and questioned, this official talked with the six women. He asked them where they were going, and they said they were all going to work in Turkey and this man had arranged everything for them.

'So then the official announced that he was there to tell them *pravda* – the truth. They were not going to work as waitresses or babysitters in Istanbul. As soon as they arrived, they would probably have their passports taken away and then be sent to some brothel and forced to work as prostitutes. They would be beaten and raped, and they might not be able to leave for a long time. And even if they did get out, they would never be paid for what they had to do. He told them all these things, and at the end, after they had listened to everything he said, each one of them told him that she was still going to leave.

'He couldn't stop them. They had passports and work visas, the Turkish man had no criminal record, and they all had tickets. So he had to let them go.'

'Where did you hear this story?'

'We've all talked about it in the IOM office, and the hotline office is just next door from the IOM.'

'Why were the women so determined to leave with him?'

'I think they just wanted to work abroad, that was all. Like everyone here does.'

I decline a lift home from the restaurant, wander slowly back through the park and have a white-wine-induced snooze on the couch. I am woken by the telephone ringing. It's Doru. He is apologetic at not having been in touch, but the TV crew have kept him busy.

'I have another woman for you to interview,' he offers, without mentioning the word 'victim'. 'She lives in a village outside Chisinau, but she is willing to tell you her story, so we can take you there, in one of our cars. Natasha can come and translate for you.'

We drive through the battered city suburbs and then another forty or so kilometres south of Chisinau, to the edge of a nondescript-looking village called Ciorescu.

The driver parks outside two squat houses fenced off from the dirt track that leads on to the village itself. The woman we have come to visit is called Anna, and she has obviously heard the car arriving because she comes outside to greet us. A slight young woman dressed in floppy black trousers and a T-shirt, she shields her eyes from the sun as she chases the hens out of the way and beckons us inside.

Her home is two concrete rooms that she shares with her son and daughter. There isn't much inside at all, except for a stove, a couch, an armchair and a huge TV that stands in the corner draped with a long, white cloth. I can't see a tap, but there are a couple of pails of water next to the stove.

Doru is talking with Anna, who is staring at him and then us and nodding, nervous as a foal. A few moments later Doru says he has to go. He and the driver will both come back in a couple of hours.

Natasha and I sit opposite Anna, who begins to speak and tremble at the same moment. She also begins to weep quietly, wiping her eyes with her trembling hands as she resolutely continues.

'Anna, we don't need to do this,' I say to her. But she shakes her head and turns towards Natasha.

'I want to tell you,' she says. 'This is my story, and I want to tell you.' She begins again back at the beginning, breaks down once more and then repeats, 'I want to tell you my story.' And on this third attempt when she launches herself into her story, it seems as though she is suddenly almost in a rush to expel it, like a toxin.

Anna was seventeen when she married a local boy called Alexandru. They had gone to the local village school together and had known each other most of their lives. A year after they got married they moved from his parents' home into this house on the edge of the village.

'We had a television and a fridge and good furniture when we moved in here,' she says, in a deliberate reference to better times. 'But even then we never had very much money, and it gradually just got worse. I was working at the local sausage factory. It was the only job I could get, especially after the children were born. But the salary was small, and my husband couldn't find any work. Eventually he had an opportunity to go to Germany, and he knew that he would be able to work over there. For a few years he sent us money regularly from Germany, so I was able to stay at home and look after the kids. My boy, Dimitri, had suffered an accident at kindergarten and he sometimes had seizures, so I really needed to be at home with him. The problem was that we never saw Alexandru. He couldn't come back to visit because he never had the papers to go to Germany in the first place. He was living there without documents. And then he wrote to me asking for a divorce.'

At the end of 1999 Anna's husband sent her a letter saying he needed a divorce in order to apply for a visa to work legally in Germany, so he could continue sending money home for her and the children. Thinking that it was in all their interests, Anna agreed to the divorce, only to have him return home a few months later with a young Moldovan woman he had met and then married in Germany.

'He came back with this other woman and insisted that they both stayed here in my house while he looked for another place for them to live. They were here for two months. We had been married for fourteen years! Can you imagine how that felt?'

I want to ask Anna why she even let him through the front door, though I can hear the answer in the squashed tone of her voice. She obviously believed she was beholden to Alexandru because he had been providing for her and the children. So Alexandru and his new wife moved into Anna's house. When he left two months later, he took the television, fridge and most of the furniture with him.

'He took almost everything, except my children. We had nothing left.' She nods her head towards the shrouded TV. 'The IOM gave me that as a donation, after what happened to me.'

I wonder why Alexandru had come back from Germany in the first place, when it sounded like he'd been having a great time over there. What had gone wrong, or who had he crossed, that forced him to return home to this impoverished corner of Europe? But Anna is already moving on with her story, wringing her hands and wiping away persistent tears as she recalls what happened next.

With Alexandru now refusing to give her any financial support, Anna had no money as well as no work. She attempted to take her now ex-husband to court but couldn't afford the fees that had to be paid in advance. She was also scared of losing her home if she lost the case. Meanwhile Dimitri needed regular medication to control his seizures, and both children needed food, clothes, books and uniforms for school.

'We were hungry and I had to do something. I went back to the sausage factory, where they paid me MDL500 a month [£35]. That put food on the table, but it didn't pay for my son's medicine, or for the school uniforms. I didn't have enough money to provide for the three of us, and after a few months I was stressed and always tired, and sick of being poor. There was nothing else I could do except to go away and work. My aunt lives in Italy, in Rome. She has the papers to be there, and I managed to talk to her on the telephone. She told me that if I could get myself to Italy, she would find work for me and I could stay with her. But she was very clear that I had to arrange my own transport to Italy.'

Anna had no money to buy a ticket to Italy, but she was resourceful. She bought a copy of *Makler* and contacted one of the travel agencies that advertised their services in the classified section.

'I rang them and told them my situation, and they said there was no problem at all. The journey to Italy would cost $1,000, and I could pay them half of the travel money before I left and the other half when I arrived. They said I didn't even need a passport to get to Italy because they had the right contacts.

'I managed to borrow $500 from my relatives. They raised the money between them because I said I would be earning good money when I was in Italy, and I even agreed when they asked me to pay them back with 10 per cent interest.'

In these harsh times it seemed everyone wanted to make money out of everyone else in Moldova, even immediate family.

I look at this thin woman, trembling and weeping in her armchair. 'Weren't you afraid of leaving without a passport and relying on businessmen that you had never met before?' I ask her uneasily, reluctant to question her while she's so distressed.

Anna shakes her head almost violently. 'No! This is what people do here. They usually go without papers. I already knew people who had done the same and were working abroad in other countries. So many people have done this and been able to send money home. The agency told me there would be nine of us leaving together. Three girls of my age, two older women and three men. There was nothing to be scared about.'

Anna did not meet her recruiter in person but made a verbal agreement with him over the telephone about where and when she would depart for Italy. On 18 July 2000 she left her son and daughter with her mother, took a public bus to Chisinau and then boarded a minibus on the outskirts of the city with the other eight passengers.

'We each handed over $500 in cash, and they drove us straight to the Romanian border. It was just like they said: there was no problem crossing the border without a passport. The driver and the woman with him had it all arranged. They took us to Bosnia and then to Serbia, and they just kept telling us we were on the way to Italy.'

I have heard this before. It sounds like a carbon copy of Olga's description of her journey. Is this what all the traffickers do here? I think to myself. Do they all hire minibuses, bribe border guards and then just speed over to Serbia? It is beginning to sound like a national collaboration. But then it strikes me that you can't get to Bosnia except via Serbia, because of the geography.

'Anna,' I say, 'you have to cross Romania and Serbia to get to Bosnia, not the other way round.'

Anna shrugs and repeats verbatim what she has just said: that they drove from Romania to Bosnia and then to Serbia. She had never been outside Moldova before and spoke only Moldovan and Russian. The only information that she had to go on was what the traffickers told her, and they had described an impossible route to her.

'After we got there, to Bosnia, the whole thing became like a film or a bad dream,' she says, and from then on she recalls her experiences in a series of flashbacks, adding place names and images in no chronological order, but as they occur to her. She seems to enter an almost hypnotic state of shock as she moves her story back and forth between countries, colouring in details seemingly at random, honing in on particular awful moments and then leaping towards the next crisis that she somehow survives or escapes.

It is impossible to track the exact sequence of events, and after a while of trying to doggedly pin down her route and the whole journey that she was taken and sometimes abducted on, I realise that I am missing the point. This chaos is Anna's story. She sounds as though she is reliving individual moments that then ignite other memories and hurtle her off on a tangent to the next definitive experience.

'We drove for days almost without stopping. We dropped the three men off somewhere and just carried on driving until we finally got to a big town. Someone told me a few days after we had arrived in this last place that we were in Macedonia. I didn't speak the language and did not have a clue where I was. I had just been taken into a bar with those two other girls my age, and then a man I had never seen before took me from that first bar to another bar in the same town, and when we got to the second bar, he told me that he had paid a good price for me. Until that moment I had no idea I had been sold. No one tells you anything: they just separated us and auctioned us between them. This man who had paid for me said that if I worked hard for him for a year, then afterwards he would pay me a percentage of what I had earned for him and allow me to take the money home with me. Then he made me dance in his bar. I had to dance there every night, but I was lucky because I was allowed to dance with my clothes on.'

Anna worked in the bar from about six in the evening until four or five o'clock the next morning. She soon found out that she was in Gostivar, a city in north-western Macedonia.

'It was terrible. Sometimes I was beaten even inside the bar, and they always kept me hungry. When I complained to Uri, the man who had bought me, he took me to a couple of other bars where the women were dancing naked and the conditions were worse. He said it would make me realise that I was lucky in his bar. Then he let me telephone my kids at my mother's house.'

Anna's tears are slowly drying up, though her hands are still shaking despite being folded together in her black lap. I try to imagine her telephoning from Macedonia to reassure her children that she was fine, and what she might have said to her mother beforehand. Maybe she fabricated her own arrival in Italy. I don't ask her about this conversation, and she offers nothing more. That telephone call home had been a privilege: a gift from the pimp who had purchased her.

'The dancing in the bar went on for months, and I began to think that I might actually be able to go home quite soon. But one night two men took me out of the bar, which happened sometimes. They would take you to a hotel room and then bring you back afterwards. I thought they would bring me back to the bar sometime that night, but they didn't. They drove me to another bar in a different town and told me that I had been sold to them. I never got any of the money I had earned from the first bar. These two men told me that I owed them DM3,000 [about £1,200].

'I was completely shocked by what they told me. I thought Uri and I had made an arrangement, but it all changed now. This new bar was very big. It was a three-storey building, and there was security everywhere, like a big prison. They held me with a group of other girls on the third floor. They locked us in and kept watch on us. Some of the girls were also from Moldova, and they told me about the fighting in Macedonia. I had seen soldiers all the time, but I thought maybe that was normal here after the war in Kosovo. The men who watched us all had guns, and they were violent. They told me there were troops from different countries in Macedonia to prevent war from breaking out, and that we were locked up because of the troubles.[2] I had never been in a place like this, and I thought that I would never see my children again.'

After two weeks locked inside this bar Anna jumped from the third-floor balcony to the second and then the first-floor balcony, and somehow escaped into nearby woods. She spent the whole night outside, dressed in a skirt and T-shirt and a pair of flimsy shoes. It was late January 2001, and the temperatures were below freezing. Anna knew she would die if she stayed outside much longer. At dawn she found a road and followed it to a small hamlet. She was looking for a church to beg for sanctuary, but instead she met a local Macedonian family of four, who brought her to their nearby house and gave her a meal and some of their daughter's clothes to wear.

'They were kind to me, but I didn't know what to do next. I couldn't stay in that village because I knew that the men from the bar would be looking for me. I had nowhere to go, so I asked to use their telephone, and I called Uri and asked him to come and pick me up.'

The Macedonian family told Uri where their house was, and he drove out to collect her. She went back to his bar and danced again.

2. Macedonia was not at war but had UN peacekeepers who were maintaining security under the auspices of the UN Preventive Deployment Force (UN PREDEP). The force was renamed UN SKOPJE on 28 February 1999.

Chapter 4

Anna Would Go Back

I have learned that the relationship between a trafficked woman and her pimp is complex. He is her tormentor and her provider. He is a brute who may rape her and probably beats her but is often the only friend that she has left in the world. He feeds her and starves her. He may show her physical affection and then rent her out to half a dozen men for the night afterwards. He is her only guarantee of personal safety but might threaten her every day. He will remind her that she is his property but may pay her a salary if she works hard enough and endures enough sex with the men that he selects for her. He decides if she can use any form of contraception, and if so what kind. He also decides when she is allowed to eat, sleep, bathe and maybe even when she can go to the toilet. He occasionally allows her to call home but might taunt her about never seeing her children again.

He is quite likely to explain that if she tries to escape from him, he will ensure that her children or parents are mutilated and murdered, and that her daughter will be raped beforehand. He will usually sell her on to another pimp but may kill her instead. Not all pimps rely on all these tactics: some are kinder and gentler than others. But a trafficked woman is still alone in a psychological minefield.

Anna never asked Uri anything about him having sold her to another bar. Instead, she returned to work and concentrated on earning enough money for him so that he would allow her to go home. She reckons that she spent another three months or so dancing at Uri's bar before she was abducted by one of his customers. This man rented Anna out for the night, put her in his car and bashed her over the head with some kind of blunt instrument. When she regained consciousness, she was in a large bedroom with several other young women.

'My head ached for a month afterwards. I don't know why he hit me; he didn't have to. I would have done what he said. But this new place was a bar run by Albanians, and they were crazy: they were even trading their own women. I saw them selling an Albanian woman who was big and pregnant to a man who came to the bar. He took her away and she never returned. Everyone who came into that bar had a gun, and we were watched like goldfish in a tank. You cannot imagine what goes on in these places.

'The only thing that kept me going was that I knew I was either in Albania by now or very near the border. I just had to get myself to the coast and then I could make it over to Italy. In this crazy bar, wherever it was, there were always a lot of customers, and some were actually quite sorry for me: poor Moldovan girl trying to save up money for her children, they used to say! They were allowed to take us out for the night too, and one of these customers told me he liked me and would help me get to Albania. So one night he took me out and drove me over the border into Albania. But he sold me too.'

The buying and selling of women like Anna has become a regional economy in its own right: traffickers who trade females have a continuing cash flow to purchase drugs, guns, counterfeit money, documents and all the other accoutrements of organised crime.

'So, I was sold to this other Albanian, and he took me to his home in Vlore. That was the strangest thing of all. By then I had lost count of how many men had bought and sold me. I had been traded like a dead body, and I felt as though I was dead by then. But in the end I was actually taken to where I needed to be! I knew about Vlore and all the speedboats crossing to Italy. I even had enough money to pay for my own crossing, from the tips those customers had given me out of pity.

'The Albanian kept me in his house, which was right by the sea. I could see the waves from the window. He kept promising to take me over to Italy, but at night he would bring his friends over to use me. I knew exactly what he would make me do in Italy. He made it very clear that he expected me to work for him as a prostitute on the street. I just had to make it over there. Afterwards I knew that I would somehow get to my aunt's place and sort out everything. I just had to get myself over to Italy. I tell you, after all this I was prepared to swim there!'

Anna and her latest pimp attempted three crossings of the Adriatic Straits to southern Italy.

'It was autumn, sometime in October, I think, and the sea was quite rough. We had to cross at night, because if we were spotted by the police, then we would all be arrested. It was very dangerous in those boats. They were crowded, and we couldn't see anything. If anyone dared to argue with the captain, he just threw them over into the sea. But we had to turn back each time because of the weather, and then I had no money left so I couldn't try any more.'

Until about the middle of 2002, the crossing from Vlore was used by a constant stream of traffickers, smugglers and migrants, all attempting to reach the south-eastern tip of Italy, between Brindisi and Lecce. The Italian Carabinieri and the Albanian authorities gradually tightened the net around them, constantly patrolling the straits in search of *gommoni*, as the renegade boats are known. Now an Interpol office has opened in Vlore, and the route is so well known and patrolled that the traffickers and smugglers have moved their operations north towards Croatia or south to Greece.

After the failed third attempt, the Albanian pimp gave up on the idea of putting Anna to work on the streets of Naples or Rome. Instead, he took her to a brothel an hour's drive from Vlore and forced her to work there, so that he could continue making money out of her. Almost everyone that Anna had met since she first left Moldova had made money out of her. But in this remote village somewhere in southern Albania, someone finally called the police.

'I was only in this village a few nights when a whole group of police barged in and took us all away. There were five of us in this bar, and we were all foreign girls. They drove us to Tirana and took us to a refuge. When we got there, this woman from the refuge asked me if I had been trafficked. She had to explain to me what being trafficked meant, because I told her that I was just trying to get to Italy. But when she explained that it was being sold and forced to work, then I said, "Oh yes, that happened to me many times." Of course I had no ID, and there was no Moldovan Embassy in Tirana, so it took three months for my papers to be processed before I could go home. I spent three months waiting in the refuge, and when my papers arrived and they finally knew for sure who I was, the police told me that while I had been away my brother had died. I had been away for more than two years. I got back home at the end of 2002. When I came back to the village, I barely recognised my own children.'

About thirty Moldovan women are assisted home by the IOM every month: one woman every day of the year. The majority of them return from within the Balkans: Kosovo, Serbia, Bosnia or Albania, though women also regularly arrive back from being trafficked to London or Moscow or even further. When they arrive at the airport, Natalia is there waiting for them, and she escorts them either back to their home or to the IOM refuge. The women can live in the shelter for a month, though a few, like Olga, end up staying for much longer. The refuge is usually full, and the IOM now has a second refuge where women can stay with their children. The Moldova IOM has now supported more than a thousand women who have survived being trafficked. Natalia has already told me that at least half the women she meets do not want to go back home or say they cannot return for fear of reprisals or shame.

Anna was brave enough to return. She has been back in Ciorescu for six months now. She is working at the sausage factory once more and lives with her two children.

'We manage because the IOM gave me some money to help me out and that has lasted for a while,' she says. 'But I am quite sick these days and don't know how long I can keep on working, and that frightens me. We have no other money coming in, and I have only just finished paying the loan back to my relatives. Living in this house doesn't help. It has bad memories for me, and in winter it's very cold in here and not good for any of us. But I have nowhere else to go, even though I don't want to be here.

'And that is the end of my story,' she announces quite formally.

Natasha leans back on the couch and sighs almost imperceptibly. Anna stretches her skinny legs out in front of her and unfolds her hands. Then she folds them back together again.

'It was terrible what happened to me,' she says. 'Things are very bad here, but out there it's worse. It's so dangerous. I just don't want to be here any more because I have nothing to hope for.' She sniffs and her voice bubbles up from her throat. 'I just wish I had made it to Italy. If I had another $500, I would try again.'

'After everything that happened, you would be prepared to do it again?' I feel almost angry with her for saying this, and for her total disregard for herself.

'Yes. Because I nearly made it last time.' She looks straight across the room at me. 'I came home with nothing. If I had another opportunity, I would go back and try again. I think I could get there next time.'

Many women who are trafficked and subsequently assisted to come back home regard themselves as failed migrants. UNICEF has published a substantial trafficking report that acknowledges this is a major reason why so many are at such high risk of being trafficked again:

> According to NGOs, it is estimated that up to fifty per cent of trafficked women who are returned leave Moldova shortly after their arrival and are re-trafficked. Without any prospect of a job or means to support themselves and their families at home, some women believe that the next time will be better and that they will be able to work abroad on their own and keep the money, while others simply do not see any other choice.[1]

Anna, Natasha and I sit outside Anna's house, waiting for Doru and the

---

1. 'Trafficking in Human Beings in South-Eastern Europe', UNICEF, 2002.

car to arrive. Anna and Natasha talk amongst themselves. I like Natasha a lot. I like the way she spoke to Olga and the way she's speaking to Anna now, as a peer. She doesn't look down on these women, or treat them as pitiful. She nudges Anna as the car rattles round the corner, and Anna stands up and dusts down her black trousers.

She asks me when I'm going home, and where it is.

'I live in Edinburgh, the capital of Scotland,' I tell her, 'and I'm flying home tomorrow.'

She nods silently, squinting in the sun.

A few weeks after I return home to Edinburgh, I receive an envelope from Moldova. It is from one of the counter-trafficking officers I met in Chisinau and contains a copy of a smeared fax, sent by a Cypriot businessman to his Moldovan contact.

Received: 23 July 2003

> PO Box 00000
> Larnaca
> Cyprus

For Attention: Nicoll

With reference to our conversation 8/1/2003, I would like to start a long-term business relationship with your agency. I would like to note that I will be requiring from your services the following points:

1. The girls you send me must be good-looking, very beautiful with a nice personality between the ages of eighteen and twenty-five. The clubs they are working in are very high class, and we only expect the best.

2. The girls must know that the job comprises of strip-tease, private show and sexual activity.

3. The girls must understand that when they are in Cyprus they are under my management and I expect respect and cooperation from them. If in any case the girls make problems for me or my business, any problems whatsoever, I will not hesitate to terminate their work and send them straight back to their country at their own expense.

4. The commission that your agency requires for each working girl is $300; that will be paid after each girl has been working for up to seven to ten days.

5. What I require from your agency *now* is passport photocopies, up-to-date photos of each girl and any medical records available (AIDS,

syphilis). I will also need your bank details, including bank telephone numbers.

6. When the visas are ready for each girl, I will send them to you by fax, and all flight tickets I will send to the airport in Moldova.

7. All paperwork must be sent to me in English and preferably sent by post.

In a few months I will come to Moldova so we can talk face to face and hopefully have a long-term relationship.

Yours faithfully,
George

Chapter 5

When the Peacekeepers Arrive

The skies in Edinburgh are grey, and I am back at work. I work part-time as a mental health outreach worker, visiting clients at home, unless they have gone back into hospital, in which case I go and visit them there instead. I have eight clients. They all have chronic mental health problems, and most of them are severely depressed as well. My job is to be someone whom they can talk to, whether it's about their health, their noisy neighbours or the voices they hear whispering inside their own heads. One of my clients has alcohol-induced brain damage: he drank so much for so long that he eventually dissolved his own short-term memory. Whenever he and I go out together I have to constantly remind him of where we are going and who I am. He is a clever, articulate and entertaining man with no memory, and he is one of the reasons that I enjoy my work. My clients are all interesting people, and my work hours are flexible, so I also have time to slowly chisel away at my trafficking research. The only problem with my job is that it's in the voluntary sector, and the pay is paltry.

When I'm not out at work, I sift through reports on trafficking in the Balkans. A lot of the material is bone-dry regional analysis, loaded with acronyms, bar charts and percentages. I know this information is necessary, vital even: it provides context, identifies trends and potential anti-trafficking strategies. But it often makes dense reading.

All the reports I have scoured identify consistently the overland journey from Moldova through Romania and on to Serbia as one of the major European trafficking routes. From Serbia, women are taken either into Bosnia or south to Kosovo and Albania.

Having already been to Kosovo, I could pick up the trail in Bosnia and attempt to track how the industry has evolved there in the last few years. The IOM were extremely helpful to me in Moldova, but this time I want to contact local organisations who are fighting their own corner against the traffickers, especially organisations from within the most severely affected communities, where the international agencies have little or no presence.

This plan, however, has a couple of potential pitfalls. I have to find these elusive local contacts, and they are probably located outside the capital cities. Also, I don't particularly want to travel alone through any more of the former Yugoslavia: I found Kosovo unsettling, and from what I've read, the trafficking situation in Bosnia sounds equally ominous. But my boyfriend has a demanding full-time career, and I cannot think of anyone else who would volunteer to come along with me. I will just have to travel carefully, and tread lightly.

Women are trafficked to Bosnia for the same reason they are trafficked anywhere else in the world: because there is a demand for compliant sex workers there. There are also 7,000 troops still on peacekeeping mission in Bosnia.[1] These peacekeepers are SFOR, an abbreviation of Stabilisation Force. Although some regiments come from non-NATO countries, SFOR are a NATO-led multinational task force. They support the United Nations Mission in Bosnia and Herzegovina (UNMIBH) from 1996 until the UN mission terminated in December 2002. The troops are still there. They have the status and privileges of UN peacekeepers, who also include other civilian personnel.

Since its inception, the United Nations has a history of protecting its own interests before anyone else's. One of the earliest UN conventions to be passed was the Convention on the Privileges and Immunities of the UN (1946), which grants the equivalent of diplomatic immunity to United Nations representatives of member states, UN officials and experts on missions. UN peacekeepers, on the other hand, are placed 'under the exclusive criminal jurisdiction of their nation of origin'. This means that any peacekeeper who commits a crime or a serious act of misconduct is liable to be repatriated and prosecuted back at home. Human rights organisations have criticised this system for decades. They claim it offers peacekeepers virtual immunity, as it relies on UN missions investigating complaints against their own staff and then deciding whether to send them home to be either disciplined or prosecuted. It also means peacekeepers are prosecuted in their own country, regardless of where the crime allegedly took place.[2]

1. The first peacekeepers in BiH (Bosnia and Herzegovina) were UNPROFOR (UN Protection Force), who were replaced by IFOR (Implementation Force) in December 1995, and in turn replaced by SFOR in December 1996.
2. This immunity can in theory be lifted by the commanding officer of a national peacekeeping contingent, thus allowing an in-country criminal investigation.

The rationale for this immunity is that peacekeepers are sent to countries where law and order have broken down, and their missions include restoration and implementation of law, order and national security. In other words, countries who contribute peacekeeping personnel to UN- and NATO-led missions are extremely unlikely to agree to their citizens being deployed in war zones if they have to worry about them being arrested or tried in courts that they (the contributing countries) have no jurisdiction over. The implication is that soldiers and staff could be arrested for trumped-up political charges and slung in prison for years to score points or gain political leverage. The UN says it deals with disciplinary matters internally, ensuring that all peacekeepers who don't toe the line are sent home and rigorously investigated. In addition to a UN-wide Code of Conduct for all peacekeeping missions (which was introduced in 1993), each UN mission is obliged to set specific terms regarding the conduct, privileges, immunity and jurisdiction of its civilian and military employees.[3] Human rights bodies like Amnesty and the American organisation Human Rights Watch are not impressed. They point out that few personnel are ever sent home, and prosecutions are rare.[4]

In 1999, Human Rights Watch began a two-year investigation into trafficking in Bosnia. Their subsequent report was published in 2002.[5] In this report, they claimed women started being trafficked into Bosnia from the end of 1995, just after the Dayton Peace Agreement was signed. By October 2002 the UN Mission in Bosnia (UNMIBH) suspected that women were being forced to work in more than two hundred and twenty bars and nightclubs across Bosnia.

Local Bosnian police officers were frequently suspected of being recruited and bribed by traffickers or rewarded with sexual favours coerced out of trafficked women. According to the report:

> Local police officers facilitated trafficking both directly and indirectly, as part-owners of nightclubs and bars holding trafficked women [. . .] as clients of the brothels and as informants to brothel owners. Trafficked women and girls reported that brothel owners forced them to provide free sexual services to police [. . .] brothel owners received tip-offs about raids and document checks from local police, allowing them to hide the trafficked women and girls before a police sweep.

Under the terms of the Dayton Peace Agreement, an International

---

3. This is the Status of Forces Agreement, or SOFA.
4. 'Does that mean I have rights?', Amnesty International report on Kosovo, 6 May 2004.
5. 'Hopes Betrayed', Human Rights Watch report on Bosnia and Herzegovina, November 2002.

Police Task Force (IPTF) was established in Bosnia in December 1995, to work alongside the Bosnian police force. IPTF monitors were professional police from around the world, deployed throughout Bosnia to improve law enforcement and analyse threats to public security. Almost two thousand IPTF monitors from forty countries were originally stationed in Bosnia. They were given the same immunity status as UN peacekeepers.

As part of their remit, IPTF monitors supervised local police raids at Bosnian bars and nightclubs where trafficking was suspected. They interviewed women and girls as young as thirteen who were being confined on premises and forced to have sex with clients, and they gathered evidence against the traffickers. But Human Rights Watch reported that a number of IPTF monitors were also directly implicated in the crimes they were supposedly investigating:

> Human Rights Watch also found evidence of involvement in trafficking-related offences by individual members of the IPTF [. . .] Deployed to promote the rule of law, a small number of IPTF monitors instead have engaged in illegal activities either as customers of trafficked women or as outright purchasers of trafficked women and their passports. Rather than request that UN Headquarters waive the immunity enjoyed by IPTF monitors in Bosnia and Herzegovina, UNMIBH has merely repatriated police monitors accused of involvement in trafficking, acting under the legal fiction that countries will prosecute or reprimand their own nationals.
>
> Eighteen monitors who purchased trafficked women, visited brothels or faced trafficking-related charges have returned home, either voluntarily or through disciplinary repatriation for 'sexual misconduct', but as this report goes to press in November 2002, Human Rights Watch has not yet confirmed a single case in which an IPTF officer accused of activities related to trafficking faced criminal investigation or prosecution.

Human Rights Watch notes that IPTF monitors from America were actually immune from prosecution back home:

> As for IPTF monitors, US law as of October 2002 did not permit their prosecution for offences committed while part of a UN mission: therefore even after they returned to the United States, US courts had no jurisdiction over IPTF monitors who engaged in the purchasing of women or girls abroad.

At the end of the 1990s an American company called Dyncorp secured a contract to supply Americans to Bosnia as IPTF monitors. Their UK office, based in the town of Salisbury, dealt with the IPTF contracts. In

1999, at the same time as Human Rights Watch were beginning their two-year investigation, Dyncorp employed an American police officer called Kathy Bolkovac to work as an IPTF gender consultant in Bosnia, to investigate ongoing reports of women being trafficked into the country. Kathy Bolkovac was extremely good at her job. She uncovered evidence of women and girls as young as fifteen being beaten and raped in brothels in front of UN peacekeepers, who stood and watched. She said she personally witnessed frightened young women being given exotic dance costumes by nightclub owners and being instructed to perform sex acts on customers, including UN staff, to pay for the outfits.

'When I started collecting evidence from the victims of sex trafficking, it was clear that a number of UN officers were involved from several countries, including quite a few from Britain. I was shocked, appalled and disgusted,' she said. 'But when I told the supervisors they didn't want to know.'

Her supervisors, at Dyncorp, not only didn't want to know: they demoted Kathy Bolkovac in October 2000 after she had filed a comprehensive dossier on the situation. She refused to refute the allegations, continued investigating the involvement of internationals in trafficking and was sacked by Dyncorp for allegedly falsifying her time-keeping records, six months later.

Kathy Bolkovac took Dyncorp to an industrial tribunal, claiming that Dyncorp sacked her because her allegations and evidence were threatening their lucrative IPTF contract. It was a long case, lasting almost two years. Eventually, in August 2002, she won the employment industrial tribunal.

Richard Monk, a former British police officer who ran IPTF until 1999, also publicly backed Kathy Bolkovac. 'There were truly dreadful things going on by UN police officers,' he told *The Times* on the day Kathy Bolkovac won her case.

One of the most bitter ironies of this case was the revelation that a senior UN official had been caught visiting one of Bosnia's most notorious brothels. Dennis Laducer was subsequently sacked and repatriated to the United States in disgrace. His employment record apparently states that he should never be allowed to work for the United Nations again.[6] Dennis Laducer was a deputy commissioner of IPTF.

One of the witnesses called to testify in the Kathy Bolkovac case was Madeleine Rees, whose work was quoted at the London trafficking training course Maggie and I attended. At that time Madeleine Rees worked as part of the UN Mission in Bosnia (UNMBH) and was ferociously critical of the links between barracks and brothels.

6. *The Natashas: the New Global Sex Trade*, Victor Malarek, Vision Paperbacks, 2004, p.164.

'There is no doubt that the sex-trafficking market emerged when the peacekeepers arrived here,' she claimed during the Bolkovac case. Madeleine Rees sounds like a straight-talker – and is apparently still working in Bosnia. I trawl around the Internet to find out if she is still working for that part of the UN. It doesn't take me very long to locate her current whereabouts. She is living in Sarajevo, and these days heads the UN Office of the High Commissioner for Human Rights in Bosnia and Herzegovina. I email her office, asking if I can visit her in Sarajevo to talk about the current behaviour of peacekeepers in Bosnia.

'You are welcome to visit, just give me a bit of notice,' she replies swiftly. It is an opening, and from her I'll try to find contacts outside the capital.

I arrange to visit Madeleine Rees a couple of months later, in November.

The salubrious-sounding Office of the High Commissioner for Human Rights in Bosnia and Herzegovina turns out to be a shoddy-looking building just outside the centre of Sarajevo. As the secretary is showing me to Madeleine's office, she asks whether I like dogs, which I do, though the question puzzles me until I step inside and see three mutts stretched out, dozing peacefully on the carpet.

Madeleine Rees is a tall, lean-looking woman with short blonde hair. I immediately notice her jewellery. She wears silver the way I imagine warriors used to wear their armour: large chunks of it strategically placed. She shakes my hand firmly and immediately offers me a cappuccino. I've been in Bosnia and Herzegovina just twenty-four hours but am learning that caffeine is akin to currency here: it is used to introduce meetings, initiate friendships, cement deals and encourage lasting peace. One of the first billboard campaigns launched in the aftermath of the three-year siege of Sarajevo featured a steaming cup and the caption 'Tolerance: let's have a coffee.'

Madeleine apologises. She only has an hour to spare – something about project reports – so we don't bother with small talk.

'How's the research going?' she says as I rummage for a pen.

I explain briefly about my trips to Kosovo and Moldova, and Olga referring to foreign troops wanting to buy sex at the Prizren brothel where she was held. I tell her I've read the Human Rights Watch report on Bosnia and want to know whether peacekeeping here is still tainted by trafficking.

The second thing that I notice about Madeleine Rees is the way she listens. She is completely silent and utterly attentive while I am speaking:

her eyes remained fixed on my face like a laser, her body poised and her coffee left untouched. It feels as though every word I say is being filed away for future reference. She hears everything and misses nothing. This has the effect of my wanting to tell her more, as though she is encouraging me to talk because she is listening so skilfully, as a good lawyer should. But I am deliberately brief because we don't have much time, and I need to hear what she has to say. Seconds after I finish she nods slightly, places one of her elbows on the table between us and starts to answer my query. She speaks in a northern English accent, with the speed and precision of machine-gun fire.

'The trafficking situation in Bosnia is complex, and it has altered quite dramatically during the last few years. Basically, from 1995 until 2000 the law was a complete mess here. It was a criminal free-for-all. Masses of Eastern European women were being trafficked into Bosnia, the borders were completely porous, and they were all coerced into the sex industry. They were sex slaves; there's no other way to describe what was happening to these women. There was no law in place to protect them, and they were being funnelled over the border from Serbia. The traffickers were simply driving them straight down the highways and holding auctions in bars and even at open-air markets, like the Arizona Market. The Arizona Market opened in northern Bosnia in 1996. Women were auctioned at night in the market, which is still open but apparently no longer trades in women. It was an appalling situation. The pimps would buy the women from the traffickers and distribute them to brothels all over Bosnia. What was even worse was that if a trafficked woman was found in a brothel by the police, she was immediately arrested for prostitution! No one was informing these women of their legal or human rights, because frankly they didn't have any. They were either imprisoned as prostitutes or else they were fined and then just dumped in the next canton and left to fend for themselves.[7] The traffickers were just left alone to carry on business as usual.'

She pauses to let this torrent of information take effect, and then speeds onwards. 'The trafficker's methodology was simple and effective. Extreme violence works for a short while. You terrify the women into complying: threaten to kill their kids and so on. As soon as you have them cowed into submission, you set up a bar or café, get them officially employed as a waitress and pay them a stipend. You create economic dependency. The women are registered and apparently legally employed, and the industry enters the mainstream. It becomes normalised, which makes it far more difficult to combat.

7. A canton is the equivalent of a constituency, or a locally administered district.

'Eventually the police began to take some action. But the way trafficking was tackled at first was a huge mistake in Bosnia. You know about the IPTF scandal?'

I nod.

'Not only were IPTF monitors being bribed by bar owners, but their military-style tactics were terrifying women who had been trafficked. These IPTF guys would kick the bar and club doors down, and after these special effects, the women would simply be taken to one side and asked if they had been trafficked. Under those circumstances, most trafficked women will deny they've been coerced, because that's what the pimps teach them to say. Sometimes they really didn't know who the hell these men turning up in the bars to rescue them were! There is no doubt that a limited number of women were released as a result of the raids, but as I have been saying for a long time now, you do not stop trafficking by kicking down doors. Firstly, you don't nail the traffickers, just possibly the pimps, and secondly, really vulnerable women are always kept out of sight, in private apartments. And that is exactly how the situation has evolved here.'

'Are more women being kept in apartments now than then?'

Madeleine nods, and drains her cup. 'Yes. Most of the bars have been closed down, and trafficking has reduced in Bosnia in the last couple of years. Some good work has been done, though there are still a number of brothels operating blatantly. Like the Kiss bar in the Lasha Valley, near a place called Travnik: it's about fifty kilometres west of Sarajevo. The police just stay away from there, and give the owners *carte blanche* to carry on renting women out to punters. Mind you' – she suddenly grins at me wickedly – 'at least they closed down that Sherwood Castle joint . . .'

'What was that?'

'Milorat Milakovic owned it, like his own human emporium. He ran a major trafficking operation from Sherwood Castle. But I heard that it's just been turned into a hotel!'

I want to stop her in full flow and ask about this man and his emporium: the name Milakovic rings a distant bell. But there's no pausing her now: Madeleine has already honed in on her next target and is aiming fire at the peacekeepers themselves.

'And as for the troops . . . you need to go up north and see what is going on up there, around Tuzla. The US troops are in Tuzla. It's a large northern town, famously liberal. Their military headquarters is the Eagle base camp, just outside the town itself. Many of the troops rent apartments in Tuzla and drive to the base every morning to clock in for work. And in the evenings, there are four or five bars where they can go to rent or purchase a trafficked woman.'

Now it is I who is still and intent as Madeleine leans back in her chair and explains what is happening.

'A US soldier can go to one of these bars, order a beer and pay for a woman at the same time. He can hire her for an hour, or the night, and then take her back to this apartment. If he can't find a woman he likes the look of, then he can order one. Yes, I mean purchase one. It will cost him about seven thousand dollars, but for that price he can stipulate exactly what it is that he wants: the hair colour, body type, weight and so on. The woman will then be trafficked to Tuzla and sold to the soldier, who will keep her in his apartment for sex and as a housekeeper. Sometimes they promise to marry them. Like the bar owners and the pimps, they deliberately create a dependency.'

'Where did you get this information?' I ask her.

'Originally from a local women's organisation, called Lara. This organisation started to make contact with women who desperately needed help to get out of the apartments. Local police have backed up this information, and I have already raised the issue, during a Rule of Law meeting we held a few months ago, at the beginning of summer. These are meetings we hold in order to discuss drafting and implementation of legislation; but I have received no response to my questions.'

Madeleine looks at me and smiles grimly. 'To tell you the hard truth, some of these women who are kept in apartments by soldiers regard this as their one chance of getting out of their own country and having a better life. And the soldiers know that. We are talking about women who come from desperate circumstances, and unless they are being severely exploited, then they won't thank us for what they see as interfering with their lives. They make decisions that you and I are never going to have to face.'

She glances swiftly at her watch. 'Very few of the women being trafficked in Bosnia are asking for assistance from anti-trafficking organisations, because frankly they are not getting the services they want or need. They are not being asked, especially by the international organisations, about what it is that they want to improve their own lives. The numbers of women staying in refuges is dropping, and anti-trafficking organisations need to seriously examine their service provision.

'Now, I'm sorry, but I am going to have to get back to work.'

My head feels like it's spinning round in slow motion as I start gathering my things and my thoughts together. Madeleine asks if I have any contacts up in Tuzla, and I shake my head gently.

'Go and see Mara,' she says. 'She runs Lara, the organisation that I mentioned. She's from Tuzla herself and manages a refuge up there, in the town of Bijeljina, right near the Serbian border. She knows exactly what's going on. She's been up there for years now. If you hang on a second, I'll find her telephone number for you.'

Chapter 6

'Well, They Sell Footballers, Don't They?'

Neither Mara nor I know what the other looks like. We both spend more than half an hour waiting in Bijeljina bus station before I finally twig that the middle-aged woman pacing in front of the bus stands has been here as long as I have. She is obviously waiting for someone too. So I go up to her and hesitantly ask if her name is Mara Radovanovic. She smiles at me through dark nicotine-stained teeth and exhales a long plume of smoke. 'Yes. I am Mara.' She has tumbledown dark-blonde hair and worn heels. Her two-piece suit is tailored but rumpled, and she must be at least fifty years old. She is not what I expect at all.

Mara guides me to her blue estate car and drives from the bus station to her office in silence, while I fidget and attempt small talk because I suddenly feel nervous and want to fill up the space. She is perfectly friendly, smiles and answers my questions, but asks nothing in return, and so I chatter on inanely until we reach a two-storey concrete building at the edge of town. It has a discreet rainbow logo painted at the top of the front door. She parks on the grass, motions me inside and then upstairs, and we squeeze into a tiny office at the top of the stairs. There is just enough room for the two of us inside. Mara leaves the door open, sits down and lights up another cigarette. She still says nothing. Moments later a woman appears in the doorway with a silver tray and sets down a large pot of coffee and two tiny cups and saucers. Then she smiles and leaves.

Mara pours us both a cup of thick Turkish-style coffee, stubs out her cigarette and says to me, 'So, what is it that you want to know?'

I clear my throat. 'About the women being trafficked across the border from Serbia, and what happens to them afterwards.'

Mara nods, fishes another cigarette out of the open pack on the table beside her, lights up and begins to talk.

'This town, Bijeljina, is one of the main trafficking junctions between

Eastern and Western Europe. The Serbian border is only six kilometres from here, and women are brought across into Bijeljina from all over the East: Moldova, Ukraine, Romania, Belarus. Before they arrive, these women are held in collecting centres in Belgrade organised by the traffickers. This is where they prepare them to become victims. The women are instructed to pose naked for photographs, and the traffickers use these photographs to make up albums that they distribute to bar and nightclub owners in Serbia, Bosnia and Kosovo.' Mara's voice crackles from years of smoking. She speaks English slowly and deliberately, taking her time and pausing to sip at her coffee and pick up her smouldering cigarette.

'The traffickers also take other photographs of the women that they use to make false identity cards. These cards often contain a woman's real name, but details like her date and place of birth are always changed. I have seen these documents. They are very good fakes, especially those for women from Romania, Moldova and Ukraine, so there is no problem with these women crossing the border. The women are given these documents, and they are taught to recite the new information on them. They learn these new details about themselves.

'Every day they are told that they cannot escape, there is nowhere for them to go, so the best thing for them to do is to cooperate and to be obedient. And while they are being kept in Belgrade, the bar owners and their clients make their selections from the photo albums and negotiate a price according to the age and beauty of the girl or woman. The most valuable women are sent straight to Western Europe, and the others are traded within the Balkans. The worst place to be trafficked in the region is Kosovo. That is what the women themselves tell us. Those who come back from Kosovo have the worst stories of all: they are treated very badly.'

She tells me that once their value has been estimated, women are moved out of Belgrade and either brought over the border into Bosnia or taken down south to Kosovo. They are driven to bars, auctioned and sold to their new owners.

'When she arrives at that first bar, the first client that a trafficked woman is forced to go with is always a friend or business associate of the bar owner, but the woman does not know this. She thinks that he is an ordinary customer, or a policeman. He may be a policeman, or he may be wearing a policeman's uniform. The woman often tells him her story, thinking that he can assist her, or she may just ask him directly to help her escape. But he repeats what the traffickers have already told her: that there is no help for her and the best thing is for her to be obedient. If she is obedient, then she will make good money, after she has earned her own price back. And afterwards, this first man tells the woman that the bar owner is a friend of his, so that she knows for sure there is nothing she can do and no one is going to help her. If she has talked to him about trying to escape, then she is punished in front of the other girls. And if anyone hears any of the women talking about wanting to get out, then this punishment is repeated.'

Mara describes the process of breaking the women down in intimate detail. I already know some of the methods that she refers to: women being kept hungry and played off against each other and bribed with pittances of money compared to what they earn for their pimps every night they work. But she sits beside me calmly unravelling the cruellest details of surviving a brothel. She tells me stories that women from her refuge have told her once they felt safe enough to talk: about being forced to cook for a bar owner and his acolytes, and then watching the leftovers being fed to his dogs; about menus listing sex acts and prices that are offered to customers at the bar when they buy their drinks. One woman told Mara that she was instructed to remove her clothes and dance on a stage in the middle of a bar while the customers bayed. She spent the rest of the night in the bar completely naked.

Meanwhile local traders visit Bosnian bars and sell flimsy articles of clothing to trafficked women, who have to pay for these clothes out of the money they earn from their pimp.

'Even these traders sell their clothes at a profit, because they know the women have nowhere else to go to buy them. When a woman is trafficked, everyone makes money from her. I have been doing this work since 1998, and at the very beginning everybody in Bijeljina seemed to think this trafficking was an easy method of making money. Even my neighbours were involved! One of my neighbours, he opened a bar too, and he said that he was going to bring women in to get rich like everyone else. "What are you doing?" I said to him. "You can't just trade women to make money for yourself, like it is an ordinary business!" ' Mara suddenly leans towards me, cigarette clamped between her stained brown fingers. 'He was just being greedy and stupid. But his bar closed down quickly, because by then Milakovic had started to run his nightclubs.'

Milakovic. That name again. I still can't remember where I've heard him mentioned before, apart from Madeleine Rees's brief comment. But here he is again, and this time I pursue him: 'Who is he, Mara? Who is Milakovic?'

Mara runs her fingers through her coarse hair and crosses one knee over the other. 'Milakovic was a Bosnian businessman. He spent a long time expanding his business, which was trafficking women. He used to hold press conferences to promote his work.' She suddenly smiles. 'He used to say that he was going to invite me to these press conferences, because he saw me everywhere else that he went. So I came to one or two of them . . .'

'Press conferences!' I am confused by the notion of a trafficker conducting his own publicity stunts. 'Why did he hold press conferences?'

'Because he was proud of his business.'

Milorad Milakovic is a fifty-six-year-old Bosnian Serb. He's from a town in north-western Bosnia called Prijedor, about three hours' drive from Bijeljina. He worked as a radio operator and as manager of a touring dance company before opening three nightclubs in and around Prijedor: Sherwood Castle, Crazy Horse 1 and Crazy Horse 2. All three of them soon became notorious as brothels, which Milakovic ran in conjunction with his wife, Milka, and their two sons, Sasa and Slavisa. Milakovic had good regional business contacts, and young women were trafficked on request to Prijedor from Romania and Moldova. The Milakovic family became big fish in a small, toxic pond. Local men and foreigners frequented the clubs in droves, and Milakovic publicly bragged that immigration officials and IPTF officers were some of the best customers he had. The growing notoriety of his small empire eventually led to a raid on his clubs in November 2000.

The raid was carried out by a group of IPTF officers. They found thirty-seven Romanian, Moldovan and Ukrainian women confined inside the clubs, thirty-three of whom alleged that they had been trafficked. The women were removed from the nightclubs and taken to a Sarajevo safe house. One week later six of the IPTF officers who had been involved in the raid were repatriated home. One of the officers had admitted to having sex with at least one of the trafficked women, and directly implicated five of his colleagues. The six of them were from three different countries: the UK, America and Spain. They were never publicly identified, and as documented in the Human Rights Watch report on Bosnia, none of them is known to have been prosecuted back at home.

Milakovic, who always claimed that he was tipped off about the raid in advance and produced a fax to back up his public allegations, was never penalized for trafficking any of the women. He simply carried on running his nightclubs.

Several months after the IPTF raid Milakovic was promoted by local businessmen to head of the Bosnian Bar Owners' Association. He began holding press conferences and was a deliberate contrarian: sometimes he would arrive at a press conference with a young Eastern European woman who would say she was happy to work in one of his nightclubs. On other occasions he argued that there was nothing wrong with trafficking women to work as prostitutes. 'Is it a crime to sell women? Well, they

sell footballers, don't they?' Mara recalls him saying at one of his press
conferences. Some of these were actually broadcast on national Bosnian
TV.

Milakovic was on a roll, confident about his power and influence in
north-western Bosnia. He was a flamboyant host, famous for the trio of
Siberian tigers that he kept in a compound at the Sherwood Castle club.
He invited journalists to have lunch with him there, next to the swimming
pool.

Andrew Cockburn of *National Geographic* shared seafood salad and
steak with Milakovic in the spring of 2003. He recalled Milakovic
describing the expense of purchasing foreign women: 'The plane, transport, hotels along the way, as well as food; that girl must work to get that
money back.'

At the beginning of May 2003, a couple of months after Milakovic had
treated Cockburn to lunch at his brothel, there was an explosion in
Prijedor. A smouldering dispute between Milakovic and a group of
disenfranchised local businessmen had finally erupted, and the Prijedor
bowling alley was blown up, apparently as a warning from Milakovic to
his business opponents. Local residents complained en masse to the
mayor of the town that it was Milakovic who was actually running
Prijedor, and said they were frightened by the atmosphere of intimidation
and violence. The mayor, who had previously been dragged from his car
and beaten by local thugs associated with Milakovic, had obviously had
enough as well. He called in SFOR troops.

Once they heard that Milakovic had finally got hold of explosives,
SFOR soldiers raided the three Prijedor clubs. During this raid they
found nine foreign women locked in one of the Sherwood Castle rooms
and explicit evidence of an international trafficking network.

Milakovic kept a comprehensive filing system in the basement of
Sherwood Castle. The troops found a stash of Romanian and Moldovan
passports, plus several large trays of index cards complete with photographs, personal details and health certificates issued by nearby Doboj
Hospital. The certificates were health clearance for sexually transmitted
diseases, presumably to assure customers that the women they were
paying to have sex with were disease free. The certificates themselves
were genuine, but the examination details and signatures had all been
forged by a hospital technician.

Milakovic was arrested at Sherwood Castle and immediately taken into
custody. His wife and sons apparently had scarpered just before or during
the raid and had crossed the border to Serbia. Meanwhile the nine
women who had been released from the club were immediately taken to
Mara's refuge in Bijeljina. They were later transferred to a safe house in

Sarajevo, where detailed statements were taken about their experiences. They all left Bosnia and returned home to their own countries before Milakovic's trial, which was held at the beginning of 2004.

None of the women identified during the SFOR raid returned to testify against Milakovic. The reasons for this have never been clearly explained, though their collective absence did prevent any further specific allegations of the involvement of internationals or peacekeepers in Milakovic's business. Fortunately for the prosecution, a young Romanian woman, who had previously been trafficked to Prijedor by Milakovic, courageously agreed to be a witness. She had been trafficked while still a teenager and had been held in Prijedor for almost two years. Her contact details had been found on one of the Sherwood Castle index cards.

In Bosnia the maximum penalty for human trafficking is fourteen years. Milakovic had such a good Bosnian lawyer that he actually managed to secure a plea bargain. He agreed to plead guilty to international procurement of prostitutes, human trafficking and smuggling of persons, but he steadfastly refused to plead guilty to sexual slavery, claiming that although he had paid for women to be trafficked to Prijedor to work in his clubs, and despite them being heavily in debt to him for their travel and living expenses, they actually chose to work as prostitutes and could have left at any time if they had really wanted to. The women released from his nightclubs had all claimed otherwise. They did not allege physical violence but said that they were all extremely frightened of Milakovic and had been coerced into working at his clubs and having sexual intercourse with his customers.

The European Union Police Mission in Bosnia estimated that Milakovic trafficked approximately two hundred young Eastern European women into Bosnia. In April 2004 Milorad Milakovic was sentenced to nine years in prison. He is serving out his sentence in Banja Luka Prison near Prijedor. Although criticised as lenient by many local organisations, his sentence set a precedent in Bosnia as a penalty for human trafficking.

The man who prosecuted Milakovic, a Canadian international prosecutor named Jonathan Ratel, said the UN was uncooperative before and during the trial: 'If the UN had their way, there never would have been a prosecution in the first place. Milakovic would have spent three or four months in custody, he'd have got out, and then it would have been business as usual in Prijedor.'

The file on the Milakovic family is still open. Milakovic's wife, Milka, and their sons are still at large. Milka, who was known for her ferocious temper, is thought to be somewhere in Russia. Sasa and Slavisa are known to be living in Belgrade. International arrest warrants have been issued for all three of them, but the Serbian government has refused to extradite the two men.

The final missing link in this complex case concerns a set of five audio tapes that Milakovic used to claim he kept as personal insurance, allegedly because they contained recordings of international police officers and soldiers visiting his clubs and renting women. These video tapes, which were supposed to be used as evidence in the Milakovic trial, have never been recovered. They are rumoured to have been either lost or destroyed during the SFOR raid on Sherwood Castle.

Mara has her own experiences of being Milakovic's adversary. 'At one time, before Milakovic was arrested, things became so very serious,' she says, 'that I also had to call SFOR. I told them that Milakovic had been saying I was causing problems for him and his business, because I was speaking out about what was happening in Prijedor. I know that the SFOR went to see Milakovic, and they told him that if anything happened to me, then he would be responsible. And it helped me.'

She lifts up the coffee pot and swirls it gently, but it's obviously empty. She excuses herself and squeezes back out of the office. While she is gone, I sit thinking about what she's told me, and her sheer nerve in taking on this swaggering kingpin whilst living here, easily within his grasp. Even though Milakovic will be banged up for almost the next decade, I don't know where she finds the stomach to continue doing this work. Bijeljina is obviously infested with criminals, and she defiantly carries on sheltering the women they want to sell to each other.

Mara comes back with a fresh pot of coffee.

'Did things change here after Milakovic was jailed?' I ask her.

She raises her hands and flutters them slightly, up and down, imitating a pair of balancing scales. 'We thought that after Milakovic was gone, trafficking would be finished in this area. He was not the only one trafficking women, but his was the major business. But we were wrong. Trafficking has resumed again. Not like it was before, because now there are fewer soldiers in Bosnia, so there are fewer women being trafficked. Many of the bars are now closed. But women are still being brought over the border for the soldiers in Tuzla.'

'So fewer women are being brought into Bosnia because there are fewer soldiers based here?'

'Yes.'

'When women are trafficked here, where are they taken to?'

'There are several places. The Mlin bar is outside Tuzla, on the road up towards Bijeljina. Women are trafficked to the Mlin: it is a notorious place. The soldiers from the Eagle base can go there and pay for women. Women are also trafficked to Tuzla so that they can be kept in private apartments. Some of them are kept by individual soldiers, and some of them are kept in apartments for men to visit: foreigners, and local men as well.'

Mara tells me she recently drove down to the Eagle base camp and saw a queue of local taxis waiting nearby. 'This was just a few months ago. And I was puzzled, because I know that soldiers don't take taxis: they have these SUV vehicles. But the local people will not be using all these taxis either. They live in this village at the edge of Tuzla, and they have their own local transport. So I went into a small restaurant, and I asked one of the taxi drivers sitting there why there were so many taxis waiting outside the base.' Her voice is still slow and calm, almost mesmerising to listen to. 'He told me that they were waiting for American soldiers to come out of the base, to see if they wanted to have a woman. If they want to have a woman, the taxi driver will take them to a woman. The local people know what is happening. Everyone in Tuzla knows what is happening. It is not a secret any more. It is a very organised business.'

'Mara, are you afraid of the people who organise this business?' I ask her. She is still and silent for a moment.

'We still have problems,' she says obliquely. 'The difficulty is that although fewer women are being trafficked now, the trafficking is managed by just a few men, who are completely above the law. They are the bosses of this area, and they do not answer to the police or anybody else.'

I ask her, hesitantly, who these businessmen are, and she gives me a name that I write down. I had to ask her this, but even as I write the name down, I know I will probably be afraid to use it. I don't want to evoke the ire of the traffickers in Bijeljina, or to put Mara more at risk than she already is.

We sit smoking and drinking the remains of the second pot of coffee, and she tells me a story about a local crook who used to drive women across the border from Serbia.

'He was a Serbian Orthodox priest – that was why he had this name, Pope – and he was bringing women over the border in a minibus regularly. For a while the border guards just let him come over with these women and do his business. But eventually the police began to ask him questions, because he was always bringing these young women over and then returning without them. And of course, when they asked him, they found out that he did not know the women but was just transporting them for some businessman. They arrested him, and he tried to escape . . .' Mara begins to laugh and cough at the same time, hacking from deep in her throat. She extinguishes her cigarette gently in the overflowing ashtray. 'And so in the end they arrested him and searched him. They even took his crucifix from around his neck. And they found that it was a hollow crucifix, and inside was a Bosnian entry-visa stamp!'

The light is almost gone, and Mara switches on a lamp and yawns quietly. I know I'll have to spend the night here because Sarajevo is more than four hours' drive away, and there won't be a bus going back this late.

When I rang her to ask if we could meet, Mara offered to book a hotel room for me, which was kind of her, but means I'm going to have to spend the night alone in a local hotel.

My attention is wavering. On the table between us there is a glossy flyer. I pick it up and glance at the shiny photo.

'This is where you are staying,' says Mara.

The flyer is an advert for a place called Motel Neno. It looks perfectly fine in a bland sort of way. Mara is finishing off another cigarette. I glance over at her, and she smiles. I've noticed she smiles a lot, a slight smile that lifts and parts her dry, thin lips.

I have tremendous admiration for Mara, and feel ashamed of my first impression of her. I had hoped she would be young and feisty, and that we could spend the evening together in a bar drinking wine, and then I could crash on her couch for the night. I hadn't expected to be met at the bus station by a middle-aged woman in a two-piece suit, and had felt a wave of slight disappointment when I first realised that this was her. Now I know that she is a Titan, and I feel foolish and judgemental. I also feel weary from the inside out.

Mara starts to gather her belongings together and lights another cigarette at the same time. I've never seen anyone smoke with quite as much dedication.

'I was called to Motel Neno one night,' she says quite casually. 'A sixteen-year-old Romanian girl had been brought over by a trafficker, and he locked her in one of the hotel rooms while he negotiated her price outside with a pimp. She was worth a lot of money because she was a virgin and was very beautiful. But she broke the window and ran to reception for help, and they called me. They know me well at the hotel because we hold our meetings with other organisations there. I brought her to the refuge, and she was safe. Nothing had happened to her. She was lucky.'

I say nothing.

Mara glances at me and smiles again. 'Motel Neno is safe,' she says.

We drive over there together in weary companionable silence. Mara knows everyone who works at the hotel, and my room looks ordinary and feels secure. The door locks tightly. I offer to buy her a beer in the large bland bar, and while we're drinking and smoking, she tells me about her garden at home, which she obviously loves. She has a large vegetable patch and grows herbs and roses as well. 'In my garden it is my time to forget about trafficking,' she says.

There is a crowd sitting in some sort of conference room next door to the bar, and we can hear various people making speeches. They get louder and more appreciative of whatever's being said, and I can't understand a word of it. When I ask Mara what's going on, she tells me it is a conference about selling woollen blankets.

We both laugh out loud together. She leaves a little while later, telling me she will collect me in the morning and take me to the bus station.

After a bowl of luke-warm soup I retire to my room, with another bottle of beer.

The next morning Mara arrives to collect me.

'Did you meet the hotel owner?' she asks me.

'No. I don't know who she is.'

Mara lights up. So do I.

'Her husband originally built this hotel,' she says. 'It was in 1998. But he ran out of money before the hotel was completely finished, and he had to borrow the rest of the money. It was a few local businessmen who lent him the money to finish it. Afterwards, he offered to pay them back as soon as he had guests paying for the rooms. But they didn't want the money back, they told him. They wanted him to do them some favour. But he didn't want to do this favour for them. So they murdered him. And now his wife runs the hotel.'

I have never been to a place like Bijeljina before. It feels infested with criminals, traffickers and murderers. I just want to get to the bus station and get out. I don't feel safe here, and I am not going to come back.

'Mara, how do you stay here?' I can hear my own voice sounding faintly shrill.

'I am used to living here,' she says calmly. 'I am from Tuzla and I know many people here. If I don't stay, the shelter will close, and then the women won't have anywhere else to go.' She stands up, ready to drive me to the bus station. 'Someone has to watch what is happening here,' she says.

Chapter 7

The Short Life of Olena Popik

An hour out of Bijeljina the bus trundles past a large signpost on the right-hand side of the road. It says, 'Mlin'. I immediately look right, and grimace. The bar is at the end of what looks like a short private driveway. It is a large mock-Disney palace, complete with half a dozen high turrets and a grand front entrance. The whole façade has been bleached white, and it looks so utterly surreal I half-expect it to rise above the trees and float away like an apparition. When Mara told me about the Mlin bar being on the road between Bijeljina and Tuzla, I presumed she meant it was actually tucked away in a glade or concealed at the end of a long circuitous dirt track, not brazenly touting for business within sight of the road. This is a quiet rural area that we are driving through, with just a few settlements of compact wooden houses and the odd petrol station cum café sustaining the traffic. Farmers are making hay and ploughing their fields. Everything that we pass by has been tinged with the coppery hues of autumn, except this hideous white showpiece.

I would like to see for myself what goes on inside this brothel, but Mara is already an hour away, and there is no way I would venture into the Mlin alone at night. That really would be stupid.

Back in Sarajevo, I find out that while I've been up north visiting Mara a young Ukrainian woman has died in Mostar, southern Bosnia. She is, or rather was, twenty-one.

Olena Popik is national news. Every newspaper-stand I pass has her name and photograph on the front page of its papers. Her death is being discussed on TV and broadcast on Sarajevo radio stations. The details I manage to glean about her are basic: apparently she had been trafficked to Mostar and died of AIDS in the town hospital a few days ago. I telephone Madeleine Rees to ask her what she knows.

'We are still waiting for final details from Mostar,' she says, 'but Olena was definitely trafficked. She had been bought and sold and pimped across the Balkans for almost three years. There she was, lying in a flat dying of AIDS, and those bastards were still renting her out to locals for sex.' Madeleine's voice is full of righteous anger. She is friendly but brisk on the phone, and it's clear she doesn't have much time to talk.

I try to find out more on the Internet, but I cannot find anything in the international press at all. It suddenly strikes me that the trafficking of a woman like Olena Popik to a country like Bosnia is not an international news story. She is just another tragic statistic of trafficking within the Balkans. Women like her are the collateral damage of regional poverty, crime and corruption.

On the surface Bosnia has undergone a transformation since the civil war I've heard referred to as 'our local world war' ended almost ten years ago. Now there is a rotating tripartite system of government in place, representing the three main ethnicities; roads have been rebuilt, buildings restructured and people have had some time to heal from the horrors they lived through. Bosnia now has a flourishing café society, a fledgling tourist industry, and a famously low rate of street crime, because people are sick to the stomach of crime. By all accounts I am safer walking through Sarajevo at night than at home in Edinburgh. I feel perfectly safe in Sarajevo, though Bijeljina gave me the creeps. But after meeting Madeleine and Mara, and hearing these headlines about the death of Olena Popik, it feels like another war is still being fought here; a war against women, who are trafficked from one place to the next like cargo, and traded like stock; the price for each calculated according to how much profit can be extracted from her afterwards. This war is being fought with different weapons, against women who are desperate to migrate in order to earn money and accumulate hope for their future and for the future of their children.

They take risks, these women, sometimes terrible risks, because they believe there is no other way of getting into the lucrative markets of Western Europe. They make hard decisions about what they are pre-pared to do, decisions which someone like me is never going to have to make. Maybe that's why news stories about women from the Balkans being 'tricked' into prostitution, and having to 'service' clients every night make me feel so apoplectic. It implies trafficking is some sort of a ruse that only a really dumb peasant girl could fall for, or be tricked into. Olga and Anna were not dumb peasant girls. They were maybe naïve, and certainly desperate; but there was no trickery involved in what happened to them. They were sold and raped and battered and used. I don't know what happened to Olena Popik, but whatever happened at the begin-ning, in the end it killed her. Liliana Gorceag, the psychologist who accompanied Olga when I met her in Chisinau, described the trafficking of women from her country in two unforgettable words. She called it 'slow genocide'.

There must be some trafficked women who escape their pimps and either return home alone or in small groups, or else manage to make a new life for themselves in a place where they cannot be traced. It is impossible to estimate how many survivors of trafficking may be scattered across Europe. I deliberately veer on the side of optimism and hope there are thousands of them, though I have no evidence whatsoever this is the case. But I have learned that trafficked women endure the unendurable. There has to be the possibility of escape for at least some of them before they are completely broken. However, there are no possibilities left for Olena Popik.

Mostar is a three-hour drive from Sarajevo. I decide to take a bus there, to see whether I can find out any more about the death of this woman, in spite of the part of me that is weary and overloaded and doesn't want to go at all.

It is mid-November, but the weather is still very mild. In Mostar there are still tourists snapping photos of each other on the new Stari Most Bridge, which spans the banks of the Neretva river flowing through Mostar. Stari Most means 'Old Bridge', and the original old bridge was built in the mid-sixteenth century. It united Mostar for more than four hundred years before being destroyed in 1993 by Bosnian Croats during the war. This new version of the Stari Most was completed just a few months ago. It provides a veneer of unison in a city that remains politically divided between the Muslims of the east bank and the Croats of the west bank.

I cross the smooth new bridge and wander through the gorgeous cobbled old town in the west-bank quarter, wondering how to make contact with any local women who might have met Olena Popik before she died.

These days the old town centre is besieged not by soldiers and militia but souvenir stalls and tourist cafés. Every keyring, plate, tea towel, postcard, T-shirt and watercolour painting is emblazoned with the arc of the Stari Most.

Towards the end of the main pedestrian drag, I pass by a bookshop called Buybook. I know this shop will sell Bosnian- and English-language books because there's a franchise of the same chain in Sarajevo. As the bookseller will probably speak English, I can ask for information in there. It has an Internet café too, which is always a good plan B.

The man behind the counter at Buybook has fine brown hair that flops over his eyes, and is very friendly. But I feel wary of asking him directly about Olena Popik, so I just enquire whether he knows of any local women's organisations. The question doesn't seem to faze him at all.

'No, I don't. But I will try to help you, wait a moment.' He picks up the phone and calls someone while I wander round the shop looking at books of black-and-white Mostar photographs, including the magnetising image of young boys joyfully plunging from the old Stari Most into the Neretva. People still pay these local boys to jump, and in summer crowds spontaneously gather on both sides of the bridge to gasp and applaud. I am so taken with these photographs that when the bookseller calls me over I'm startled by the loud sound of his voice. He is clasping the telephone, obviously mid-conversation.

'There is one international women's organisation called La Strada who have an office here. You can meet with their director, Fadila Hadzic, in two days. She is very busy right now, because of this case of Olena Popik. Is that what you want to talk with her about?'

His face is open and curious. I find myself smiling at him warmly. So much for my reticence.

'Yes, I do want to talk to her about Olena Popik.'

He nods, finishes his phone conversation, scribbles down an address and gives me directions to the La Strada office. When I thank him profusely for saving me so much work, he begins to blush at the neck, and then I feel tongue-tied and shy for a moment. These small acts of kindness mean an awful lot when I am alone in someone else's country. We stand at either side of the counter in fumbling silence for a minute.

'Terrible,' he says suddenly. 'What they did to her was terrible.'

I remain silent, waiting to see if he'll continue, but he doesn't say anything else, just gently presses the paper with the La Strada address scribbled on it into my hand.

On 2 November Fadila Hadzic was at a local restaurant, celebrating her birthday with her family, when someone from the Mostar La Strada office called her mobile to say she was needed at the hospital.

'We had heard some rumours before about a young Ukrainian woman who was being shared between several pimps. I did not have any details, but I told the police what I had heard, and so when Olena was brought to the hospital, the police called us.'

'Did you see her at the hospital?'

'Yes.' She nods. 'I saw Olena just a few hours before she died. One of the traffickers had dumped her at the front door of the hospital at three o'clock in the afternoon. He drove off without saying anything to anyone. As soon as the hospital staff found Olena, they knew that she was very ill.

They put her into an isolation ward because they were afraid of contamination. But I was allowed to go inside and speak to her for a few minutes.'

'Could she speak? What did she say to you?'

'She only said a few words to me. She knew that she was dying.' Fadila sighs wearily, her chest wheezing slightly as she exhales. 'Olena was young and she was very frightened. But they couldn't do anything for her: her body had been completely ruined by disease. She had AIDS, hepatitis C, syphilis and tuberculosis. It was like every part of her had shrivelled up. Even her skull was tiny, and most of her hair had already fallen out. The public prosecutor had been called too, and he wanted to try to take a statement from her. But she was much too sick for that. I wasn't with her for very long after he left. The nurses had to attend to her, so I left her with them. It was a terrible way for her to finish her life.' Fadila's voice doesn't break, but she tells me all this with a leaden sadness. 'There was a policeman guarding the door of her room because we knew she had been trafficked and used, and she still needed protection from them. She died at eight o'clock that night.'

Fadila tells me what else she knows about the short life of Olena Popik. Olena was from a village or town somewhere near Krivoy Rog, in the south-east of the Ukraine. When she left the Ukraine she was nineteen and apparently already had two young children, who now live with her mother and sister. Fadila doesn't know if Olena was trafficked straight out of Ukraine, which seems likely given her age and the fact that she came from a country renowned for the trafficking of its young women, but she may also have left on her own to search for work.

Her journey has been tracked by her passport, which travelled with her throughout the Balkans and appears to be a genuine Ukrainian passport. No one knows whether she was allowed to keep her own passport, though it was with her when she was dumped at the hospital.

'We know from her passport that she travelled from the Ukraine to Hungary, and from there to Belgrade and then Slovenia,' says Fadila. 'We think that she was sold to a bar in a Slovenian town called Celje, and from there she was trafficked to Imotski in Croatia. There have been newspaper reports about her in both these countries, because she died of AIDS. Olena had many clients. Before she was brought to Mostar, she had also been sold through bars in the north of Bosnia, and she was in the town of Zenica, and then in Sarajevo too.

'We think she was brought here to Mostar by another Ukrainian, a woman who paid for her in northern Bosnia and sold her to a local pimp. Olena was already sick with AIDS so the woman sold her for a cheap price. The pimp who bought her kept her in an apartment in the south of

Mostar. She was here for six months before she died, and during that time he rented her out to clients, and he sometimes allowed other pimps to rent her out. He also delivered her to birthday parties as a "present" and she had to have sex with the men at these private parties.'

'A woman from her own country sold her?' It immediately makes me think of mercenaries during wartime: logic at its most brutal application. A knock-off price for a sick trafficked woman, because the conditions are so rough she'll die on the job anyway.

Fadila nods without speaking. She is rotund and soft-looking. I can picture her as the matriarch of a large, boisterous family. But she looks drained right now and has already told me this is her fourth meeting of the day. The short life of Olena Popik has temporarily taken over her own.

Fadila tells me that Olena was forced to continue working even when she became very weak. She was apparently addicted to some sort of narcotic, which meant she could endure long hours of work, yet put even more strain on her ravaged immune system. As she became sicker and weaker the price for having sex with her dropped.

'In the end, just before she came to hospital, she was having sex with very young men,' says Fadila. 'They could afford to have sex with her because it was so cheap, and no one else wanted to. It was costing them just a few KM to abuse a dying woman.'[1]

Since Olena died, there have been appeals on Bosnian TV and in newspapers for the men who had sex with her to volunteer for HIV tests. Fadila thinks many of them are too scared of being publicly identified to come forward. 'They don't want the shame of being in the paper,' she says, her voice sounding blank. She calls through to the office next door for more coffee for both of us, but I think I need to go soon and leave her in quiet if not peace.

Fadila has a cardboard folder in front of her. She opens it and pushes two photocopied photographs across the table towards me. They are both of Olena. The first is a grainy newspaper photograph: I've seen it before, on the Sarajevo news-stands. Olena is on her knees and bending backwards, arching her back. There is a lap-dancing pole just behind her; she's wearing underwear or a bikini and is obviously in a nightclub. You can't actually see her face, but her body looks strong and supple. I haven't seen the other photograph before. It looks like a passport photo: artificially lit with no discernible background. Olena Popik stares out. Her hair is a long, dark-brown mane. Her mouth has been painted such a hard red it looks varnished. And her eyes are fixed on whoever is standing in front of her taking the photograph, as if daring them to pity her.

1. The Bosnian currency is the konvertible mark, or KM.

We both look at the photographs without speaking, and when I slowly pass them across the table to her, she returns them to the folder labelled in black marker with the name Olena Popik. It is almost empty.

We sit back and smile quietly at each other, and during our silence my eyes drift slowly around the room. There are eye-catching campaign posters on the walls, a computer hums from one corner, and the desk is strewn with papers and leaflets. This is a hive of activity.

Fadila stands up stiffly, reaches over to the desk and hands one of the leaflets to me. La Strada, it says, is a network of nine independent human rights NGOs, with offices across Eastern Europe and headquarters in the Netherlands. It aims to 'Prevent trafficking in human beings, especially women in central and Eastern Europe. The primary goal is to improve the position of women and to promote their universal rights, including the right to choose to emigrate and to work abroad and to protect them from violence and abuse.'[2]

The team who run this La Strada office between them also have a small refuge for trafficked women and operate a hotline phone number that women can call for help.

Fadila is being patient and courteous, but I think she has told me as much as she knows. No one has been arrested in connection with Olena's death: the case is wide open, and a police investigation has started. But there is one earlier detail that I need to clarify.

'Fadila, why do you think the trafficker brought Olena to the hospital?' I ask her. I can't figure out why a pimp callous enough to work a woman almost to death would take her to hospital at the last moment. 'I thought he would have just left her to die in the flat or abandoned her on the street,' I say.

Fadila sits forward and clasps her hands in front of her on the table. She looks at me as though surprised by my naïvety. 'It is simple,' she replies. 'If he had not brought her to the hospital, then he would be held responsible for her death.'

2. www.un.org/womenwatch.

Chapter 8

The Useful
Women of Albania

When I return home to Scotland, life resumes its daily pace. But the women I've spoken to in Moldova and Bosnia linger in my mind: I remember the way Olga fiddled with her glasses case when she was sitting in the IOM meeting room, Mara's stoic defiance, and the resigned expression on the face of Anna, stranded back home in her village after being trafficked to Albania.

I particularly remember Anna's descriptions of Albania: its chaos, violence and seeming lawlessness. From recent reports in the British press ('Albanian Mafia Steps Up People Smuggling', 'Sex Trade Gang-master Jailed for 11 Years', 'Slaves in Soho'), it sounds as though Albanian gangs are taking control of the British commercial sex industry: trafficking women from all over Eastern Europe, including their own country, into Central London. My plan is to visit the 'major sending countries' first, to find out as much as I can about how people are recruited and transported, and then follow that up by examining what happens once they actually arrive in 'destination countries' like the UK. In light of the almost pathological reputation Albanians have earned for running organised crime syndicates, it feels impossible to write a book about human trafficking in Europe without visiting Albania.

This, I promise myself, will be my final trip to the Balkans because then I will have traced one of the major routes from Moldova to Western Europe, and I won't need to return to this part of the world. Even though I honestly felt safer walking around Sarajevo at night than I do in Edinburgh, I never totally relax in the Balkans.

Meeting Mara Radovanovic convinced me that local organisations have their ears closest to the ground. However, I have no Albanian contacts at all. I call Amnesty International to see whether they have any suggestions. Sian Jones, who works on the Balkans team, is generous with her information: she offers me a number of leads, including an Albanian woman living in Brighton who has an MSc in migration studies from the University of Sussex.

When I track down Julie Vullnetari and explain what I'm doing, she tells me she is returning to Albania in a few weeks' time and will be spending the next few months with her family in their village in south-eastern Albania. She is about to start her PhD and is doing part of her initial research in the area where she grew up.

'If you would like to come and stay in the village with my family, then you are very welcome. Our village is very near the Greek border, and there are migrants crossing back and forth over the mountains. I've also done some research on trafficking, so we have plenty to talk about!'

'Thank you. That would be great.'

I'm startled by this immediate open invitation. I've never even spoken to this woman before, but it feels like the decision to visit Albania has just been taken out of my own hands. I know I can't afford to turn this invitation down. I arrange to stay in touch with Julie via email and to call her when I arrive in Tirana.

A week later a friend of a friend introduces me to an Albanian woman who lives just a few streets away from me. Alma, who is from Tirana, married a Scots musician and has settled over here. She has a host of contacts back at home and puts me in touch with a local women's NGO called 'Useful to Albanian Women', who have an apartment above their Tirana office where I can stay as a paying guest before visiting Julie Vullnetari and her family.

Alma also emails her friends in Tirana, who immediately offer to take me out on the town. This trip somehow seems to sort itself out without me doing very much at all.

Albania has just over three million inhabitants, though almost another two million ethnic Albanians live in bordering Kosovo and Macedonia. It secured independence from the Ottoman Empire in 1912, but through-out its first thirty years as a fledgling sovereign state was invaded and occupied by all of its neighbours, including Italy. Germany also invaded during the Second World War. The Albanian Communist Party, which took over in 1944, was led by Prime Minister Enver Hoxha, who con-trolled and isolated the country for forty years. Hoxha died in 1985, but his cronies clasped on to power until the beginning of 1991, when anarchic student-inspired strikes finally forced multi-party elections and effectively opened Albania to the outside world. Six years later, in 1997, the country erupted into a brief, brutal civil war after the devastating collapse of ill-advised pyramid investment schemes, which bankrupted hundreds of thousands of people who were already struggling to sustain themselves. International peacekeepers were drafted to Albania, and political stability gradually resumed in 1998.[1] Slightly wealthier than Moldova, Albania is still classed as one of the poorest countries in Europe'. Transparency International, who rate countries in terms of corruption, has no chapter on Albania, as it has been unable to 'identify a sufficiently broad-based impartial network'.[2]

Alongside evolving as a fledgling democracy, Albania rapidly also became notorious for systematic corruption and organised crime, both of which have gone from strength to strength. One theory about the rise of the so-called Albanian Mafia is that mass arrivals of ethnic Albanian refugees (including Kosovans) in Italy at the beginning of the 1990s led to Italian Mafia members employing young itinerant Albanian males as criminal cannon fodder and literally training them on the job. As Angelo Loconte from the Brindisi Serious Crime Unit famously commented, 'The Italians were the brains, and the Albanians became their hands.'[3]

Some of the first wave of Albanians to seek sanctuary in Italy were convicts who had either just been released or broken out of Albanian jails, as well as thousands of Kosovan men who had been brutalised and bullied by the hardline nationalist regime of Slobodan Milosevic.

Albanian criminals have also been very strongly linked with the Italian Mafia in the US, have carved out their own substantial portion of business in the States and, like the Cosa Nostra, their success has been credited to an intricate code of honour and almost impenetrable family networks. Albanians traditionally adhere to the law of Kanun, a sacred code of ethics that hinges on *besa*, or word of honour. In some parts of northern Albania crimes are still avenged through Kanun codes, with families murdering each other in 'blood revenge' if honour has been violated. They also have the distinct advantage of a language that most other people don't speak or understand.

Albanian criminals (who originally looted their arms from former government stockpiles) have cultivated a reputation for extreme violence, pose a serious challenge to both Italian and Turkish Mafia groups and now apparently control a substantial portion of the heroin trade from Asia into Western Europe. They trade weapons and are also brutally efficient traffickers of humans, including their own people. You cannot put an exact figure on trafficking rates in Albania, or anywhere else for that matter, but the UN estimates that between 1991 and 2001 approximately one hundred thousand men, women and children were

1. *Albania: the Bradt Travel Guide*, Gillian Gloyer, Bradt Travel Guides, August 2004.
2. 'Albania: State of the Nation', International Crisis Group Balkan report, 2003, no. 140.
3. www.balkanspeace.org.

trafficked from Albania to other Balkan countries and to Western Europe.[4]

Gus Xhudo, a criminologist at the University of Pittsburgh, has written extensively about the rise of organised crime in Albania. In his analysis: 'Once scattered, disorganised and working for others, the Albanians have, in the last five to ten years, moved into independent operations, established a vast network of mules and troubleshooters throughout Western Europe, coordinated activity with supportive émigré communities and managed to consolidate their operations on both sides of the Atlantic.'[5]

It is mid-March 2005 when I fly from London to Tirana. The Useful Albanian Women have kindly arranged to collect me at Rinas Airport. When I walk into the arrivals hall, two of them are holding up a large banner with my name scrawled on it. I feel bashful, and totally charmed.

Several years ago the Mayor of Tirana, Edi Rama, who is also a professional artist, decided to give his city a facelift. The result is a kaleidoscope of spirals, rainbows, waves and stripes painted across the front and sides of many city-centre buildings, some of them seven storeys high. The paint still looks fresh now, and these eclectic murals brighten the whole centre of Tirana. The roads, in contrast, are diabolical. The tarmac is wracked with potholes and craters, and that's on the good stretches. Many streets look as though they've been disembowelled. We drive along several side streets where rubble is just piled up against the pavements, and the car has to manoeuvre its way through slowly, tilting us from one side of the back seat to the other.

The Useful Albanian Women have their (unpainted) building on a dusty backstreet just off a central boulevard called Kavajes. It's quite a lovely place: there is a community café in a vine-covered courtyard, with a drop-in centre next door, the offices upstairs and, above the offices, a guest suite where I am staying.

The director of the Useful Women is Sevim Arbana, a handsome blonde, with a rather fierce look in her eyes.

'We can't talk here in my office, it's too damn busy!' she exclaims when I ask if we can meet to discuss her work. 'Tomorrow morning we'll go out, for coffee.' I quickly realise that Albanians are as dedicated to caffeine and nicotine as the Bosnians. They like their coffee strong and their lungs black in the Balkans.

---

4. 'Safe for Whom?', Asylumaid, June 2004, p. 61.
5. 'Men of Purpose: the Growth of Albanian Criminal Activity', 1996.

*

The next morning Sevim takes me to the Sky Tower; it's one of those glassy modern structures that have become symbols of affluence in numerous capitals, and hence look totally ubiquitous. The lift glides silently up a transparent shaft, and we perch in an open-air café above Tirana. The view, which stretches to the pale, glinting edge of the Adriatic, is quite magnificent.

While we're waiting for our cappuccinos to arrive, I ask Sevim about the recent history of trafficking in Albania and the current status quo.

'We still have trafficking in Albania, no doubt about it,' she says. 'But not like it was before. Trafficking was very big business in this country from 1993 until 2000. During that time there were huge numbers of young women being reported as trafficked. Albanian women were being taken to Italy, and women from other Eastern European countries were also being trafficked through Albania and forced to work in the Italian sex industry.

'We set up our organisation in 1996 to assist local women, and at the end of the 1990s we wrote the first national survey about this trafficking and sex-work phenomenon. We identified three groups of Albanian women who were most vulnerable to being trafficked: poor rural women including Roma and other minorities, waitresses and girls working in clubs or bars who were already being sexually exploited by their bosses, and university students who were away from home and needed to earn money.

'During this whole period we had very serious economic problems in Albania. And from the beginning of our work, we told the international donors that it is not enough just to campaign against trafficking and open shelters for women when they are deported back from Italy. You have to address the issues underneath. If you want to address trafficking, then look at our opportunities to migrate. Women are trafficked from Albania because they are desperate to leave in the first place!

'We have done anti-trafficking campaigns in my organisation: warning girls and women about the dangers of wanting to work abroad, or having a boyfriend who says he is going to take you to Italy to get married and have a wonderful life. But' – Sevim leans forward across the table to emphasise her point – 'if all we are doing is warning women not to leave, then I don't believe in these campaigns, and anyway, they will never work. If we don't give them reasons to stay in Albania, then of course they will try to leave! Some of them are trafficked. But the other reality is that if women are living here in poverty and they have nothing, then they will sell the only thing they can make money from: their own bodies.'

This isn't what I expected to hear at all. I thought Sevim would talk about a continuing trafficking crisis in Albania. But she's worked as director of the Useful Women for nine years, and as we sit at the top of the Sky Tower, she reiterates her belief that the number of foreign women being trafficked into Albania has reduced, and chronic poverty is meanwhile continuing to coerce local women into domestic and international sex work.

In 2001 Daniel Renton wrote an extensive report for Save the Children on child trafficking in Albania, which also examined the trafficking of young Albanian women.

> Albania has been a major source country for the trafficking of women and children since the collapse of Communism in 1991. It is estimated that there are thirty thousand Albanian prostitutes abroad [. . .] However, the picture is a complicated one. There is a steady rise in emigration for voluntary prostitution abroad in order to escape poverty and bleak futures in Albania. It is difficult to determine who leaves willingly and who is forced to leave for prostitution. But according to Italian NGOs, many Albanian voluntary prostitutes are unprepared for the harsh reality awaiting them, and often end up being trafficked, exploited and victimised when abroad.[6]

According to UNICEF, this trend of prostitution due to chronic poverty has also expanded the domestic sex industry in Albania. In its most recent report on 'Trafficking in Human Beings in South-Eastern Europe', the agency observed that:

> In 2003 there was more information, and more cases of internally trafficked women, some of them under eighteen, than in previous years. There appears to be a growing internal prostitution market, and more local women are engaged in prostitution, replacing the former trend for women to be sexually exploited in Albania on their way to Western Europe.[7]

Sevim tells me her organisation used to run a refuge for Albanian women who had been trafficked abroad. 'We are negotiating opening a new shelter with a Greek NGO for women who have been trafficked over there. But now I am clear that I do not want to be involved in any refuge if the women are not allowed to run it themselves. We can support them, but it has to be their project. Otherwise, we are just taking money from the donors to keep the victims in refuges. And we have to offer them

---

6. 'Child Trafficking in Albania', Daniel Renton, Save the Children report, 2001.
7. 'Trafficking in Human Beings in South-Eastern Europe', UNICEF, March 2005.

training programmes for professional jobs, so they can help themselves and have a future: otherwise, these refuges are just bullshit.'

She looks at me sharply. 'For many internationals, anti-trafficking work is a very lucrative business. These big organisations have been working on this problem for the last ten years – and tell me, what has changed?'

I want to find out whether resident international organisations agree with Sevim. I call the Tirana IOM office and arrange a meeting with their counter-trafficking programme officer, a friendly American woman called Ruth Rosenberg. She tells me she arrived in Tirana just a few months ago, though the IOM itself has been here for the last seven years. She and I and her Albanian colleague Silvana talk in Ruth's tiny oblong office on the second floor.

'The patterns of trafficking have definitely changed here in the last couple of years, and we are aware that not so many foreign women are being trafficked into and through Albania,' says Ruth. 'It's partly because it's now easier to reach Western Europe direct from Romania. Romanians no longer need a Schengen visa to enter the EU. But it's also because Albania has better border controls, and this in turn has affected the routes traffickers use in and out of Albania. People are now trafficked through Macedonia into Greece, or else through the north of Albania, via Kukes and then up to Kosovo. The most organised networks, though, secure the right papers or have good forged documents, and they just take women straight through Rinas Airport.'

Ruth does not agree that fewer Albanian women are being trafficked and tells me the majority of IOM 'beneficiaries' (trafficked women assisted by the organisation) are young Albanian women who've been trafficked abroad, usually to Italy or Greece, though the IOM has also seen an increase in women being trafficked within Albania itself, which is classed as 'internal trafficking'. They believe the main recruitment method is fake marriage proposals from Albanian men. IOM helps fund a reintegration centre where women can be sheltered, supported and receive training for work when they are ready.

'Our centre is full, and we are assisting more women at the moment, not less,' she says.

Thinking of Sevim's comment about training, I ask Ruth what sort of work Albanian women are offered at the reintegration centre. She says there are several different options: English-language training, hairdressing or dairy production.

'For a lot of women, though, it's difficult to hold down an apartment and manage even a fairly menial job after what they've been through.

Many of the women do end up sharing a subsidised apartment between them and working in the local shoe factory.'

'The local shoe factory?' I try not to sound sarcastic as I repeat those four words back to her. 'Doesn't that just put them right back in the same menial existence that drove them out of Albania in the first place?'

'Not all Albanians want to leave this country,' comments her colleague Silvana. 'Many people have close families and communities here. I certainly don't want to leave Albania.'

'Silvana, how much do you earn a month?' I can't help asking her this. Maybe this is a cheap shot, but I'm taken aback about the shoe factory and want to make my point now.

Silvana glances at me silently. She looks pissed off and does not reply.

'You work for an international organisation,' I say, stating the absolutely obvious, 'and no doubt you make a good salary. Of course you don't want to leave. But a lot of other Albanians do. Isn't that why women are trafficked in the first place?'

Trafficking is a minefield. When I first started thinking about this book, I thought finding research material would be a major hurdle: how wrong I was. There are so many organisations producing so much material – analysis, thematic papers, information packs, annual reports, etc. – that it is impossible to keep up with it all. It's not in the least surprising that organisations have diverse views about human trafficking. Every organisation has its own agenda: local NGOs have sound local knowledge, and maybe also want to assure investors and donors that they're doing their work properly and the situation has improved; international organisations are wealthier, far less constrained by local corruption and politics, but motivated by international (i.e. Western European) agendas, and may be ignorant, or oblivious, to underlying local dynamics. What you excavate on a research trip depends almost entirely on with whom you choose to speak, and I don't speak Albanian, which limits me even more. I remember the confusion I felt in Kosovo, trying to work out what was actually happening, as opposed to the views being expressed to me by people with their own vested interests. How in hell can I expect to unravel what is happening here in just two weeks? At best this is educated guesswork on my part.

Ruth Rosenberg did not have any recent IOM statistics to hand but has graciously agreed to send me the figures the organisation has most recently collated on trafficking, which may add clarity, or confusion, to my attempts at understanding trafficking in Albania. In the meantime I decide to call a couple of Alma's friends in Tirana, and Julie Vullnetari in her village. Maybe once I am out of the city things will become more illuminated.

Alma's friends invite me to join them for a drink that evening. Then I call Julie on her mobile.

'We are expecting you,' she says, her voice echoing down the line. 'Take the bus to Korca tomorrow, and I'll meet you there and bring you to the village.'

The public bus is basic. It has lumpy seats and dirty windows. The journey south-east to the town of Korca is beautiful, though. Once beyond the battered suburbs of Tirana, we drive south through rugged mountains that eventually lead down towards the shining waters of Lake Ohrid. The lake is a part of the long border snaking between Albania and Macedonia. It's one of the trafficking routes in and out of Albania that Ruth mentioned. Snow-capped mountains glint across the water.

I have a seat to myself and am perfectly content to sit and stare out of the streaked windows for the six hours or so it takes to reach Korca. En route we pass dozens of wooden villages and small towns. Just beyond one of these settlements, a young woman stands alone at the side of the empty road. Her skirt is short and her hair dyed violent yellow. She sneers at the bus.

I only know our bus has actually arrived in Korca when the driver pulls in at another bus station, and this time everybody gets off and no one gets back on.

I clamber down the steps into brilliant sunshine, and the first thing I see in front of me is a man strolling down the street with a large brown bear. I stand next to the bus, staring. I am aware my mouth is slightly open. The man is dressed in a brown suit with breeches and knee-high laced-up boots, his bear ambling alongside him, tethered by a lead. I can't take my eyes off them.

'Hello. Are you Louisa?'

A small woman with pale skin and thick tresses of flame-coloured hair is standing beside me, smiling enquiringly.

'Just look at that,' I say, gesturing at the bear, still mesmerised. A second later I realise who she is, and smile apologetically. 'Sorry! You must be Julie.'

She follows my gaze. 'He's Roma. His bear is his business. People pay to have their photos taken with him, or maybe he makes the bear dance for them. By the time he has beaten and trained the animal, it's hardly a bear at all.'

*

Julie and I take a small local bus a few miles, to the point where her village, called Cangonj, meets the road. This region, she tells me, is called Devoll. As we wander up the hill to her house, she explains that she lived here until she was eighteen. 'Now my father lives here with his mother, his second wife and my little brother.'

Ahead of us, Cangonj is wrapped around the hillside in tight terraces interspersed with twisting, narrow mud lanes. Hens peck in fenced yards, while dogs and children roam. There is a main street, with a few half-empty shops, a local bar where the men drink in the evenings, and a large, empty-looking school. A mosque stands alone on the opposite hillside, its silver crescent reflecting shards of sunlight.

I stay with Julie and her family for five days. They are all very kind to me, though I can exchange only the most basic of Albanian pleasantries with them. Her little brother is learning English but is too shy to say more than a breathy 'Hellohowareyou?'.

Julie's father, a large, solid man with thick, dry hands, has recently retired and spends his days pottering around the house, doing minor repairs and planting vegetables in the garden, which looks out across the small valley. His wife tends to Granny, who is clad from head to foot in widow's black and almost bed-ridden, but smiles and laughs aloud in company and sings quietly to herself when she is alone.

Over the next few days Julie and I drink coffee, wander around the village, sit on the front steps of her house and talk a lot. We take our time, exchanging life stories and political opinions. We talk about our travels, our love lives, Albania, England and Scotland. She is an intense and friendly woman who has lived abroad for a long time but comes back to Albania at least once a year, and has done so ever since she first left, back in 1989.

Julie is a 'regular migrant'. She studied in Romania and Holland before moving to Brighton. After finishing her MSc at the University of Sussex, she's now just about to start researching her PhD on 'the dynamics between internal and international migration in Albania'.

She and I are sitting in the garden. I am in the sun, and she's deliberately in the shade, as her skin burns easily. She's explaining her work to me.

'My PhD is about why people choose to migrate within or out with their own country: for instance why people choose to move to Tirana or else decide to cross the border and work in Greece.

'My own experience as a migrant and part of this community is that people want to leave as they don't believe they have a future here. Almost half the population of Albania still works on the land. Their income is totally dependent on the usual climatic conditions, and people often still plough their fields with horses and donkeys. You'll see, when we go out of the village. The easiest crop to produce is wheat, but it's just a subsistence crop. In this region the soil is fertile, and you can also grow apples, potatoes and tomatoes and sell your excess at local markets. But since we joined the World Trade Organisation in 2000, there has been no customs tax levied on imported food, and we've been flooded with cheap food from Macedonia. So rural communities are struggling, and young people are leaving. Life in Devoll is actually not so hard: we have one of the highest standards of living in Albania, and people are not starving here. But even so, one in four adults has migrated either to the city or abroad. And if they go abroad, it's often without documents, because there are very few other options. Migrants want to work, and their remittances keep communities alive, and the money goes directly into the local economy.' She glances upwards. 'Look at my house. We have cable TV and a washing machine, all from my migrant remittances.'

Remittances from Albanian migrants currently make up more than 20 per cent of GDP. According to the World Bank, Albanian emigrants send back more than $500 million a year.[8]

'Migration is a continuum: the very poorest and very richest people often stay at home. The very poorest can't afford to leave, and the very richest don't want to, because they're doing very well!' She smiles. 'Some people here are doing very well! But the EU countries that working migrants want to reach all have huge shortages of skilled and unskilled labour, which these migrants are needed to fill; yet obtaining a Schengen visa here still costs about two thousand euros, which is comparable to an annual rural salary.'

It is a salient point. In the UK we have been recruiting migrant NHS, agricultural and construction workers for years. Often it is to fill short-falls in labour, but increasingly migrants are being brought in because they will work harder, more cheaply and endure appalling pay and conditions that UK residents simply won't tolerate.

Every Albanian whom I've spoken to so far has told me how tricky it is to obtain a foreign visa, unless you have the right connections and the money to pay a backhander. Corruption lubricates the Albanian econ-omy: everything from getting visas to seeing a doctor involves paying some sort of bribe.

Julie is in full flow now. 'Like migration, trafficking is also a con-tinuum,' she says. 'It incorporates many experiences, and in order to understand it, we have to be prepared to examine all of them. Women are

8. 'Trafficking in Human Beings in South-Eastern Europe', UNICEF, March 2005, p. 102.

abducted by traffickers; there have occasionally been abductions here. But many women also approach smugglers and traffickers because they decide to enter the commercial sex trade in order to make money to survive, and there are no other viable ways for them to migrate.

'As an Albanian migrant, I find it really offensive when middle-class white women in anti-trafficking projects patronise women from countries like mine by implying that we are all naïve victims. The assumption is always that men are smuggled and only women are trafficked.'

UNICEF, who have written some of the most reliable and consistent research on trafficking, reported back in 2002 that:

> In some cases there are also situations of forced migration, when traffickers have a contract with a family and a girl or woman is taken abroad to earn back the money lent to the family, or a woman is kidnapped and taken over the border by force. However, such cases of forced migration are rare – there are enough young women sufficiently desperate and willing to take their chances with traffickers.[9]

Julie tells me she and her father are planning to visit relatives and friends in several local villages and asks if I'd like to join them. I say I'd be delighted. The three of us spend the next couple of days crisscrossing Devoll. The visible contrasts in wealth and poverty are astounding. We pass by dozens of peasants bumping along in carts pulled by knarly old horses, while our taxi is passed by several glinting Mercedes Benz. In villages of mud streets there are grand, elaborate houses and cramped-looking shacks built literally side by side. It's a snapshot of migration incentives, the remittances of successful migrants on show for all to see.

In each house that we visit, which are mostly beautifully furnished, elegant homes, people ask me why I have come so far from Tirana, and when I tell them I am writing a book about trafficking, they are surprisingly open with me. In every village I am told stories about two or three young local women who left home a few years ago to work in Italy. Most of them have never come back, and the families of these missing women hope for the best, worry about the worst and have no way of making contact with their daughters.

The women who have returned to these villages are, almost without exception, seriously psychologically damaged. They are frightened of strangers, or else lash out at people they know. They are paranoid and disturbed. Some of them, unable to cope with being marooned amongst people who don't know what to say to them, or who are embarrassed by their behaviour, have left once more. Others have simply withdrawn into

9. 'Trafficking in Human Beings in South-Eastern Europe', UNICEF, 2002.

themselves: they stay in their homes and are rarely seen outside in the village streets. I am told these women are ashamed of what has been done to them and cannot face the world beyond their door. Their lives shrink, and they imprison themselves inside their bedrooms and rot away silently.

I hear these stories from neighbours, relatives and friends of the women, who talk quietly while we are sitting in their homes. Julie translates these stories for me. She tells me she is familiar with these stories, and though none of these women are friends of hers, she knows whom the villagers are talking about.

A local doctor tells us about one woman who came home with such severe mental health problems that he has to sedate her regularly. 'What happened to her drove her mad,' he says, 'and her family has also suffered terribly. I know of several mothers who are sick with grief because they do not know what has happened to their daughters. My own daughter is sixteen, and at school she sits next to a girl who was taken to a town near the coast, Fier, by a man who promised he wanted to marry her. When they reached Fier, she heard him talking with his friends about putting her to work on the streets in Italy, and she managed to escape by telephoning her own family, who came to Fier ready to avenge this act violently, and they took her back.'

I ask the doctor what happened to the trafficker, and he shrugs his shoulders and says he really doesn't know. That is the strangest part of these stories: apart from this one comment from the doctor, no one mentions the traffickers themselves – who they are or how they get away with these crimes. Julie does not mention them either. The Mafia and organised criminals I read about before I came here seem to be invisible: huge networks trading just beneath the surface, where someone like me cannot even hear them at work.

Research by the IOM and other organisations has highlighted that most people in this country are trafficked by someone they know: a friend, acquaintance or relative. The crime of trafficking carries a maximum fifteen-year sentence, and the US State Department report on Human Rights Practices in Albania states that during 2004 more than two hundred and thirty trafficking cases went to court, resulting in 362 convictions. Some convictions resulted in long sentences: for instance, two pimps who trafficked a teenager to Italy received seventeen and nineteen years in prison.

However, the report also notes that, 'Authorities often released arrested traffickers because of insufficient evidence, or if they were prosecuted, charged them with lesser crimes or gave them less than the minimum sentence for trafficking.' And it pulls no punches with regard to police complicity, stating that, 'the [Albanian] police were often involved directly or indirectly in trafficking.'

Julie tells me that a few years ago she and a group of local women set up an organisation called the Moravia Foundation. They wanted to secure safe housing for trafficked women who had returned to Devoll. They had the idea of offering these women the equivalent of foster homes in villages far enough from their own to give each woman some anonymity and privacy, but they couldn't secure any funding.

'We are a well-connected network of local women who know this area better than anyone else, but because we didn't have an office with a fax machine and a long-term business plan, we couldn't get backing from a mainstream national or international organisation. It's a shame because I think it would have been very good for some of these women languishing here.'

I hesitantly ask her whether she thinks it might be possible to speak to one of the returned women, and she shakes her head. 'No. I really don't think so. They don't want to speak to anyone about their experiences.' Like Sevim, she's very straight with me, and I immediately wish I hadn't asked her about this. I don't want to be the equivalent of a bloodhound, sniffing out trafficking 'victims' for interview.

The day after our last village visit, I leave Cangonj. Julie comes back to Korca with me, and we say goodbye at the bus station. I tell her I'm sorry to leave and glad I came, and we say we'll keep in touch. I keep an eye out for the bear and his keeper, but they are elsewhere today. After Julie has left, the bus is delayed for an hour, so I wander around the market and find an Internet café on one of the main streets.

Ruth Rosenberg has emailed me from the IOM office. She has found the most recent trafficking figures they have. In 2004 the Albanian branch of the IOM assisted sixty-four Albanian women who had been trafficked and nine foreign women.[10] This number doesn't prove anything, except that in Albania the IOM are assisting fewer trafficked women than in previous years. It does not mean fewer women are being trafficked, but maybe fewer of them are asking organisations such as the IOM for assistance.

The other detail Ruth has forwarded comes completely out of the blue: the Albanian authorities have started apprehending 'irregular Chinese migrants' at the Greek and Macedonian borders. To date, just small

10. According to UNICEF, the IOM assisted 141 Albanian women in 2002/2003 and forty-eight foreign women. See 'Trafficking in Human Beings in South-Eastern Europe, UNICEF, 2005, p. 101.

numbers had been apprehended: eight migrants last year and eleven so far this year, but they had all been debt-bonded and were en route to Italy. Most of the migrants apparently had 'reservations' about going back home because of their debts to their smugglers/traffickers (who were apparently not apprehended), but they declined to apply for asylum and were swiftly removed back to China.

Chapter 9

Burrell

Burrell is a town of some twelve thousand people, set amidst the mountains of northern Albania, three hours' drive from Tirana. The setting is spectacular. The town looks bleak. It would look bleak even in sunshine, but in this rain that has been lashing down for the last half-hour, it's especially grim.

The streets are pitted, the tenement blocks are grey, and there is crap everywhere. I am standing on a street corner waiting for a woman called Natasha to arrive. In the meantime I watch half a dozen adults rummaging through several overflowing bins and skips. After they've left, clutching armfuls of God knows what, a pack of dogs arrive and rummage in there too. A large cat hisses its way into one sodden heap and joins the burrowing scavengers. I shiver in the rain and wonder whether the people always get to the bins first.

When I got back to Tirana from Cangonj yesterday, Sevim was in the office, scowling and stomping around the place like she'd had a very bad day. I told her briefly about Julie, and about the insane minibus driver who had raced from Korca to Tirana at breakneck speed, refusing to stop even when three people were simultaneously throwing up out of the windows. I said I was thinking of going to Vlore for a few days. Vlore is a large town on the south-west coast, famous for its pristine turquoise waters: this is where the Adriatic and Ionian seas divide. It also used to be a criminal hub. Italy is just 75 kilometres away, and migrants, smugglers and traffickers regularly used to run the gauntlet between the two coastlines. When things went wrong and boats were intercepted, the migrants were often just tipped in the water to drown as the smugglers and traffickers sped away. It was a bad situation. This is the town where Anna was eventually held for a month after being trafficked out of Moldova. Since Interpol opened an office in the town, and a local NGO set up a refuge for trafficked women and girls, things have improved considerably. I wanted to see if I could arrange to meet the refuge staff, and maybe also persuade the Interpol office to talk to me.

Sevim listened to all this in silence and then glared straight at me. 'Why do you want to go to the south, Louisa? The south is paradise. Do you want to see what is really going on here, how the poor people live? Then you go to my project in Burrell. I was there two days ago. They have nothing in that place, and that is why the adults are all desperate to leave, and so the children are left like orphans. You know, they ask for bread from the lunch table in our children's centre, just to have some-thing to eat in the evening. You go there instead!' She threw down the gauntlet, angry and frustrated.

'Then help me get there,' I retorted, 'and I'll write about it.'

Albania is a country where things can be fixed in moments if the spirit is willing, and well enough connected. Sevim picked up her phone, and within fifteen minutes my trip to Burrell had been arranged.

At six o'clock this morning, I clambered into the back seat of a sleek Land Rover, driven by a barrel-stomached man called Tonin. His wife and their three kids came along too. After a stunningly beautiful drive along an increasingly wretched road, they dropped me on this corner of this sorry-looking place and set off to visit their relatives somewhere further up north. As soon as they'd departed, it began to rain.

Now, I hover from one foot to the next: I'm starting to shiver. Ten minutes later a middle-aged woman in a red raincoat walks up, peers at me through the drizzle and shyly introduces herself. This is Natasha, who runs the Burrell children's centre that Sevim referred to. Moments later we are joined by her teenage daughter, Albina, who goes to university in Tirana but is back home for the weekend. Albina is about nineteen, speaks fluent English and has come along to translate for me.

'I am so sorry about the weather,' apologises Natasha, as though she has cast the rain down herself. 'If the weather was good, we would take you to the mountains for a picnic.' Instead, she and Albina take me on a tour of the local slums.

Two young brothers live in a boxroom at the top of a flight of worn concrete stairs. Their home is lit by a light bulb that fades, brightens and then fades again as the current surges and falters. They have hacked their way into the local electricity supply. The ceiling is obscured by large squares of sagging cardboard, and there are scraps of rancid lace stretched across the windows.

Natasha introduces me to the younger boy first. He is a dark-skinned twelve-year-old, stunted and extremely thin. His name is Manuel, and his lanky eighteen-year-old brother is called Arjan. They live alone here now, in this one room that stinks of piss and stuff rotting. Their mother left a decade ago, when Manuel was just two. Her husband, his father, used to knock her about when he drank too much, and one day she'd obviously had enough because she took off for Italy. Apparently she's married to an Italian and doing very well these days, though no one knows for sure; like the women who have disappeared from the villages surrounding Cangonj, she has never been back.

The boys' father has left too: he got on a bus going to Kosovo just a few days ago, to look for construction work. Kosovo needs reconstructing, and he needs the work. Albanians don't need visas or permits to live and work in Kosovo. It's one of the few places in the world where they are actually welcome. The boys manage between them by scouring bins and skips for discarded aluminium cans, which they sell for scrap to a local merchant. They cook their food on what looks like a brick with live wires wrapped around it.

'Manuel comes to the centre every day to eat lunch,' Natasha says in her hesitant English, as we carefully clamber back down the steps.

'What about his elder brother?' The boys looked hungry, and their home was pitiful. It has just dawned on me what I've really let myself in for, coming here to Burrell.

'We cannot afford to feed him. We can take children only under fourteen years, because we already have seventy-five children coming to us every day.'

Natasha is, ironically, from Vlore, the southern paradise Sevim mentioned. She moved up here after getting married to a local teacher and has lived in Burrell for the last fifteen years. She used to be a primary-school teacher herself but now manages the children's centre, where poor and destitute kids get a free cooked meal and basic education skills.

'The state schools don't like to teach hungry children, because they learn more slowly and don't bring their own equipment,' she tells me as we attempt to avoid puddles and marauding stray dogs at the same time. She is quite reticent with me, often turning to her daughter to supply the words that she can't think of, rather than risking getting them wrong herself. Albina, on the other hand, is confident and chirpy and tells me several times how wonderful university life in Tirana is. After growing up here, I'm sure Tirana would be bliss. There's something quite heartbreaking about this ragged, dirty town being surrounded by beautiful mountains and clean, high air. It just highlights the desolation.

*

We spend the rest of the morning visiting half a dozen more families, who live in single-storey concrete blocks on the outskirts of town. They are all farming families from the surrounding mountains who migrated to Burrell in search of work, and instead ended up in the backstreets sharing virtually nothing between them.

The buildings they occupy look like old coal cellars to me: draughty and low, and dark inside. Some are more decrepit than others, and some are actually not too bad, if you can say that about seven or eight people sharing two rooms and, as far as I can see, one bed between them. None of them has running water. The kids fill up pails at a communal tap jutting out from a dripping wall. But each family has hacked into the electricity supply, and almost all of them have TVs: great big old black-and-white sets that sit on wooden boxes or tables with rickety legs, projecting flickering pictures and hissy words.

In one home that we visit, it is actually the gnarled old grandfather sitting in the only armchair and smoking his ornately carved pipe who is the main breadwinner. He owns a handcart that he pulls around the streets, like a two-legged beast of burden. Locals pay him to pile their belongings on to the cart and then drag it wherever they need to go next. The money he earns feeds and clothes his nine children, grandchildren and great-grandchildren, who all live here with him. His sinewy arms are dark as hardwood, and the veins stand out like cables inserted beneath the skin. His only son, a stocky man in his thirties called Ilir, helps out when business is brisk, and also makes some extra money in summertime by playing the clarinet at local weddings. Ilir's teenage son in turn accompanies his father on a large handheld drum.

Ilir asks if we would like to hear them play, and Natasha nods enthusiastically. They produce their instruments and begin to play raucous Albanian wedding tunes, while the rest of the family sit and smile as Natasha gets the kids up to dance with her.

I sit there amidst this sudden celebration. Part of me is still in that first room with Manuel and Arjan, and I can't get that miserable image out of my head. But we are here now, with a large family who support each other and live in visibly better circumstances. It's all very surreal, particularly this musical performance. Natasha has known these families for years and treats every single member with absolute respect. And here she is, dancing energetically round their threadbare living room with their kids and grandkids in tow, her face glowing and suddenly vivacious.

After thanking the family for their music and hospitality, we go on our way, and Natasha and Albina take me to a nearby café for lunch. Natasha orders piles of food, and we feast on several platters of roast chicken, chips, salad, bread and bottles of beer and some luminous, fizzy orange drink. I sense that Sevim is footing the bill for this spread. The slightly queasy guilt at eating so well here of all places doesn't manage to spoil my appetite, and between us we polish off most of the food. Natasha wraps the remains in our napkins and stuffs them into the bottom of her handbag. 'Someone will enjoy this later,' she says.

I think maybe we will visit the children's centre in the afternoon, but Natasha has several more families for me to visit. She is looking for one boy in particular, a lad called Aldon, and has already asked several other children if they've seen him today, but apparently no one knows where he is.

We visit a different slum now, at the back of a large tarpaulined market. It is made up of several low-rise white buildings, which, once we step inside, conceal a warren of passageways and narrow doors. We make our way down a dim passageway, one at a time, Natasha leading. We turn left then right, and she bangs on one of the doors.

Pjeter and his wife, Alma, have four young children and have lived here for five years. They left the mountains when the land that their home was built on was suddenly sold to a private owner, who immediately evicted them.

The kids happily clamber over us, while Alma brews Turkish coffee and Pjeter talks and smokes. Albina translates.

'By the time we left the village there weren't many people living there, anyway,' he says. 'Most of the younger people have either come down here or moved to Tirana. The old folk are left, because they don't want to move to the city. They have spent their lives in the mountains, and they are too old to do anything else now.'

In contrast to the other homes we have visited, this one is bright and quite well furnished. The walls look freshly painted; there are several rugs on the floor, and an electric heater is keeping the room warm. It is the end of March. There are still odd banks of gritty snow in the streets outside, and the mountains surrounding Burrell are clad with drifts.

Pjeter has no job, nor does Alma. They rely on Alma's brother to provide for them. This brother of hers sends money a few times a year, and they eke it out until the next donation arrives.

I ask him where this wealthy brother lives.

He responds with a wry smile. He has a fleshy gap between his front teeth, and eyebrows you could scour pans with. 'He is in England. Oxford. I don't know what he does, but he makes a good salary and sends money to Alma's sister too.'

'Is he there without papers?' I've got so used to asking this question that I forget Pjeter might not want to admit that Alma's brother is living in my country illegally.

'Of course he's there without papers! We have no other way of getting there!' Pjeter starts talking more loudly and leans forward in his chair, gesturing emphatically with his bony fingers. I can't tell if he's angry or passionate or both, but he obviously wants to talk.

Albina's brow furrows as she translates rapidly between us. 'He says most of the people who leave Burrell try to go to England. They know where to find each other and can help each other to find work and places to live.'

'How much does it cost to get to England?'

'Seven thousand euros.'

'How does anyone from here get hold of €7,000?'

Pjeter shrugs. 'No one has €7,000. They have to borrow the money from someone who's already abroad, or else pay some of it up front before they leave and then owe the rest when they arrive.'

I decide to push my luck and ask Pjeter about the route to England. To my surprise, he is quite upfront about it.

'They go north' – he gestures with a skinny index finger – 'up to Croatia and then over to northern Italy by land or boat. The smugglers are all from this area, so they know the best routes. After Italy people travel in the back of lorries, or on trains. It takes a while, but it's the only way they can get into your country. We cannot go over to Italy from Vlore any more, though people from up here usually left from the north, anyway.' He nods towards Alma, who is bringing in a tray of steaming cups of coffee, 'Her brother went via Croatia. He has been in your country for eight years now.'

'Has he ever been back to visit?'

Pjeter shakes his head and leans back in his chair. He is suddenly calmer, more relaxed. For some reason the tension has lifted from the room, and he rolls a cigarette thoughtfully between his thumb, index and middle fingers. 'No. He can't come back. That is the problem of going without papers, or on a false passport that expires some months after you arrive: you have to stay. You can't come home to visit your family, because officially you never even left in the first place.'

I sit on the couch, a minute cup of Turkish coffee balanced on my knee, and ponder what he has just said. I don't know anything about Alma's brother, except that he lives in Oxford and is apparently doing very well for himself. They haven't even told me his name, but he sounds like a regular immigrant, just trying to make a life for himself and work in order to earn enough money to send home to his family. Then it suddenly strikes me that whatever type of character he is, this man is now forced to live like a fugitive.

There are hundreds of thousands of migrants stranded across Europe without documents. They are our invisible labour market: cheap, discreet and often totally vulnerable.

People usually migrate so they can make better money than they do at home. Many undocumented migrants who make it to Britain do very well in their own terms. They're unlikely to earn the same as regular workers but often make more money than they could at home. Others, however, are ruthlessly exploited, even if they are entitled to work in the UK. Tracts of Britain, such as East Anglia, have become notorious for the dire pay and conditions imposed on its working agricultural migrants.

Last year a large group of Greek migrants spoke out against 'slavery-like conditions' at a daffodil farm in Cornwall, in a case that highlighted another industry thriving on abysmal pay and conditions. Nineteen-year-old Chrisovalandou Mandela told the *Independent* about being forced to work long hours in freezing weather, being beaten, starved, denied wages and sleeping in tents or unheated sheds. One of her colleagues said the group were given cans of dog food to eat. When they complained, they were threatened at gunpoint and told they had to pay €1,500 each in lieu of travel expenses before they would earn anything. The group, who were all ethnic Romany, had been recruited directly from their villages in northern Greece and were working legally. Some of the flowers they picked were for a major flower supplier to retailers including Sainsburys. They escaped their gangmaster only after managing to telephone their village and request help. They were escorted from the farm by an Orthodox priest living in Penzance and a representative from the Greek Embassy in London. Environmental health officials described conditions on the farm as 'atrocious and inhuman'.

The gangmaster in charge of the migrants denied starving and mis-treating them. The group were driven to Heathrow Airport under police escort, and after examining the case, Customs and Excise said none of them had made a formal complaint, and no further action would be taken.

More than five thousand migrants are employed on Cornish daffodil farms annually. They earn about six pence per bunch of dozen stems, which are all picked by hand.[1]

We finish our coffee and stand to leave. Pjeter and Alma thank us for visiting them, and we thank them for hosting us. I wish them luck, but I

1. *Independent*, 14 February 2004.

don't really know what else to say. There aren't many options left in Burrell.

It is only about three o'clock in the afternoon, but it has already been a long day, and I am feeling worn out. I hope this was our last visit. But as soon as we step outside, Natasha tells me we have one more visit to make.

'We have to go back to the first building, to find Aldon,' she says. 'That is where his house is.'

I really don't want to go back there and know this reluctance is expressed all over my face. 'Natasha, please can we make this the last visit?' I ask her.

She nods. 'Yes. After we have met with Aldon, we will go back to my apartment and rest.'

But not before then. Natasha has her own agenda going on here: she is relentless in her determination to show me the worst this place has to offer. She wants me to remember Burrell and the people in these slums and take it all back home with me. I have to admire her bloody-mindedness.

So we walk slowly back to the first flight of stairs we climbed this morning. We trudge back up and walk through the dank, stinking corridor, turning right at the door to the boxroom where Manuel and his brother, Arjan, live. There is another door just along the wall. It's blue. Instead of knocking, Natasha pulls gently at the wood, which is so damp one of the planks bends back like sinew, and she can see straight through into the room beyond.

'He is here.' She knocks.

The door is opened, and Natasha leads the way inside. The first thing I see is a large double bed that sags heavily in the middle as though there is an immense invisible weight lying on top of it. Even in this bad light I can see how stained the bedclothes are. There's a puddle of some dark liquid on the floor that we step over on our way into the room beyond.

Aldon leads us into this second room, sits on one of the couches and silently resumes eating what looks like a bowl of burnt macaroni. The naked light bulb suspended above him mercilessly illuminates the surrounding filth. There are two couches. The one Aldon is sitting on is bare, the other strewn with matted blankets. The curtains look as though they were previously set on fire. There are potato peelings on the floor and a single dry crust on the shelf next to where I'm standing. At the side of the crust is a photograph of a young woman in a high-neck white blouse. I instinctively pick it up to look more closely. She is smiling confidently at the camera. It must be his mother.

Natasha is talking to Aldon, who is nodding at her and murmuring his reply. Albina translates as I bend my head and roughly wipe my eyes, furious with myself for the tears. I have never seen a hovel like this.

'His mother left two years ago,' says Natasha, turning back towards me. 'She went to Kosovo, and she has been back several times, to visit the boys and give her husband some money to look after them. She was here just a few months ago, at the beginning of the year.' She turns back to Aldon.

'When is Mummy coming back, Aldon?'

'Not yet,' he says, though God knows how he would know because he is only five years old.

Natasha shakes the remains of our lunch on to his plate and talks with him quietly for a while longer before sitting down on the edge of the other couch next to me.

'He lives here with his father and two brothers. His father drinks, and his brothers are both thieves. None of them can read or write. When Aldon's mother went to Kosovo for the first time, I asked his father why she had decided to go there. He just told me that she went there alone to find work.'

'What do you think she is doing there, Natasha?'

She shrugs. 'We do not know for sure. But . . .' She pauses for a minute before adding carefully, 'I do not think that she was trafficked. I don't think that there is trafficking in Burrell any more; this woman, she worked here as a waitress before she went, and she was a kind of local prostitute. She got paid for what she did, and I think she has gone to Kosovo to find better paid work. It is a pity her husband didn't go instead, because he is no good to the boys. He drinks whatever money there is, and you can see how they live.'

Aldon suddenly interrupts Natasha to ask if we want to watch TV, and begins to fiddle with the live wire that goes from the TV straight into the wall.

'No, no, don't do that. We don't want to watch TV.' Natasha shakes her head at him, and he drops the wire on to the floor and goes back to eating the remains of our lunch.

I sit beside her, remembering Mara Radovanovic in Bosnia and what she told me about women who were trafficked to Kosovo: that the stories these women had told her were the worst cases of physical and sexual violence she had ever come across.

Natasha stands up and brushes down her skirt. It is obviously our cue to leave.

'When she comes back next time, I am going to try to talk with her, and see if she will agree to stay here even for a little while,' she says. 'There is nothing for the boys here: their father does not provide anything for them, and I want to see them having more of a life than this. So I will try to meet her when she comes back from Kosovo next time. She is the best hope that they have now.'

Chapter 10

Article 18

I sleep on the couch in Natasha's living room, and the next morning she and Albina show me the children's centre that Natasha manages. It is a large, draughty old building that was a theatre in some former life. The children who come here are all from the slums. A few of them are neatly dressed, many others are clad in threadbare cast-offs. Most of them, like Aldon, are small for their age: stunted by insufficient, poor-quality food. He is here amongst them, little Aldon, tucking himself into corners next to the heaters, and being found and fussed over by the team of affectionately stern women who run the centre between them. There is not enough room in the dining area for all the kids, so they eat their lunches in shifts. For many, this is their only full meal of the day, and Natasha tells me proudly they serve meat twice a week at her centre. We eat plain boiled macaroni served with bread and fresh tomato salad, and the children practise their English greetings on me while we're dining.

Just before we leave the centre, I take a solitary prowl around the dark, unused quarters of the building, open an unmarked door and suddenly find myself standing on stage. In front of me is an audience of empty wooden chairs nailed to the floor, behind me a backdrop of faded crimson curtains made from heavily lined velvet that moths began feasting on long ago. Spectral light filters through several grimy windows and skylights, lending the whole auditorium an expectant twilit atmosphere. I look up at the ceiling. There are still a few old spotlights suspended up there, like huge blind eyes gazing back into the past.

That afternoon, Albina and I go back to Tirana together. Natasha waves us off, hugging both of us before we clamber into the minibus.

'Thank you for coming to Burrell,' she says to me.

'Thank you for showing me Burrell, Natasha.'

I admire her tremendously. This must be a harsh, often sad place to live in, especially during winter. I have only been here overnight but feel physically relieved to be retreating to the capital.

On our way back, Albina tells me more about her life at university. She can't afford to live anywhere near the city centre, so she spends two hours a day commuting from her room in the suburbs to her classes and then back again by public bus.

I ask her whether she thinks she'll return to Burrell after finishing university.

Albina thinks about this for a minute or two before saying, 'If I could find a job like the one my mother does, then I would go back. I want to be near my parents: I am their only child, and they miss me. But if you can't work, there is nothing in Burrell. Tirana is the place to have a future.'

I am leaving Albania tomorrow morning. There is a boat sailing from the nearby port of Durres up the Dalmatian coast to Trieste, where I have already arranged to meet the Comitato per i Diritti Civili delle Prostitute, which translates as the 'Committee for the Civil Rights of Prostitutes'. They are a group of activists who support local and migrant sex workers, as well as women who have been trafficked into the Italian sex industry. I'm particularly keen to meet them because the committee was originally set up by Italian sex workers themselves, and I want to hear their views on trafficking. I found their contact details on the Internet, and they emailed me back and said they'd be happy to meet me if I came to Trieste.

One of Sevim's colleagues, Fabiola, is giving me a lift to Durres. Fabiola is a statuesque woman with a crimped mane of dyed auburn hair. She drives a BMW that has no windscreen wipers because someone has just stolen them. Car crime is in a league of its own in Albania. A few days ago someone told me that so many stolen cars are brought into this country it is very difficult to buy one here that hasn't been nicked.

The windscreen-wiper theft was a badly timed crime. The weather erupts into a torrential rainstorm just as Fabiola and I are setting off for Durres. Nevertheless, Fabiola speeds down the motorway towards the port, peering through the windscreen and cheerfully admitting she can hardly see a damn thing in front of her.

'What do you think of Albania?' she hollers above the din of the rain beating down on the car.

'I like it very much!' I holler back. 'Even though it's very corrupt and the drivers are crazy!'

Fabiola responds with a guffaw, her hands clenched around the steering wheel. 'Yes! We have too much corruption, and even the Italians say we drive like lunatics!'

Everyone I've met in Albania has acknowledged the scale of corruption in their country, and how it has created a regime of bribes, favours and organised crime. When I asked how the rot set in, several people, including Sevim, gave me the same reply: that after more than forty-five years of totalitarian regime people still have very little experience of challenging authority and there is no established culture of peaceful protest or lobbying the government. Albania's recent history has been dominated by dictatorship and anarchy.

Fabiola and I arrive in Durres unscathed and in plenty of time. As we head for the port, butterflies begin to flutter against the lining of my stomach. This ferry takes twenty-four hours. I've chosen to sail rather than fly to Trieste because it's a cheaper and more leisurely journey, though once I am actually on the ferry I will be confined until Italy. The ferry doesn't stop en route, and I don't expect there will be any tourists on board: the end of March is too early in the holiday season.

I wheel my suitcase through to the almost deserted passport control, have my passport glanced at and wander slowly up the quayside towards the ferry itself, trying to look forward to this journey.

As soon as I am aboard, my passport is taken from me by the purser, who exchanges it for a cabin key and a square of cardboard with a number on it. My cabin is three floors below the main deck. It has two narrow bunk beds, a tiny sink that rattles when I turn the tap on and a blindingly bright wall light. I stash my suitcase under the lower bunk and leave immediately.

Every person I pass on the way back up to the main deck is a man, and I feel them glancing back at me curiously. The corridors are well lit but narrow, and I construct a mental map of the most direct route as I ascend the metal stairs.

The rain has just about ceased, and the ferry begins to judder into life. I stand on deck looking back at Durres. The city high-rises are painted in the same brilliant colours and gaudy patterns as in Tirana. They look ridiculous and beautiful. The port is stacked with cranes, loading equipment and other huge weights of machinery that grind and roar into the wind. As the ferry begins to push away from the quayside, I feel incredibly lonesome and vulnerable.

When I got back from Burrell yesterday, Sevim told me that twenty-seven Albanians had just been arrested outside Durres. They had been attempting to cross over to Italy on an inflatable dinghy. The weather suddenly deteriorated, and the crossing was being abandoned when the police pounced.

These 'irregular migrants' later told police they had each paid €3,500 to be smuggled over to Italy by the owners of the dinghy, who had assured them they would be met en route by another vessel and guided over to a safe cove on the Italian coast. The smugglers took their money and vanished just before the police arrived. The migrants were taken into custody, their money gone, their troubles just starting.

From the outset, the odds are so utterly stacked against migrants without documents: everyone has a vested interest in them either failing to get out or being completely expendable once they have been smuggled to their destination. But after visiting Burrell, I understand why they still tenaciously keep attempting to slip through the nets.

I muse on deck until Durres has receded into a grey and orange industrial haze. Afterwards, I climb back down to my cabin to collect a book. That will be my shield for the evening against glances and attempts to question me.

The cabin door opposite mine is open, and a short, elderly, white-haired man is sitting on his bunk. He springs up when he sees me and greets me in Italian, though he is obviously an Albanian.

I reply in my few words of Italian. He starts gesturing: asking me if I am travelling alone and then demonstrating that if I have any problems at all, I am to bang on his door and he will sort it out. He is standing upright on slightly heeled shoes, but still does not quite reach the height of my shoulder. His seniority, however, carries its own gravitas, and he has obviously decided to look out for me. I thank him and promise to let him know if I need his help.

'*Sono Pjeter.*' He thumps his own diminutive chest as he introduces himself, disappears back into his cabin for a second and then thrusts a can of warm beer into my hand. He bows and returns to his bunk, quietly pushing his door half-shut. He gives me courage.

In the main lounge upstairs, my fellow passengers are watching TV and buying drinks from the bar. There are a few women amongst them, who all seem to be travelling with toddlers, except for three nuns sitting together in one corner, engrossed in a quiet, hilarious conversation. They look as though they're having a better time than anyone else on board.

I instinctively look round for any young woman being escorted by someone who looks like a cross between a businessman and a pimp, but cannot see anyone who qualifies. I find a seat and open my book.

The next day I am standing on deck, watching Croatia slowly slide by. The sun is out, and the sea sparkles and foams across the Adriatic. Occasionally I spy the veneer of a white city sprawled along a stretch of coastline, or stacked atop distant hills or mountains. I have never visited Croatia, and it looks distantly beautiful.

Below me, on the working deck, the ferry crew are all identically dressed in Guantanamo Bay-style orange boiler suits. They are a mixed bunch of black, brown and white men working together. Some of them are obviously from the Indian subcontinent; others look Filipino. There are also two black men and a handful of Slavs. They look up at me, and I look back at them. We are mutually curious. A couple of them wave, and I wave back. The only people I have spoken to on board so far are Pjeter and the male cashier at the self-service restaurant. But as I lean against the rail with my eyes closed and the sun full on my face, a different voice greets me hesitantly.

'Hello.' One of the crew is standing at my side. He wipes his hand on the midriff of his orange boiler suit and offers it to me. 'I am Valentino,' he says.

'Louisa. Nice to meet you.' I shake his outstretched hand. We smile at each other.

'Where are you from?' His English is tentative but clear.

'England. And you?'

Valentino is Romanian. He is a large, gentle-looking man. As we stand in the sun, he tells me he has worked on this ferry for nine years now, sailing from Albania to Trieste and back again twice a week.

He goes home to Bucharest whenever he can, to visit his elderly parents. He was married, but his wife met someone else whilst he was at sea and left for a new life in America. She took their daughter with her.

'My daughter was young: only four years old. I have seen her one time in three years. I think she does not know who her father is now.'

'I'm sorry,' I say, feeling momentarily lost for words: partly because I know the rest of the crew must be scrutinising us from the deck below.

I ask Valentino about this multinational crew. He says they come from nine different countries, including India, the Philippines, Tanzania, Albania, Romania and Croatia. Some of the Asians have been working on board longer than him and know the boats very well. But the Europeans always get paid more than everyone else, even though they all do exactly the same jobs. When I ask him why this is so, he shrugs.

'This is the method. I know I am lucky because this is good work for me, but I am tired of sailing.' He is staring at me through small, shining eyes. 'Are you married?'

When the ferry docks in Trieste, we all assemble by the purser's office to reclaim our passports. I have lost my numbered square of cardboard but am waved over by the purser, who hands me my passport.

I queue-jump by default and am one of the first to leave the ferry and wander on to the quayside, where there is a bus waiting to convey us to the customs hall. As I lift my suitcase into the boot, my name booms down from the bridge. I look up and see an orange figure waving farewell from the upper deck. I wave back at Valentino, smiling up at him and to myself. It hasn't been such a bad journey at all.

Some other ferry must have just docked in Trieste too, because there is a thick snake of people waiting to have their passports checked and luggage searched in the customs hall. Suitcases, sacks, bags, satchels and boxes are being hauled up on to huge white tables and slowly emptied and searched by officials in blue uniforms. One of them is using a dagger to slice through the lining of an elderly man's suitcase. I am waved through the EU channel, my passport is glanced at once more, and I wheel my case straight into Italy. I wonder how long it will take the Albanians to clear customs.

The next morning I take a taxi to Androna degli Orti in the backstreets of Trieste, to meet Carla Corso. She is one of the founders of the Comitato per i Diritti delle Prostitute. A smartly dressed woman in her mid-forties, she could easily pass for a banker or city councillor, except her blonde bob is flecked with a shower of fluorescent-pink highlights.

'My English is very poor,' says Carla, before introducing me to her translator, a young woman called Hermine, whose skin is the colour of coal.

The three of us sit down in the main office and attempt to talk amidst phones ringing and other women having discussions of their own whilst they clack away on keyboards. But it's too noisy and distracting, so we make our way upstairs and eventually find a small vacant room. It is white and bare-walled. The only pieces of furniture in it are a small, round, white table with four chairs and an empty medicine cabinet. For some reason, it reminds me of a convent.

'So . . .' Carla sits down heavily and crosses one knee over the other: 'What do you want to know for your work?'

I explain about my book, and Hermine translates as Carla listens, nodding occasionally. When I have finished, she nods once more and gives me a brief history of the Comitato. It was set up more than twenty years ago, in 1982, by a community of local female sex workers, including Carla Corso, who was once described by an Italian journalist as 'the most famous prostitute in Italy'.

'We wanted to have a meeting point and a sexual health drop-in clinic, where we could pick up condoms, have regular health checks and talk to a doctor in confidence, especially about HIV prevention. After we opened the clinic here in Trieste, we talked to women working in Torino, Bologna and Venice, and we gradually opened offices and clinics there too. We also campaigned to have the law on prostitution changed so women could work together and be safer.'

Working as a prostitute is not against the law in Italy. But, like Britain, the laws governing the sex industry are paradoxical. In Italy prostitutes cannot work 'off street' in a private apartment or together in a brothel, and migrant sex workers have to carry their documents with them at all times when they are working, or else risk arrest and detention.

'From the very beginning of the committee, most of our work was out on the streets,' says Carla. 'When we weren't working ourselves, we were still often outside, visiting prostitutes in other areas, distributing condoms and information and just talking to the women. I've been involved in the committee since it started, and I've seen the changes in the Italian sex trade because I have spent twenty-three years talking to sex workers.

'In this country our sex industry has always been street-based. Women sell sex in nightclubs and private apartments, but that's the expensive end of the business, and more sex is still sold on the streets. The difference is who is working the streets now.'

Carla pauses, leans back in her chair and then leans forward again, her hands clasped loosely together. The dark circles ringing her eyes are almost concealed beneath a thin layer of cosmetic foundation.

'At the beginning of the 1990s almost all the prostitutes working in Italy were Italian. There was a small minority of foreign prostitutes, and trafficking was not a problem. The women had their own rules about where they worked and how much clients had to pay. They did not undercut each other, and a lot of women were well established in the industry: they worked the same streets for years.

'The first wave of foreign sex workers to arrive came here in the early '90s. They were women and transgender prostitutes from South America: Colombia and Brazil. Migrant sex workers, all of them. A year or two later we started meeting women from South-East Asia, mainly Thailand, who also moved here to work as prostitutes because they could make more money in Italy than back at home. During the wars in the Balkans women fled over here from the old Yugoslavia, and they worked on the streets just to have the money to survive. Gradually, more and more foreign women started arriving. There had always been a few African women working here, but most of them did not come over until the mid-1990s – and that was the turning point in the Italian sex industry. Nineteen ninety-five was when things really began to change.'

Carla and her colleagues had closer contact with the sex workers than anyone bar the punters, and soon noticed the change in demographics, and atmosphere, on the streets of northern Italy.

'Of course, we immediately noticed the Africans! They were

considered very exotic at first, and so they were very popular. A lot of the Italian prostitutes were resentful because they started to lose a lot of business. But at the committee we had always said we would support any migrant sex workers, so we tried to make contact with the African women.

'But whenever we approached them on the streets, African women were very reluctant to talk. It was extremely difficult to make contact with them, and it wasn't just language: these women were withdrawn, and we could see they were scared of what they were doing. We often had no contact with an African until she came to us because she was pregnant and didn't know what to do. They didn't know anything about contraception!' Carla throws up her arms in a classic gesture of exasperation. 'They were out on the streets every night and knew nothing about protecting themselves! There were women who had four abortions in one year! These were not voluntary sex workers: they were being trafficked into Italy and forced to work as prostitutes by the men who brought them over. They had no documents of their own and were too scared to tell anyone else what was happening to them. More and more began to arrive from Africa in 1995, especially Nigeria, and young women were also arriving from all over Eastern Europe.'

The Comitato supported as many trafficked women as they could and, alongside other activists, lobbied the Italian government to do something to provide for and protect these women. Three years later, in 1998, the Italian government introduced a new immigration law, which contained Article 18. This article provides a renewable six-month resident permit to severely exploited foreign migrants, including trafficked women, who are at risk because they have escaped their situation. Article 18 is the only provision in Europe where a migrant does not have to agree to testify against their trafficker or exploiter in order to be granted a temporary resident permit. A woman who manages to escape her trafficker in Italy is legally obliged to give a basic statement to a police officer in order to obtain her permit, but no more than that. She can give this statement to a social worker or a registered NGO, who will pass it on to the police on her behalf. Although Article 18 states severely exploited migrants are not obliged to cooperate any further with the authorities, or to testify in court in order to obtain temporary residency, human rights lawyers and NGOs claim that in practice residency is often issued as a *de facto* reward to migrants who do agree to cooperate further, or testify, which the majority apparently do. In 2004 more than eight thousand migrants were granted temporary resident permits in Italy.

People who receive the Article 18 permit are, however, obliged to take part in social assistance and reintegration programmes, which are now

run across Italy by various NGOs and community projects, including the
Comitato per i Diritti Civili delle Prostitute.

'We set up a project for trafficked women in 2000,' says Carla. 'This is
called Stella Polare ['Northern Star']. We work with psychologists,
educators and cultural mediators from six countries. Because we now
have funding from the government, we have a mobile unit, so we can
drive around the streets at night, distribute condoms and lubricant to the
women, and they can easily contact us if they do need help. We now have
three refuges for trafficked women, where they can stay for up to one
year. They have time to rest and recover and then to look for work. They
can also get legal advice and take classes in Italian. Under our Article 18, a
woman who was trafficked can stay in Italy for up to eighteen months,
and if she can find regular work, she is entitled to continue staying here.
Eventually she can apply for permanent residency.'

The Stella Polare project has brought the Comitato far more into the
political mainstream. These days they work alongside police officers,
magistrates, social workers and, Carla tells me, her eyes suddenly twink-
ling, nuns and priests.

'Yes! Some of my best colleagues are nuns. The Church has good
networks across the country for women who want to get off the streets.
We work well with these Church partners because we are usually prepared to listen to each other. I have been out on the streets many times
with nuns from the Church, making contact with women on the streets.'

My mind immediately conjures up an image of Carla, with her pink
highlights, strolling downtown alongside a nun clad in ankle-length black
robes. They would make quite an impression, wandering through the
streets of Trieste together.

I have one last question. 'What difference has Article 18 made?' I ask
Carla.

'It has been very good in providing for some of the most vulnerable
women and giving them protection when they are being badly abused and
exploited,' she says. 'There are fewer women on the streets now than two
years ago, but there is still a demand for foreign prostitutes here, and new
women are still arriving, especially from Eastern Europe: now women are
being trafficked from Bulgaria, and there are Roma women too, from
very poor communities. Many of the Africans are struggling. For a while
they were considered very exotic, but now the men want young white
Eastern Europeans. On the street a woman needs ten clients a night, and
the Africans tell us they are lucky to have seven or eight. There is more
supply than demand on the streets at the moment, and the women are in
competition with each other.

'It is difficult to say exactly how many of them are in this situation, because women who make the decision to work as prostitutes also have to use a facilitator: there is no other way for them to come inside Italy.

'When they cannot migrate, they will arrange to be smuggled, and some of the smugglers are traffickers; these things are all tied together. For us' – she smiles broadly and shrugs her shoulders at the same moment – 'if women were allowed to migrate legally and safely this would definitely help to prevent sex trafficking. Why should women not be allowed to migrate into sex work if they have made this decision for themselves?'

On my way out, Carla hands me a bundle of leaflets and papers to peruse. She shakes hands with me quite formally. Hermine smiles as she waves goodbye, standing quietly next to Carla. I would very much like to have heard Hermine's story, but she avoided telling me anything about herself. I asked her where she came from; she told me she is from Benin. And I left it at that.

I wander slowly back towards my hotel, find a vacant table outside a side-street café and order a cappuccino. I flick through the bumph Carla has just given me. There are leaflets on sexual health and the Stella Polare project and booklets in several different languages, which use cartoon strips to illustrate how women can best protect themselves whilst working on the street. Finally, there is a small green flyer with a telephone number and a short accompanying text printed in pidgin English, so as many women as possible can understand the message.

If dem force you make dey do prostitution
we fit help you comot this bad trade O . . .
Make Una Call Us Now For
800-290290

Chapter 11

On the Streets
With Franco

I met my Italian friend, Alessia, when she used to live in Edinburgh. Now she has moved back home to Vicenza, which is two hours' drive east of Trieste. Vicenza is a classic provincial town of a hundred thousand or so, and as the textile centre of Italy, it's a fairly well-heeled place. After my meeting with Carla Corso I board the train to go and stay with Alessia and her family for a week. They live on the edge of Vicenza, at the point where fields meet the town. Alessia takes some time off work, and we take day trips to nearby towns like Verona and Bassano del Grappa, where we stroll through piazzas and then loiter in warm twilit streets drinking *aperitivos* before late dinner. It is bliss. I exhale slowly, drink lots of wine and sleep very well.

During the week Alessia introduces me to her friends, some of whom I already knew from previous visits. One of them, Christian, has started volunteering for a local Catholic organisation called Papa Giovanni, which does social work with destitute people and outreach work with the sex workers of Vicenza. I have already seen the sex workers: they line the streets at night, especially the highway that leads north-west from Vicenza towards Verona. Alessia and I have driven past them several times on our way home.

I wonder if there is any way of making contact with them. I think that just stopping the car and attempting to speak to one of the women would be pretty futile. As Alessia says, we would just be stopping her from working.

I mention all this to Christian, and after a few late-night glasses of wine in one of the Vicenza bars, he generously volunteers to ask whether Alessia and I can spend a night out on the streets with one of the Papa Giovanni outreach workers. So Christian speaks to someone, who speaks to someone else, and negotiations go on for a few days, until halfway through dinner one evening, we get a call from Christian.

A volunteer called Franco is willing to meet us tonight, in about an hour. Apparently he has been out on the streets regularly for more than ten years, offering advice and support to women who either want to get out of the sex trade or stay in it as safely as possible. We can meet Franco at eleven o'clock in front of the Church of St Josephina, which is near the beginning of what locals now refer to as the '*Putan* Tour'.

Alessia and I get to St Josephina just before eleven. Franco is already there, leaning against his car. A street lamp casts a pool of waxy yellow light around him and the car. He looks as though he's in his fifties. He has a short, thick white beard and is wearing an Arran-style sweater and a striped sunhat that is pierced with a medley of badges and motifs. Introductions are brief and to the point. My Italian is rudimentary, and Franco obviously wants to get to work.

He instructs us to follow his car to a lay-by, where we can park our car and then climb into his, so we can drive along the highway together. By the time Alessia and I return to her car, Franco has already sped off, and Alessia, who drives like a demon at the best of times, has to put her foot to the floor to catch up with him.

Fifteen minutes later we are in Franco's car. He is driving through the centre of Vicenza, talking in growling, staccato Italian as we head to the highway.

'I do this run two or three times a week. I know most of the girls by sight and many by name now. Some leave and others arrive, but I keep up with the changes. My job is to keep an eye out, see who is around, spot the new arrivals, find out if any of the girls have gone missing and offer a room in a shelter for any who want to get off the street.'

Just outside the town centre, we see the first young woman, loitering alone on the street corner.

'She's Albanian,' says Franco, slowing the car down as we drive past. 'She's been here for a while. She works to support her family: she's got a lot of brothers in Albania who are unemployed. That one, just over there, she's a Romanian. New here. That blonde girl is also Albanian, and so is the girl she's standing with. Those two usually stand together. The Africans are further along the road, before the transsexuals. You'll see.'

As we drive on, I ask him if he knows whether these women have been trafficked.

He snorts loudly. 'No! That first one, she makes good money here and sends it home! She's already got a day job, so this is extra cash for her. The others are newer here, but they're doing quite well too. Not like the African prostitutes, they're struggling. Not exotic any more. Used to be, but these days the men want white girls, or transsexuals. See over there, those two. They're both transsexuals.'

On cue we pass two athletic-looking women with hugely inflated breasts, who leer loudly and give us the finger as they cackle wildly together.

'The men like them because they are half and half. That's why they are the most expensive to hire. Where are they from? Brazil. No, we can't stop and talk to them, because they're crazy. Mind you, that's because they get beaten up. The punters desire them and despise them at the same time. Wait a while, and we'll see if we can get one of the other girls to answer some questions.'

Tonight is Wednesday. This is usually the quietest night of the week on the street. The mid-week lull. I'm surprised how many women are out here when even the traffic is sparse.

I ask Franco about this and he shrugs. 'This is average. On a Saturday night there can be a hundred and fifty prostitutes lining this road. There are certain petrol stations and roundabouts where punters go for certain types of sex, or a girl from a particular country.' He brakes suddenly, almost veering and then gestures towards my side of the car. 'You know what that is?' He laughs out loud, making a sound like a bark, and I see the reflection of Alessia nodding through the driver's mirror, though she isn't laughing. 'It's Vicenza Police Station!' he barks again. 'This strip goes right past it!'

We drive past the lit-up station. Several women are standing right opposite, alone or in pairs. Those who are alone stand at regular distances from each other, within sight but out of earshot. Occasionally I see a black and a white woman standing together, talking and smoking, but it's mostly women of the same colour who are side by side. We drive past one white woman standing alone beneath a street lamp, her coat open and breasts bared to the road.

'Why do they end up here, Franco?' I ask him. 'What happens to them?'

I want him to explain why there are so many women renting themselves out on either side of a police station. I've seen women selling sex on the street before in several other cities, like my own, Edinburgh, but not lining the roads like this.

Franco scratches the back of his head underneath his hat, wipes his dry nose, then checks his mobile phone. He is constantly in motion: energy crackles around him. 'There are girls who do this for the money: it's just business for them. They get themselves over here, become established, find steady clients and know their way around. Nobody owns or pimps them. There are other girls who are controlled by their boyfriends, who are their pimps. These guys bring them here specifically to work on the street, and they don't usually beat them. But they're mean to them. It's psychological, you know. They threaten them: tell them that if they don't earn enough, they'll have their kids disfigured or something like that. Then they don't need to beat them anyway, because the girls don't believe they have any choice about being on the street. The girls who do the cars are the younger ones, and they only last two or three years at most anyway, because it's rough.

'The worst off are the prostitutes in the apartments. That's where the real money is made. It's only €30 for sex in a car, but the men pay €100 or more in an apartment, and it's become big business in the last couple of years. And inside those apartments is where you find the real *schiavi*, slaves. They are off the streets, where the police can't find them, and we can't keep an eye on them. Those girls have no one looking out for them.'

He adds that Papa Giovanni now ask him to visit private apartments to try to locate the off-street trade. 'I make appointments via the Internet, which is where most of the off-street trade is advertised. I get the addresses, visit the apartments and talk with the girls inside about the services we offer.' He turns his face to me and grins. 'I pay, but I don't purchase.' His expression is not a leer. I don't quite know what it is.

He's a maverick, Franco. Blunt as a cosh. No time for jargon or carefully chosen words. He refers to all these women as prostitutes, whether or not they choose to be here apparently selling sex at the side of the road, and moments later he rails against people who regard them as victims.

'These campaigners who want to stop the sex trade, they will tell you that every one of these prostitutes is a victim who wants to get off the street, and that's bullshit. We have helped more than six hundred girls off the streets so far, and we've got thirty-seven of them in different shelters at the moment. I also check up on them in the shelters, and we try to get them into work afterwards. But some of them choose to stay, and even for those who try to get out, it's hard to stay off the street. They make better money working as a prostitute than doing some shitty menial job. They get training as seamstresses or cleaners or in a shoe factory, but the money is no good. And if they've already worked the streets and some guy offers them €50 for sex, most of them are not going to turn it down.'

Estimates about the number of sex workers in Italy vary. Some journalists claimed there are more than seventy thousand women working in the Italian sex industry. Carla Corso believes there are around sixty thousand female and transgender sex workers, and that more than three quarters of them are migrants.

We are well out of Vicenza now, driving along a stretch of wide, dark road with intermittent street lights. We've been out for more than an hour, and Franco has barely paused for breath.

'I've been doing this work for twelve years, and I've heard a lot of stories. I've even had some of these girls stay in my own house because they've been in trouble.'

Before I have a chance to ask Franco about bringing troubled girls into his own home, he turns sharp right off the highway into an unmarked road, then almost immediately right again into a narrow, dark lane. He drives on slowly for a couple more minutes, until we come to a dead end. Then he does a slow, wide U-turn and winds down his window.

'You can't see anything now, but these are all fields where some of the men bring the girls. It's a free-for-all here, and you can fuck like a Turk.'

I glance back at Alessia in the back seat, and she meets my eyes. Without exchanging a word, we agree that he is an oddball, but he doesn't feel to either of us like a weirdo or a predator. We both feel quite safe with him, and that is what we care about right now.

On the way back to the main road, Franco slows the car down to a crawl in front of a young black woman standing alone on the junction corner.

'Let's see if she'll talk to you. Her name is Raisa. Offer her €20 if you want to ask her a few questions. These Africans are more likely to talk to you. The Eastern Europeans will tell you to go to hell. They don't trust anyone.'

I wind the window down, and Franco calls out something from his side of the car that includes her name. Raisa looks at the three of us and immediately backs off into the shadows. Franco shrugs and drives off.

'Why didn't she want to speak?' I ask. I assumed that she would be willing to talk to another woman, especially as Franco was with us.

'I don't know her very well, and there are three of us in the car,' he says, turning back on to the highway. 'Like I said, it's rough work on the street. She doesn't know who you two are, and she's scared of being beaten.'

We drive slowly along the highway and stop a couple more times in front of other women standing at the side of the road, but they also back off straightaway.

I feel increasingly tense every time we pull up: I don't like the way we're hassling women when they obviously don't want to speak to us, or are afraid of what they think we might try to do to them.

Franco's isn't fluent in English, so Alessia and I talk quietly between ourselves and decide to tell him that we don't want to approach any more women. But he has already stopped once more, in front of three black women standing on another corner, by a wide, dark, grassy verge. Two of them immediately retreat to the other side of the road, but the third woman holds her ground.

I instinctively wind the window down and ask her if she speaks English. She nods. 'Yes, I do.'

'Can I ask you a few questions?'

She nods again.

'Where are you from?'

'Liberia,' she says, looking around jerkily.

She tells me her name is Angela and that she travelled overland across Africa to Europe.

'We came across the river and arrived in Spain,' she says.

'Which river?'

'The one between Africa and Spain. The wide river.'

She is frowning and nervous, but I persist, because she has started to talk. 'What happened when you got to Spain?'

'Spain was nice. I didn't have to work in Spain. We stayed there for a few weeks, and then we came here, and he made me work outside on the street.'

'Who is he?'

She looks at me as if I am completely stupid. 'My boyfriend. He brought me here. He makes me do this. I don't like it here: it's dangerous, bad work. They can beat me, and if I don't make enough money, he beats me now too. Are you going to help me get out?'

Franco leans right across me and talks directly to her. She nods a few times as he speaks, visibly irritated.

'Yes, I know about your Papa Giovanni,' she says to me afterwards, when Franco has retreated back to his side of the car. 'I just need to get my papers in order. Are you going to help me?'

'Do you want to go back home, Angela?'

I am deliberately fending off her question, because I am not going to help her. I don't know how to help her. She doesn't want whatever it is that Franco has just offered, and I have nothing else to offer her but some euros. I feel like a punter myself right now: thanks for the info, Angela, I've got the gist of your wretched story, so I'll be off. Here's €20 for your trouble.

Angela is glaring at me. 'Of course I want to go home! But I can't. I've got nothing: no money and no documents. I can't go anywhere. Are you going to help me?'

'I'm sorry; I don't know what to do to help you. But I can give you some money. Thank you for talking to me.'

I hand €20 out of the window, and Angela says thank you back as she takes the money. Franco revs the engine and slowly turns the car round, back towards the highway. As we are pulling out, the other two women join Angela, and they stand together talking.

The three of us have nothing to say to each other for the next few minutes. When Franco does begin to speak again, his voice is slower and softer. 'Girls like her have no money and no papers. Officially they don't even exist. They are completely at the mercy of the men who drive up and take them away in their cars, and every time they get into a car they can disappear. I've spent a lot of time talking to these girls, and I've also met a lot of their clients, and some of them, they do things to these girls they would never do to their wives or girlfriends.'

He drives us silently back towards our car.

Chapter 12

God's Work

The morning after our night out with Franco, I start packing to go home. I plan to take a train south through Tuscany to Rome, stay in as cheap a hotel as I can find for the next couple of days and then fly direct to Scotland, courtesy of Ryanair. However, my homeward plans stall when Italy is brought to a sudden, inevitable standstill by the death of Pope John Paul II. As the tidal wave of a million mourners surges towards Rome, I retreat from joining them and spend an extra week in Vicenza, waiting for the papal funeral to be conducted, and for an available flight back home.

Alessia has to return to work, so I spend my afternoons in her sunny attic room, writing and staring out of her window across the fields, which begin at the edge of her garden. The days are long and bright. I've been away from my home for more than a month now and am definitely ready to return to my own familiar corner and take stock of this journey. But the Internet is a devilish device, and I lose track of the hours as I trawl through cyberspace, unable to resist the idea of trying to find out just a little more before I leave.

I email various Italian organisations that work with trafficked women, refugees and undocumented migrants in Rome, and receive one reply. Signora Franca di Lecce heads a small refugee organisation with an office in Rome. She writes that though she may not be able to give me the information I require, she knows someone who works with trafficked women and will try to contact him on my behalf.

I visit Signora di Lecce the morning after I arrive in Rome. Her office, just off Via Roma, is at the top of a mountain of dark, cold stairs. But she is there, waiting for me with a cup of coffee and a warm smile.

By the time we have drunk our coffee and talked for an hour, I am not going home any more, at least not for another week or so. After leaving her office, I go straight into the first travel agency I see on the street and book a one-way flight to Palermo, Sicily.

*

Vivian meets me outside the main Palermo *posta*. I am sitting on the wall outside, enjoying the brilliant Sicilian sunshine when he pulls up in his rackety old blue car. We signal to each other by waving. His appearance is a bit of a give-away: a tall, bearded Nigerian with onyx skin. Mind you, I hardly look Sicilian myself. We shake hands politely as we introduce ourselves, and he asks how I am, whether I had a good journey and if I like Sicily. I tell him I'm fine, the flight was fine too, and this is the first time I've been here. I arrived yesterday, in the early afternoon, and found an English-language guidebook in the airport bookshop, which listed a small B&B in the old town centre run by a 'friendly Dutch woman called Marjolein'. Both her guest rooms were full last night, but she said I was welcome to stay on the roof terrace. Swathed in blankets and surrounded by flowering cacti, I drifted off to sleep as bats flittered across the indigo skyline.

'I think Sicily is gorgeous,' I say to Vivian, as he opens the passenger door for me. 'How long have you been living here?'

Vivian Wiwoloku is from the city of Lagos. He graduated as a pharmacologist and also trained as a Methodist minister before leaving Nigeria. He originally came to Palermo fifteen years ago, in 1990, to do the equivalent of a PhD and work as a preacher with the resident Nigerian community.

'In between the weekly services we also held regular prayer meetings at houses in the Noce district of the city, and some of the ladies began to attend these meetings. They were in spiritual crisis and came to our meetings to ask us to pray for them and give them the strength to leave the street. We prayed with them, and these ladies came back the next week so that we could pray for them again and give them more strength to leave.'

He looks over at me and nods twice as though to confirm this information, then slowly turns his attention back to the steering wheel and the crowded road. All of his movements, speech and gestures are slow and considered. Vivian drives placidly through the streets of Palermo, whilst the Sicilians speed around us, horns bellowing, as though hell-bent on revenge.

The ladies he is referring to are African women who have been trafficked to Sicily and forced into street prostitution in lieu of their 'debt'. Vivian tells me they come from West Africa, usually Nigeria.

'When we began to meet with the ladies every week, to support them in prayer, we realised that even when they had the courage to leave the street, they had nowhere to stay. So we set up our project, Pellegrino del

Terra ['Pilgrim of the Earth'], so they would know where to contact us when they needed somewhere to stay.'

He offers to take me on a tour of Palermo and says we can eat dinner later at the small café Pellegrino del Terra has also opened, partly as a fund-raiser, and partly to employ several of the ladies who have come off the street. I immediately agree, wondering what he will show me as this obviously isn't going to be a sightseeing tour.

Vivian drives through the centre of Palermo, turns left at the Quattro Canti crossroad and down Corso Vittorio Emanuele towards the port. Palermo is deafening. The street traffic is a constant roar, fuelled by the additional power of laughter, music and crowds of people talking and calling out to each other. The buildings are tall, elegantly ruinous, blackened by exhaust fumes.

We turn right at a roundabout, and the road briefly becomes an underpass, a concrete corridor flowing with ribbons of traffic. It has a narrow raised strip of pavement.

'This is where many of the ladies have to stand at night,' he says as we are driving upwards, back out into the sunlight.

'They work in this tunnel to pay off their debt.'

We come off the main road, bump through a labyrinth of backstreets and he stops outside a large church. This is Santa Chiara all'Albergheria. It's Sunday afternoon, and there's a large crowd buzzing outside, formally dressed in suits and hats, as though they've just been at a service. Everyone seems to be African. People constantly greet Vivian, and he says he is well, 'thanks be to God' a dozen times before we climb the steps.

He explains that Santa Chiara is also a reception centre for newly arrived migrants and refugees. He shows me the huge courtyard at the back.

'We have dormitories here, where migrants can stay when they arrive. They can have food and find advice about what to do next and how to arrange their papers.'

Later, Vivian and I have our dinner at the Pellegrino del Terra café. It's quiet this evening, with just a few customers eating and drinking, though Vivian says they have regular Saturday-night parties. 'Sometimes they have to beg the customers to stop dancing and go home!'

While we're eating, I ask him more about the ladies: how many of them are here, and who traffics them to Sicily in the first place?

'There are maybe three thousand Nigerian ladies in Sicily,' he says, putting down his fork. 'More than one hundred of them have come off the street completely, and we are in contact with more than a hundred and fifty others who are still on the street. They come to Sicily because they think they will have a better life in Italy. Often they think they are actually going to work in Rome or another big city. The madams lie to them and then force them on to the streets—'

'Madams?' I interrupt him. 'Are the traffickers women?'

He nods. 'Yes. I think all of the ladies have been trafficked by Nigerian women. They trust the madams, you see, when they assure them that there is good, honest work waiting for them in Italy.'

He has met a number of these madams over the last ten years. 'They even come to find me sometimes,' he tells me calmly.

'What do they say? Do they threaten you?'

'No. They just ask me why I spoil their business. Because they know that sometimes our project receives calls from ladies who want help to leave that night, and that we visit the ladies to pray with them, and they also come to our prayer meetings. The madams ask me to leave their business alone. You have your work at the church, they tell me, and we have ours. Let us leave it like that, and then we won't have to bother you again.'

'And what do you say to them, Vivian?' I have a sudden terrible urge to laugh at the absurdity of this situation: female traffickers visiting a local preacher, asking him to please stay away and leave them to rent out their girls in peace.

'I tell them the ladies need to know they have somewhere to come when they are ready to leave the street.'

After our meal, Vivian introduces me to the two young Nigerian women working in the café and unexpectedly asks them if they will talk to me about their experiences. They both shake their heads, one smiling shyly at me, the other looking down at the floor, sullen as a teenager. I tell him it's fine if they don't want to talk. Vivian is a gracious man and has said he wants to help me. But after Albania, and especially after just being on the streets with Franco, I've realised asking a woman questions about her experiences of being trafficked is pretty invasive.

Over the next few days Vivian and I meet several times. He is late on every occasion, sometimes hours late, because someone who needs his help has called his mobile and he has to go and tend to them first. Half of Palermo seems to have his mobile-phone number. I try not to let this endless waiting drive me crazy, because I admire and respect him.

When we do eventually meet, he shows me the small Pellegrino del Terra office. It's a cramped room on a side street, with a fridge, a table and chairs, but no telephone. Run by three Nigerian women, it's open every weekday for any ladies who want to come in for advice and information, as well as for refugees, migrants and anyone else who needs help. Destitute Sicilians come to the door too, asking for food and shelter, and are always welcome inside.

After leaving the office, Vivian and I walk through the old city of Palermo together, meeting some of the many people he knows. We visit the young Sudanese refugee who made it to Sicily alone after God knows what happened to his family. Now he works in one of the corner shops where people make cheap international calls back home to Africa. Vivian introduces me to Bangladeshi traders, Moroccan restaurant workers and a group of other young North African men who have just returned from one of the large inland farms, where the hours are long, conditions hard and the pay minimal and non-negotiable; but it's still the best deal they are going to get in Sicily.

In the late afternoon we meet a middle-aged Nigerian with crazy bright eyes, who blurts out his story to me while Vivian is taking another call on his mobile. Wole used to be a TV cameraman in Lagos but fell foul of the Obasanjo regime because he also filmed opposition politicians. Warned on the quiet that he was going to be detained, he spirited himself over the border at night and slowly made his way overland to Libya.

'Many of us were there, waiting for the chance to come to Europe.'

Eventually a group of them managed to secure a boat from one of the Libyan smugglers.

'It cost me everything I had to share a leaking vessel with twenty-five others. We nearly died out there. The engine packed up, and we had no water left, and then the boat began to leak! It was fishermen, you know, who saved us. They spotted us and called the Navy, and we were towed into Lampedusa. You see dead bodies floating in the sea: people who lost their way.'

Lampedusa is a barren outcrop of an island, 200 kilometres south of Sicily. The most southern fragment of Italian territory, it's a magnet for African immigrants (*clandestini*) desperate to reach Europe. It is also, perversely, an upmarket tourist resort, because of its pristine beaches and fabulous diving. A large detention centre has been built at the end of the airport. Officially it has the capacity to hold 200 detainees; on occasions ten times that number have been packed inside. Wole was one of the lucky ones. He was brought to Sicily and managed to find a good immigration lawyer. Now the Italian authorities are flying most *clandestini* straight back to Libya: regardless of what they've been through, there is no chance of claiming asylum in Europe. Instead, the Mayor of Lampedusa, Bruno Syracusa, has asked Sicily for more boats to patrol the waters, and scoop up the dead bodies.

Wole has made it to Europe, but at a price. There are flecks of foam either side of his mouth. He looks physically sick and mentally unsteady.

'This is not Italy!' he roars, opening up his arms expansively. 'This is a refugee camp for Africans!'

After saying goodbye to Wole, and later to Vivian, I stroll through the backstreets towards my B&B, pondering as I wander. The smugglers, traffickers and Sicilian Mafia seem to have carved up business neatly between themselves here. The smugglers control the boat runs from north-east Africa, charging, according to Wole, the equivalent of €2,000 per head for the chance to reach Europe in a leaky boat with a dodgy outboard engine and a compass for directions. Older Nigerian women have taken over the business of trafficking young Nigerians into street prostitution. And the Mafia? They oversee just about everything else in Sicily. There are far fewer murders these days, but it's still reckoned that 80 per cent of stores in Palermo pay *pizzo*, protection money, to the Mafia.

Vivian has arranged to meet me at the Pellegrino del Terra office at ten this morning. He wants me to meet some nuns who work with the ladies. He arrives at a quarter to twelve, and we set off in his car. Half an hour later he parks in a nondescript-looking suburb of large modern buildings and blocks of flats.

The convent is surrounded by a high wall. The sign outside says, 'Buon Pastore', the 'Good Shepherd'. We are buzzed inside and met by a nun clad in white, who leads us to a large, ornate living room and leaves us to wait.

It is very quiet. There is, bizarrely, a vending machine in one corner. I ask Vivian if he wants a coffee, and he shakes his head. As the thin beige liquid is trickling into the plastic cup, another nun arrives and escorts us to an office to meet Sister Maria Rita.

She is a very round, beaming nun. Vivian translates as she explains this order, the Catholic Sisters of the Good Shepherd, provides refuge for ladies who have just come from the streets. Vivian and his small team of volunteers are out in Palermo several nights a week, reminding the ladies at the underpass, and elsewhere, they have refuge waiting for them when they are ready. There are several places they can stay, and this is one of them.

'Many of the ladies are not prepared to come off the street until their debt is paid,' she says. 'They are frightened they will be found by the madman, or of what will happen to their families back at home. Even when they owe nothing, there is the risk they will stay on the street, because they become used to this life, and they still need money to live. Unemployment is a huge problem in Sicily. You know, we are 5 million people on this island, and we are the poorest part of Italy too. We have to find better work for these ladies than cleaning or looking after children, or they will be tempted to go back to the street and make better money.'

Vivian has already told me that once their debt is expunged, the Nigerian ladies are actually free to go. It is a curious principle in this mercenary business. Everywhere else I have visited, the debt either just keeps increasing or as soon as it is paid off, the woman is immediately sold to another pimp.

While Sister Maria Rita is talking, two teenage girls casually push the door open and wander in. One of them lights up when she spots Vivian. 'Mr Vivian!' She flings her arms around his neck. Vivian looks rather embarrassed at her joy in seeing him. I feel quite choked up as she embraces him. The two of them then plonk themselves down amongst us. The slightly older-looking of the two, Yvetta, takes over translating, and when I ask her how she finds the convent, she smiles at me.

'It's fine. You know they have these rules, but you can mostly come and go as you want. They ask to switch your mobile phone off for the first few weeks, so Madam cannot find you, but after that you can start to study, and they will help you decide what to do afterwards.'

Yvetta wears thick glasses. Whilst on the street she was beaten with a bottle by a punter, and is now blind in one eye. She has lived here for six months and is employed as the convent's cultural mediator. The other girl, who is so delighted to see Vivian, arrived just two weeks ago and says only that she is safe and happy.

'I want to be here,' she says to me. 'Believe me, I want to be here.'

Yvetta and Sister Maria Rita offer me a tour of the convent. It's a large building with several floors, including a semi-independent third-floor wing where the ladies have private rooms, a lounge and several kitchens where they cook for themselves. We climb up to the third floor, and Sister Maria Rita stands at the door of one of the kitchens, beckoning someone forward. A woman comes out, holding a wooden spoon. She is wearing an extremely tight and very low-cut crimson dress that stretches from her breasts down to her calves. Her lipstick is streaked across thin, dry lips; her lower lip has a thick scab hardening on top of a swelling that palsies her smile. Her skin is blotchy, and she looks as rough as hell. She doesn't say anything, just smiles at us, revealing a mouthful of broken, missing and stained teeth.

'This lady, Rosa, has just come from the street,' says Yvetta, as the woman retreats back into her kitchen.

She must have turned up with just the clothes on her back, and here she is, safe in the convent, cooking her lunch. This place is quite something.

Yvetta and Sister Maria Rita introduce me to half a dozen other ladies who have been trafficked to Sicily and taken refuge here. Most of them meet my eyes and say hello cheerfully; a couple of them obviously don't want to speak to me and stare down at the floor. They are all Nigerian, except for one young woman, from Kosovo. She was trafficked to Sicily for organ 'donation' and managed to escape before one of her kidneys was stolen from her body. She has been living here for three years now but still looks shell-shocked. Kosovo, I think to myself: once visited, never forgotten.

Yvetta, Sister Maria Rita and I end up in the communal lounge. There is another young woman in there, sitting alone and reading. When I apologise for the interruption, she beckons me over.

'No problem. Come and sit down and talk to me.'

Her name is Bright. She is very small and slender, and has tiny, narrow feet. While we all sit, Bright and I talk. At first she says very little about herself: only that she's been in Italy for 'a few years now, and I think I will be staying for longer'.

Sister Maria Rita interjects to say she's sorry but she has to go; there is work waiting for her, and Yvetta says she is busy too. When they stand to leave, Bright asks me to stay a while.

She asks me a lot of questions about myself, and she's a good listener. She seems comfortable, self-confident, quite joyful, really. Her eyes have light in them: she is healing from whatever has happened. I forget Vivian is waiting downstairs for me, and when one of the other sisters comes up to collect me, because it's now mid-afternoon, I am sorry to be going.

'Why don't you come back tomorrow afternoon?' says Bright. 'Come back and we can walk in the garden and talk some more.'

Vivian is busy the following afternoon, so I take a taxi back to the Buon Pastore to visit Bright. She's waiting for me in the hallway.

'We are lucky, because today is beautiful, thank God, so we can go and sit in the garden!' She beams at me and leads me through the quiet, clean convent to a large, well-tended garden, where sets of picnic chairs and tables are set out on a wide lawn.

We sit in the sun and carry on talking. I have already told Bright why I am in Sicily, and I know why she's staying here, but there is an unspoken agreement between us that she will talk to me about what happened if and when she's ready.

A while later Bright goes inside to fetch orange juice. In her absence the silence is reassuring: the trees screen sounds from the road. I remember what Carla Corso said about nuns being some of the best people to work with. She seems to be right. I hadn't expected the convent to be like this at all.

Bright comes back with juice and biscuits, and we pick up where we left off. The time passes easily. When the air begins to cool, Bright invites me inside for a cup of tea. We return to the empty lounge, cupping the hot mugs in our hands, and she finally says to me, 'You have to understand how this terrible thing can happen to a girl from Nigeria. I know how it can happen, because it happened to me.'

Bright grew up on a farm in eastern Nigeria, outside Benin City. She has seven brothers. She attended primary and secondary school, but her parents couldn't afford to send her to university. Bright was restless and didn't want to be confined to the farm, so she arranged to stay with a relative in Benin City for a few weeks, to see whether she could find work there instead.

'I found work in an office. It was basic, and the pay was a poor local salary. But as soon as I started to work, I paid for night classes and learned how to type quickly. That was how I got a better job and stayed living in Benin City. I was living in my aunt's place because I could pay her rent and that was good for both of us, and I could also send money home. It was my aunt who introduced me to this woman, a friend of hers, who asked me if I wanted to come and work in Rome. That was how it all started.

'You know, my life was good in Benin City. I was not deprived, not at all. But this woman, she knew what to say. "There is good work waiting for you in Italy," she told me. "They need hard-working Nigerians like you. They will train you as an auxiliary, and you will clean the hospital, help the patients, and the money would be good." I don't remember exactly how much, but it was more than I could ever earn in Benin City.

'I spent all my savings on buying the plane ticket, but it wasn't enough money, and so this woman paid the rest. I signed a paper to say I would repay her. I remember she said to me, "Don't worry, after a few months working in the hospital, you will have paid me back everything, and you will forget who I am because you will be earning good money and having a wonderful life!"

'I know there are lots of very clever people who think they would not make this mistake. All I can tell them is "Go and live in Nigeria! Try life over in my country and then say that you would not be willing to take the risk of coming to Europe to earn good money." These clever women, they ask you to sign a contract, and you sign it gladly, even if it states that your own home will be at risk. "It's just a formality," they say: "Nothing to worry about." I know why these girls take these risks: I understand how they are tempted, because these madams who bring them over here, they tell you exactly what you want to hear.'

Benin City is the capital of Edo State, one of the poorest states in Nigeria. The majority of Nigerian women who are trafficked to Europe come from Edo State. Research from the Benin City Women's Health and Action Research Centre has concluded that around a third of young Nigerian women in Benin City have received at least one offer of working abroad.[1] The combination of domestic poverty, historic trade relations with Italy and widespread corruption of officials, especially police and immigration, has opened up business for traffickers to transport young Nigerian women to Italy. Researchers have traced Nigerian women being trafficked into the Italian sex industry since at least the mid-eighties, though the trade has undoubtedly burgeoned since 1995. There's never been a precise explanation for why so many of these women come from Edo province, which is poor, but not the poorest part of Nigeria. Poverty, discrimination against females and the lure of migrant remittances have all been cited. Female emigrants have returned to Edo State from working abroad, built fine homes and easily recruited young women to work in Italy. Some of these young women know they will be working in the sex industry; many others are unaware. There are now thought to be up to ten thousand Nigerian sex workers throughout Italy.

It was the summer of 2002 when Bright travelled from Benin City to Ghana with her aunt's friend, and then they flew together from Ghana to Rome.

'It was all legal. I had my passport, and she got the visa for me and came all the way with me herself. The journey was easy, and I was very happy. When we arrived in Rome, she took me to an apartment, where she introduced me to another Nigerian woman who was going to be looking after me. Then she asked me politely to give her my passport so that she could register me with the police, and that was the last time I ever saw her, or my passport. She just vanished.

'This madam, she had half a dozen girls in her apartment. We were all Nigerian. And she told me straightaway that I owed her a lot of money, and that the only way I was going to be able to pay back this money was to go on to the street. She said my debt was €40,000.

'"You are joking," I said to her. "I am never going to work on the street. No way." And for almost a month I refused. Most of that time I stayed in the apartment, and she left me alone. She cooked for me, and she waited for me to change my mind. For those three or four weeks she

1. www.migrationinformation.org, Jorgen Carling, 2005.

did not mention the street. But one day out of the blue she told me she wouldn't feed me any more, because I wasn't earning any money for her. She said I could go out and earn money any way I wanted, but I had to make €150 a day to continue staying in the apartment. "What are you going to do?" she said. "You have no passport, but go to the police if you like. They will arrest you and put you in prison, and prison in Italy is very dangerous. You don't speak this language, and you have no rights here. Eventually, after prison, they will deport you home to Nigeria, but you will still owe me money, and I know where your family live. I will find you and them and tell them everything about you, and I will collect my money."

'She was never violent, and she never used voodoo on me. You know, the voodoo can work on some girls and make them easily controlled, like frightened animals. But Madam, she knew I was a Christian and those things have no effect on me. But she was still not going to let me have a roof over my head unless I worked for her. I was frightened, sure! I was very scared of going to prison and what might happen to me there, because she was right: I had no papers, and with no papers you have no identity. But you know the strangest thing of all? It was the other girls who persuaded me to go on the street. They said, "Look, it is not so bad. You get used to it. You can earn good money, and after one year she will let you go. You can pay back this debt, make some money for yourself and then go home with your head up." So, this is how I ended up working on the street in Rome.'

These voodoo rituals have received more than their fair share of press attention, with lurid reports of young women being daubed in chicken blood and terrified by local witchdoctors. But research carried out in Nigeria indicates that the ritual itself is a formal pact between the young woman and her 'sponsor'. The young woman promises to repay her sponsor in full and in return is guaranteed safe passage. This pact is often sealed by an *ohen*, a traditional priest, who functions as the equivalent of a local magistrate.[2] He assembles a small parcel of nail clippings, locks of hair and other small 'protective' personal items collected from the young female. This ritual is deemed to protect her, and most of them are willing for the *ohen* to seal their pact. Christians sometimes make similar emigration pacts in Pentecostal churches. These are all public acknowledgements of the opportunity and responsibility being given to the young woman and are taken very seriously. The trafficker will only threaten to unleash the power of the *ohen* if the young woman challenges the pact by

2. Jorgen Carling (International Peace Research Institute).

wanting to leave before she has paid back her 'debt'. Anti-Slavery International has, however, spoken to *ohens* who acknowledge the ritual can be manipulated, and that traffickers sometimes deliberately use an accomplice to impersonate an *ohen* and perform these rituals in order to gain psychological control over the women.[3]

'Nobody tells you what it is like working on the street at night. How bad it is. You have to earn this €150 or else you sleep in the park that night, and the park is very dangerous, and anyway, you still have to pay her all the money next time you go home. I never had to sleep in the park, but I have seen girls crying and begging each other for money because they didn't earn enough to go back to the apartment.

'Madam buys you street clothes, but you know you have to pay her for them. You stand there on the side of the road in these clothes that she bought for you and wave to the cars to catch their attention. The first car stops, and maybe the man shouts, "Hey, whore! Suck my cock for free!" But you don't shout nothing back, because you don't know if he's drunk or crazy. So he drives on. When the next car stops, he asks you how much, and when you tell him, he wants you to do it cheaper for him. But you need the money, so you smile and say, "No, this is my price," and he drives off too. By the time the third car stops you are feeling a little desperate because you haven't made any money yet. And when this guy pulls up and shouts, "Let's go!" you get in the car without negotiating how much it will be, because you need to work, and you don't want him to drive off like the others.

'Maybe he drives you a little out of town, somewhere you don't know, or to a park, and then he parks in the dark and says, "How much?" And you don't want to say too much, because he might refuse to pay, or get angry, and you don't even know where you are. So you have to ask him what he wants and how much he is willing to pay. Any maybe he wants to come in your face, or have sex without a condom, or anal sex without a condom, and you have to try to persuade him that you don't do that without a condom, but still get him to agree a price. Sometimes they say, "Hey, don't hassle me. I'll pay you later. Let's just see how it goes." And they mean that if you are good enough, they will pay you. They often refuse to wear a condom, and some men say they will put the condom on, and then they break it on purpose, so they can release themselves inside you. And afterwards maybe they insist on paying you less, saying it wasn't so good, or ask for it gratis, because they say you are a whore and this is

3. 'Human Traffic, Human Rights', Elaine Pearson, Anti-Slavery International report, p.165.

what you do anyway. Or maybe they beat you and steal your money, or leave you in this park and drive off without you.

'I was lucky. I never had my money stolen, and I was never beaten. But a lot of these men, they don't like women. They want to use them and just leave them in the street or the park afterwards, like a piece of trash. Even when you are back in the car with him and he has paid you the money, it's not safe yet. I stood on the street with women who were just thrown out of cars afterwards. These men opened the passenger door and kicked them out into the middle of the road while they were still driving. The women were all scraped by the fall and had to roll out of the way of other cars.

'Sometimes we stood on the side of that road and young men drove past – they were almost young enough to be boys – and they threw cups of piss at us for sport. Just for sport.

'I tell you, I was actually lucky on the street, because I always earned my money and could go home to sleep in the apartment afterwards and bathe. And every night when I got back, I thanked God that I had survived that night.'

It takes between one and three years for a trafficked Nigerian woman to pay off her debt. Research from the International Peace Research Institute encapsulates the dynamics involved:

> The strength of the Nigerian trafficking networks lies in the element of reciprocity between traffickers and victims. The religious and legal sanctioning of the pact [. . .] gives the majority of victims a strong motivation to comply. As a result, Nigerian trafficking networks are less reliant on the use of violence than their Eastern European counterparts.
>
> The victims' commitment to the pact makes it particularly difficult to combat this form of trafficking. In several European countries authorities have 'rescued' women from their traffickers, but they return to prostitution to fulfil their obligations.[4]

Once the debt has been paid, some women leave, while others begin to work for the madams as supervisors of the new arrivals, or return to Nigeria and recruit another batch of young women to work in Italy. This is what researchers call a 'self-regulating and self-perpetuating model'. It creates a chronic cycle of victims becoming perpetrators and feeds the industry.

Bright suddenly smiles at me. It's an unexpected smile. 'I almost forgot to tell you that I was arrested on my very first night,' she says. 'After all those

4. Jorgen Carling, International Peace Research Institute, Oslo, 2005.

threats from the madam, the police caught me one hour after I started on the street! The girls were shouting, "Run! Run!" But I didn't know who from: I didn't even know what the police looked like. I had hardly been outside before. I tried to run and just fell over, and they caught me.'

'What happened when they caught you?'

'Nothing much. I tried to explain to them what had happened to me, but they didn't speak English, and I didn't speak Italian. They put me in this cell for one night and just released me the next morning – really. She was waiting for me outside the station, the madam. She knew exactly where I was. "I told them," she said to me. "I told them you were working for me, and they let you go." Now, of course, I know she was just making it all up. But something happens in this situation, and you stop believing yourself. She told me these lies, and instead I believed her.'

After several months of working on the streets of Rome, the madam unexpectedly told Bright that she was going to work for another madam. Bright has no idea why she was passed over to someone else. The second madam, another Nigerian woman, brought her to Sicily. She installed Bright in a private apartment, not in Palermo but in Catania, a resort on the east coast.

'It was the *centro historico*, the old town, where the tourists come to visit.

'Because I am small and I look young, she let me work mornings and afternoons, before they got drunk and aggressive, so I didn't have to go with the drunks and the stinking old men. And even though I hated it, I knew my situation was actually better now, thanks be to God. I was in that apartment for more than a year when one man came inside who was very nice to me. From the very beginning he was very kind. He understood I didn't want to be there, and soon he talked with my madam. She told him how much she had paid for me, and he agreed to pay her the money, so I could be free from this work.' Paying for sex is commonplace in Italy. The Italian Interior Ministry estimates that up to 45 per cent of Italian men pay for sex at least once a year. This has created enormous demand for migrant sex workers, including trafficked women and girls.

When Bright was released from her trafficker, her friend contacted Vivian, who offered her a place at the Buon Pastore.

'I was glad to come here,' she says. 'For a long time I didn't want to go outside. I was very ashamed, and I was always afraid that people would know what I had been doing and would shout, "*Puta!* Whore!" at me in the street. I have lived very quietly for a year, but now I am ready to leave.'

She talks about what has happened with a detachment that implies she has mentally processed her experience and is poised to move out, and on.

'Where will you go?' I ask her, curious about what she'll do next.

She smiles at me quite openly. 'I am going to stay with my friend, the one who helped me in the first place.'

For some reason this doesn't surprise me. He was a punter, who paid to have sex with Bright, then paid off her debt and bought her freedom.

Bright leaves this hanging in the air for a moment and then changes the subject. 'I know a few girls who are on the road or working in these nightclubs. Some of them can't get out because of their debt, and for some of them now, it is their life. This woman I know still dances at a club in Catania, even though her debt is paid. She called me recently and asked me how much money I am going to earn when I start work. When I told her my salary, she laughed herself silly. "Why don't you come and work with me?" she said. "You can just dance around a pole and wiggle at the men, and you can earn good money. And you can keep it all. Now you don't have to pay no madam." "No thanks," I told her. "I know how I want to earn money. You do your job if you like it, but I don't want this club money."'

'So what's your new job?' I ask her. 'Where are you going to work?'

Bright is going to start working in the Pellegrino del Terra office. She is also planning to go to university to do a diploma in social administration, so she can work with ladies and immigrants who have just arrived in Sicily. 'I think I could be useful there,' she says.

I can't help asking her about the madam who brought her to Sicily and whether she is still pimping girls out in Catania.

Bright shrugs and says she doesn't know. 'But I imagine she is still there,' she says. 'These madams have a very good business.' Then she asks me a question back. 'Louisa, what about the ladies in your country? What happens to them?'

That's a bloody good question, I think to myself. But I don't say that to Bright. What I say to her is 'I don't know very much about them, to be honest. I've been researching what goes on elsewhere. I guess it's time I went back and had a look.'

Bright walks me downstairs to the front door of the convent. She gives me a small square of paper. She has scribbled her email address on it.

'Stay in touch and let me know,' she says. 'Good luck with your book, and may God bless you.'

Chapter 13

Whose Side Are You On?

The most striking difference between the sex industries in Italy and Britain is where most of the women work.

In Italy, I saw foreign sex workers lining the streets. It is heavily ironic that the country that has the most comprehensive provisions for trafficked women and other severely exploited migrants in Europe also has one of the Continent's most blatantly visible sex industries. From Trieste to Palermo, thousands of women are on the streets every night selling sex to unpredictable male punters. It's a minority of women who work off street in private premises.

In Britain, however, it is the off-street sex industry that's flourishing.

Street workers are still predominantly British women, while foreign women are almost exclusively based in saunas, massage parlours, walk-up flats or private houses, away from casual glances and very often removed from easy contact, except for the punters of course.

I used to live in London and have returned to look at the sex industry and talk to people who work with sex workers and trafficked women. Human trafficking has been a specific offence with a maximum fourteen-year penalty in this country since 2002.[1] Prostitution, on the other hand, has never been illegal in the UK, though many of the activities surrounding it are criminal offences. There are some thirty prostitution-related offences, from kerb-crawling to brothel-keeping and 'controlling prostitution for gain'. The sex industry is a legal, political and ethical minefield. It's also extremely lucrative: one recent estimate put the value of the UK sex industry at £770 million a year, with street prostitution accounting for just 5 per cent of the total.

Although London was my home for more than seven years, I don't know much about its sex industry, and so I start my search in as obvious a place as possible: Soho.

---

1. Section 145 of the Nationality, Immigration and Asylum Act 2002. This act only refers to traffic in prostitution.

*

Soho has always attracted foreigners, whether migrants or tourists. Immigrants started moving into its narrow streets back in the eighteenth century, and by the turn of the nineteenth century it was truly cosmopolitan, and colonies of artists, writers and political activists had also set up home there.

William Blake was born in Soho, and Karl Marx lived on Dean Street for years. Towards the end of the nineteenth century Soho began to establish itself as the epicentre of London's nightlife, and by the 1960s it also had a burgeoning resident sex trade, which still famously thrives. Almost fifty years later, Soho remains the most obvious red-light district of London. In Berwick Street, where the open-air market has traded cheap fruit and veg since the 1960s, cafés and clothes shops are interspersed with sex shops selling varieties of porn, venues advertising fully nude pole dancers, clip joints, where punters are infamously ripped off to the tune of hundreds, sometimes thousands of pounds, and the walk-up flats, where men buy cheap, quick sex like fast food.

The flats are called walk-ups because they are situated at the top of flights of narrow, steep stairs. At the street-level entrances, there are uneven hand-written signs advertising 'sexy oriental model' or 'French Chloe, new in town'. Inside the small flats, prices for sexual acts are typed on menus that are tacked on to the wall. Prices fluctuate, especially if the woman is desperate to make up her money on a particular day, but sexual intercourse, which lasts about ten minutes, costs around £20. The price doubles if a punter wants unprotected vaginal or anal sex. Punters are also charged an extra £10 if they want the sex worker to use a specific position. Workers also sell combinations of oral, anal and hand jobs.

Sex workers in Soho have to work extremely hard as the rents are extortionate. The walk-ups cost at least £250 a day in rent, and the sex worker has to pay her maid too.[2] Maids earn £80 a day, plus tips, but this is negotiated between the two women. In order just to break even, a Soho sex worker needs to earn around £350 a day, which means seeing at least eighteen punters a day. Some flats have different women working in them on different days. If a sex worker doesn't make her quota for the day, the debt is transferred to the next day or to her next shift, and she will then have to see more punters. The pressure to earn as much money as possible is intense.

Wandering along Berwick Street Market, I notice several of the walk-ups have lamps displayed in the windows. When a woman is having sex

---

2. A maid is a receptionist who screens punters for a sex worker and provides security at the flat. Often a former sex worker, she knows the industry and how to manage the punters.

with a punter, a red light bulb is lit, which flickers against the thin curtain fabric. To describe these walk-ups as part of the Soho landscape doesn't begin to convey how completely ubiquitous they've become. They are spaced at regular intervals, almost as though on a grid system.

Since the mid-nineties, the Soho sex industry has radically altered, as more and more foreign women have started working in walk-ups. The sex industry has also expanded right across London. Swathes of new brothels, in all their guises, have opened from one side of the capital to the other, including in suburban residential areas. According to outreach services, as supply and demand are shifting outside the city centre, prices in Soho are gradually being pushed down and it is beginning to lose its high earning potential.

Soho sex workers used to be predominantly British women, but nowadays there is general consensus that 80 per cent of the women selling sex across Central London are foreign nationals, predominantly Eastern European and South-East Asian women. That much is agreed between police, campaigners and outreach services. But what is still fiercely contested is how many of these women have been trafficked into the sex industry and how many are migrants who have deliberately come to London in order to earn money as sex workers.

It was at the end of the 1980s that police in London first became aware of South-East Asian women being trafficked into brothels controlled by gangs of triads. The Chinese triads are descended from seventeenth-century Shaolin monks. Originally from mainland China, they moved south, and eventually established themselves in Hong Kong, where they are known as 'Black Societies' and triad membership remains a serious crime. In the early nineties, Charing Cross Clubs and Vice Unit (also known as CO14 or Commissioner's Office 14) gradually began to gather further intelligence about South American and Thai women being trafficked to the UK. By the mid-nineties CO14 was also identifying Russian and Eastern European women who were being trafficked into Soho and forced to sell sex.

In 2000 two researchers from the University of North London (now London Metropolitan University) published an influential report called 'Stopping Traffic' in which they estimated that somewhere between 142 and 1,420 women were being trafficked into the UK every year.[3]

In their report summary, Liz Kelly and Linda Regan suggested the British government ensure that 'a well-resourced NGO providing support and advocacy to trafficked women exists in the UK within the next eighteen months'.

3. 'Stopping Traffic', Liz Kelly and Linda Regan, Police Research Series, paper 125, 2000.

A year later, at the end of 2001, a women's housing association in London called Eaves began to provide refuge for a small number of trafficked women. Eaves took these women in because they (the women) had nowhere else to go. Having survived the trauma of being trafficked, they had no money of their own, no access to public funds and were facing utter destitution. When I first met the director of Eaves, Denise Marshall, in the autumn of 2002, she still had no funding to house these women but was damned sure that she wasn't going to turn them out. Finally, in March 2003, after a blaze of media publicity about the plight of Eastern European 'sex slaves', the Home Office began to fund a pilot project at Eaves. Twenty-five beds were allocated for trafficked women, under the name of the Poppy Project.

The Poppy Project is not a building: the twenty-five Home Office-funded beds are dispersed across houses that Eaves Housing already managed in London.

Originally, the project was piloted for just six months. Funding has continued, but in spite of the constantly high rate of referrals, the number of bed spaces has not increased.

Natalia Dawkins has been the manager of the Poppy Project since March 2004. In a previous life she was a Camden social worker, and also used to work for Chelsea Women's Aid. I meet her at the Eaves Housing headquarters in Kennington. She is a friendly, energetic and outspoken woman, and talks me through the basics of the project at almost break-neck pace.

'Every woman who's referred to us has four weeks to consider her options; it is a four-week period of reflection. If she wants to carry on staying with us after that, then she has to cooperate with the authorities – that's police and immigration. She's got to be prepared to provide the police with intelligence that could lead to the arrest and conviction of her trafficker, though she's not compelled to give evidence in court.'

The Home Office has placed other stipulations on which women are eligible for the project. In order to qualify, a woman must have been trafficked into the UK (as opposed to coming here voluntarily and being exploited afterwards); she must have been forced to work as a prostitute within the last thirty days and have identified herself as a trafficked woman to the authorities. Another stipulation – that women who made claims for asylum could not subsequently stay at the project – was dropped in the early days of the project, after the Home Office was heavily lobbied by campaigners and human rights organisations; the Poppy Project staff also stuck their necks out over the issue. Women who have been trafficked into Britain from outside the EU are now advised by Poppy to consider claiming asylum. Forty per cent of the women Poppy has supported to date have been from Eastern Europe, but they've also supported women who have been trafficked from as far afield as Pakistan, Jamaica, Ecuador and Mongolia.

A year after the project opened, Poppy published a report that spells out the levels of brutality many trafficked women are subjected to: '77% of the women we work with have been beaten, often with objects (chains, sticks, screwdrivers, bottles and household implements were all mentioned). Women also mention being burned with cigarettes, thrown from moving vehicles, locked in the boots of cars and threatened with firearms.'

During 2004, 146 women were referred to the Poppy Project, totally beyond its operational capacity. They could only accommodate twenty-five of them.

'Housing women who have been trafficked is very complex: they've got a huge range of physical, psychological and practical needs. You can't just give a trafficked woman a room; she needs a refuge in the literal sense of the word,' says Natalia. 'People have a classic "shock and sympathy" response towards women being trafficked, but there are huge gaps in public awareness and service provision. Even though this is the only government-funded project for trafficked women in the UK, we've still had no confirmation of long-term funding. In emergencies we do refer women to other refuges. But the grim reality for a woman who's been trafficked to this country, then forced on her back and made to have sex with twenty or more punters a day, every day, is that if we don't have a space for her when she does finally get away from her trafficker, then there is very often nowhere else for her to go.'

While I'm talking with Natalia, Denise Marshall appears at the door. She is the driving force behind Poppy. She says hello, then sits down on the nearest chair, frowning heavily.

'I've just been to a conference on trafficking. You know what, there's a whole industry out there of overpaid consultants going to expensive conferences and coming up with language and jargon to describe what we already know. I'm not interested in jargon, and I couldn't give a toss about strategic initiatives. I care about the women we work with and what has happened to them. I care about the woman who came to us after she had been gang-raped in this country by eighty-eight men, one after the other, in one day; it was on Christmas Day, actually, a couple of years ago. This woman knows how many of those punters raped her because she counted every one of them. That's what I care about.'

A few minutes later Denise stands up to leave. I ask her what the name Poppy stands for. Without drawing breath, she replies, 'It stands for "Pissing Off Ponces and Pimps, Yeah".'

The Poppy Project has done its own research into the UK sex industry. 'Sex in the City', by Sandra Dickson, was published in late summer 2004. Focusing on off-street prostitution, where most trafficked women are confined, it mapped the scale of commercial sex in London. The research team identified more than seven hundred flats, massage parlours and saunas selling sex across London (excluding some of the walk-ups), and more than a hundred and sixty escort agencies. They calculated that up to 8,000 women were selling sex, not only in Soho and Central London, but right across London's thirty-three boroughs, and that 80 per cent of the women working off street were foreign nationals.

The report also identified clear evidence of separate off-street premises being linked by telephone numbers, implying a high degree of organisation in the off-street trade. Sandra Dickson concluded that up to a thousand women were being regularly moved between premises. Moving women between premises keeps them isolated, disoriented and unable to access any support services.

Even if they do manage to pay off the debt imposed by their trafficker, and even *if* they are then free to go, many women are still often subsequently stranded in London without documents, money or assistance.

> The range of ethnicities mapped and the comments made by the Poppy Project users both indicate that the sex industry in London has areas with a high concentration of trafficked women, including women who have paid off debts to traffickers and are still working in the sex industry. [. . .] Without exit strategies and resources in place, closing down sites selling sex will not result in fewer women involved in prostitution, but could simply result in women being sold on, or having to move to another flat, parlour or sauna to continue working for themselves in the sex industry.

One of the recommendations of the 'Sex in the City' report was that support services working directly with sex workers be extended, in order to help women stay safe whilst working, and to directly assist those who want to get out of sex work.

The Praed Street Project is situated in a quiet off-street square near Paddington Station in west Central London. It opened seventeen years ago, originally as a mainstream sexual health research project, but now works exclusively with 'women associated with the sex industry'.

The women who attend the sexual health clinic and use the drop-in service are based around the vicinity of Paddington, Bayswater, Westbourne Park and Mayfair. Jane Ayers is the project's outreach services manager. She has been with Praed Street for the last twelve years and has seen the sex industry in this part of London transform in that time.

Back in the early 1990s Praed Street supported a lot of street sex workers. These were mainly British women, though there was always a minority of foreigners amongst them, mainly women from Thailand and Africa, plus small groups of Australian backpackers who would supplement their round-the-world trips with sex work.

The Australians left years ago, though the Thai and African women are definitely still here, and towards the end of the 1990s the project also started making contact with Brazilian women who were migrating to the London sex industry.

'The influx of Brazilians was the turning point for us,' she tells me when I meet her at the project office. 'I tried to get mainstream services interested in working with migrants, because they were becoming a larger part of our client group, but back then no one was very interested. They all wanted to work with vulnerable young people. Now of course everyone wants to work with migrant sex workers!'

The arrival of the Brazilians also marked a gradual reduction in the number of British women working the streets.

'The streets started clearing about seven years ago,' she says, 'and more of the migrant women started working out of flats, so we needed an outreach service to make initial contact. We started a Friday afternoon outreach service seven years ago, and it's still going strong.'

Ninety per cent of the women who now contact Praed Street are migrants. The last time the project counted, they'd worked with eighty-six different nationalities. The biggest single majority is still Brazilian women.

In contrast with the Soho walk-ups, many sex workers in west Central London work from unadvertised basement flats. They used to advertise with small shiny flyers, called 'cards', which they paid 'cardies' to distribute in public phone boxes. But the cards elicited mass complaints, and in 2001 carding became a criminal offence.

In 2002 Diane Taylor reported in the *Guardian* that women who continued advertising with cards were being visited by undercover police officers posing as punters, who would warn them to stop using the cards. The police were sometimes accompanied by immigration officers, who would also apparently check the women's immigration status.[4] Jane believes this change in the law had a huge effect on migrant women working from flats.

'Whatever you think of the ethics of carding, they allowed women to work independently. When carding was criminalised, it all went completely pear-shaped. The women who still use cards are now at risk

4. Diane Taylor, *Guardian*, July 2002.

because they can be easily identified by the police and immigration, but no one cares if the women are removed nowadays, because they can be so easily replaced.'

'Why can they be so easily replaced now?' I ask her.

Jane leans back in her chair and is silent for a moment. She has talked resiliently about the sex industry until now; I don't know whether this is a deliberate ploy, but I sense no anger, resignation or pity in what she says.

'The industry here is completely saturated,' she states. 'There are flats opening and closing all the time; some of them have half a dozen women squashed inside, all competing for business. We used to have a stable list of clients, but now our project worker has to recreate our client list every couple of weeks.

'The overall result is the industry has fragmented. There have always been clear divisions between work on and off the streets. Sex work has always been violent for the women working on the streets, but indoors, in the flats and saunas, it was different. There were well-established rules and boundaries between women and the punters, which kept most of the women in the flats safe. Both sides knew the score. But these boundaries have crumbled, the rules have completely gone to pot, and as a result, sex work is far more unpredictable.'

She tells me this fragmentation has had a direct impact on the sexual services now being offered. Whereas, for example, punters used to have to go to certain places to pay for anal sex, it's become a mainstream sexual service, and there's more pressure on women to offer it.

'Women are not all forced to have anal sex, but "O and A without" [oral and anal without a condom] has become a sex-industry catchphrase, and a high proportion of women are now offering some services without condoms.'

Jane tells me the sex workers aim to make £40–£50 a punter in the flats, plus a £10 tip for the maid. When I remark this is double the going rate in Soho, she nods. 'Yes, I know. The women round here regard themselves as more up-market sex workers. They see Soho as the bottom of the barrel.'

It's known that many women are initially trafficked into Soho, and then moved into other parts of London, or dispersed across the UK.

At Praed Street, the project workers now support many more women whose entry to the UK has been 'facilitated'. Jane believes the vast majority of these women know they will be working in the sex industry, but that many of them have no idea of the realities of sex work and the conditions they'll have to tolerate.

'There is a whole spectrum of facilitation,' she says, 'and trafficking is at one end of it. To be honest, we've changed our approach to trafficking—'

'What do you mean, changed your approach?' I interrupt her.

'We were a bit defensive about the whole issue at first, a bit fixated on sex workers *not* being victims. Now we acknowledge that trafficking is a real issue in the sex industry. But it's complex. You can't simply claim every migrant worker is a trafficking victim; it's not as simple as that.

'What has changed is that a lot of women now arrive in London already indebted; some of them work to pay it off, and then they're free to go, but some women are definitely not free. The most vulnerable are constantly moved around, kept deliberately disoriented and work alongside different women all the time, so they can never have the chance to form alliances. Their mobile-phone numbers are constantly changed, they are very isolated, and they work extremely long hours.'

'Where do these women come from?'

'Eastern Europe or Thailand. I have never yet met a Brazilian woman in London who has been trafficked.'

She tells me many of the Eastern Europeans speak very little English, which makes it extremely difficult to support them. Some women fit a classic trafficking profile; they are brought over here by a trafficker, informed they have a debt to pay off and confined inside a flat to sell sex. The debt, of course, is unpayable, because it's continually inflated: women are charged for food, accommodation, hot water and every other single thing they need to survive. They are charged money for having periods or being ill.

Other women have been recruited from inside London; these are often young women from recent accession states like Hungary and Lithuania who are already employed in bars or cafés, deliberately targeted by men who become their 'boyfriends' and offer them better paid work, and have no idea of how their situation is going to escalate. These pimps, who are both Eastern European and UK residents, use a combination of physical and psychological force to coerce these women into sex work. Sometimes they impose a debt on the women; other times they simply assume ownership over them.

If they are registered with the Home Office Worker Registration Scheme and have been legally employed for a full year, A8 nationals then become *de facto* full citizens of Europe and are entitled to public funds, including full welfare benefits. But women who have not worked here for a year, or who have not been registered on the scheme – either because they have been working illegally in the UK, or because their employer hasn't provided them with the necessary paperwork – are vulnerable. The benefits rules are complex. Though legally entitled to be in Britain, if they lose their job they may well be stranded without money. From a trafficker's point of view, these particular women are an easy target because they are already over here and may well be unaware of their rights and entitlements. This may be one of the reasons so many women from the recent accession states are now being identified as having been trafficked.

For Thai women, the situation is quite different. Their facilitation into the London sex industry has gone on for so long, their experiences now follow certain well-established patterns.

The Thai women arrive in London in groups. They enter this country on six-month tourist visas, so they are not entitled to work. Every new woman is heavily debt-bonded and owes around twenty thousand pounds to her facilitator.

I have heard constant rumours that gangs of triads still dominate this trafficking route, though there is speculation that other criminal organisations may also be involved. But there are extensive networks of organised criminals, and people get nervous. I've spoken to another project worker in London who has regular contact with foreign sex workers; she described Thai women owing thousands of pounds to triad gangs, and having to pay off the debt with sex work. Afterwards, she repeatedly insisted I mustn't use her name or refer to the organisation she's employed by.

Jane has done outreach work with Thai sex workers for a number of years now. She says every new group of arrivals has a leader, a woman who has worked in London before and who increases her own status by recruiting new sex workers.

It takes up to six months for a Thai woman to pay off her debt by sex work. At this point her tourist visa will be expiring, and unless she can somehow negotiate an extension, it's only a matter of time before she'll be identified and removed by immigration. Consequently, the women have to work extremely hard almost every day of the week. And there are a lot of other women to contend with in this saturated sex industry. Nevertheless, Jane is clear that some of the Thais with whom she has regular outreach contact regard their debt-bonded facilitation as a sound economic decision.

'For some Thai women, coming to London and working in the sex industry is a decision that definitely works for them; they are articulate and confident, and know that as soon as they pay off their debt, they can start earning their own money. These women do not regard themselves as victims. I've had Thai women say to my face, "Look, this is working for me. I can buy a small farm back at home with the money I make here and support my family. Back off, and let me get on with it." These women feel patronised if you go around offering to save them. Some of them do definitely go on to become part of the whole system of bringing in new women; others leave London and then make the choice to come back and work here again.

'But there are other women who find the whole experience completely traumatic; they are vulnerable, have no resources to cope with the realities of the sex industry, and are treated extremely badly. These are the women moved from flat to flat and never allowed out alone. Their passports are taken away, and they are checked up on half a dozen times a day. The experiences that Thai women have here are extreme.'

I ask her whether the project has exit strategies for women who either want or need to get out immediately.

'You cannot have one exit strategy, because individual women's situations are very different. I would be very cautious about suggesting any woman left her work, unless she was being very damaged or she told us that she wanted out. But there are warning signs, and if a woman is clearly being traumatised and damaged, then I would suggest she leaves, and we can offer her assistance. We can refer women to the IOM if they want to go home, and they'll support them to return through their Voluntary Assisted Return and Reintegration Programme. But in my experience, although many women want support and a safe space to talk about what is going on for them, not a lot of them actually say that they want to exit the industry.'

'And the British sex workers who've left the streets, where have they all gone?' I ask, remembering what she said earlier about the streets beginning to clear about seven years ago.

'To tell you the truth, in many cases I really don't know,' Jane replies. 'There are still English women working both on the streets and in flats and saunas, though there's an awful lot of places where they can't get a job for love nor money because of the competition. But you have to remember that this is an industry where women do disappear.'

In an attempt to find out whether the sex industry has also become saturated outside London, I contact Manchester Action on Street Health, or MASH, a sexual health project for women working in Manchester's saunas and massage parlours, as well as those working on the street. There are more than ninety saunas and massage parlours in Greater Manchester, which has earned the city the onerous title of 'Sauna Capital of Europe'.

Tina Threadgold has been the manager of MASH for the last five years. She tells me the number of foreign women working in the city-centre parlours and saunas started steadily increasing about eighteen months ago, and reckons there are now at least a third more women working indoors. She agrees with Jane Ayers that indoor work has traditionally been self-regulated and fairly safe for women, as they've worked side by side, looking out for each other, and for risky punters. But she is also concerned that many of the recently arrived women cannot speak English, beyond identifying themselves as Polish or Czech (which are both accession states). Others claim to be Greek. Tina does not believe they are Greek and thinks most are Eastern European.

'We are in a very delicate position with these women. As a sexual health service respecting the right of women to decide to work in the sex industry, there's a real issue around assuming they have been trafficked simply because they are migrants. But these particular young women are very vulnerable, because they can't negotiate with the punters, or anyone else for that matter.'

I ask her how a woman who speaks no English can get herself a job in a massage parlour. She says she's not sure herself, but some of the women have apparently arrived at parlours accompanied by English-speaking women.

'We've also had quite a few calls from local sauna owners. They tell us they are being approached by men offering them women to work in the saunas. They describe some of these women as physically frightened, and a lot of the men as physically intimidating.'

Tina says the off-street industry has recently expanded to the point that saunas and parlours are now stridently competing for punters.

'Would you describe the Manchester sex industry as saturated?' I ask her at the end of our conversation. I don't want to put words in her mouth, but am hoping to obtain some kind of comparison with London from a similar front-line sexual health service.

'I can tell you this,' she says, 'the off-street industry is definitely reaching saturation point.'

The policy of Manchester City Council is to 'minimise the adverse effects of prostitution on areas of the city and divert prostitutes into better lifestyles once they're in the court system'. According to Tina Threadgold, the police have historically had a fairly 'hands-off' approach to the sex industry, though the off-street trade is now being more closely monitored, and the National Criminal Intelligence Service (NCIS) is gathering intelligence on trafficking. NCIS, which started life as the Home Office National Drugs Intelligence Unit, gathers and analyses information in order to provide criminal intelligence for police forces and 'other law-enforcement agencies'.

Glasgow City Council, by contrast, has a zero-tolerance stance on all forms of prostitution, regarding it as violence against women. Services for sex workers are therefore explicitly oriented towards supporting women to exit the industry.

Base 75 is a city-centre healthcare service for women involved in street prostitution. It's been running since 1989. Ying Zhang, a researcher at the Base, tells me the number of street workers registering at the service and the number attending the drop-in have both dropped significantly in the last two years.

I ask her where these women have gone, and she echoes Jane Ayers, saying, 'In many cases we really do not know.'

Some of these women may have left sex work, but in Glasgow 90 per cent of street workers are thought to be cocaine-, crack- or heroin-addicted, which means that as long as they are addicts, they have to work relentlessly.

Meanwhile, Scottish police admit they have 'scant' intelligence on trafficking, and there have been no convictions for human trafficking in Scotland.

Bronagh Andrews is employed by the Scottish Executive to assess the scale of trafficking in Scotland and develop an appropriate response service if needed. She tells me that to date there have been few confirmed cases of women being trafficked into the Scottish sex industry. These confirmed cases have involved women from recent accession states and several women from Africa.

'We don't have a great deal of information about the off-street sex industry in Glasgow,' she says, 'but from what we have gleaned, the off-street trade is flourishing.'

A weekly sexual health clinic for women working in Glasgow's saunas has to date been attended by women of twenty-eight different nationalities. This in itself is no proof that Scotland has a major trafficking problem. But the pattern seems to be consistent across the country: British sex workers are disappearing, whilst more and more migrant women are working invisibly indoors. But these issues, like the industry itself, are complex, and undoubtedly related.

We live in a culture saturated with the sexual imagery of women and obsessed with the principles of acquisition and immediate gratification. Female bodies are used to sell everything from cars to clothing, exotic holidays to mobile phones, and the underlying principle is always the same: women are products for sale and consumption.

And what about the men who pay for sex? Little is known about punters; they've remained conspicuously absent from the controversies of the commercial sex industry.

No one knows for sure how many British men pay for sex, though recent published research did cast some light into this particular corner. The research was undertaken by Helen Ward and colleagues at Imperial College London. After two surveys involving almost eleven thousand men, they suggested that twice as many men are now purchasing sex compared with ten years ago, and that just under one in ten men living in Britain has paid for sex in his lifetime.

There were no links between ethnicity or social class and paying for sex, but apparently the men most likely to pay were Londoners aged between twenty-five and thirty-four.

Helen Ward encapsulated the findings by telling the BBC, 'There are more men with money and more women looking for this type of work.'

The figure was seized upon by the media as proof that the sex industry is rapidly expanding and that men paying for sex has become both more mainstream and more widely accepted. There is no doubt that some of these men are paying to have sex with women who are forced to have sex with them, and other men, on a daily, often hourly, basis. Police working in the vice industries cite the Internet as a major contributor to the expansion of all forms of commercial sex in the last ten years. Women are frequently advertised on-line, and traffickers are known to insert web cams into brothels, so they can film women being forced to have sex and sell the footage on-line.

Nowadays, men who pay for sex can also log on to the Internet to share, compare and rate their experiences online. Punternet was set up seven years ago by an Englishman who lives in the States, probably northern California,[5] and has given himself the online pseudonym 'Galahad'. Within Punternet, he has created an index of 'field reports' in which punters fill in details about the cost, presentation and value for money of the sex they purchase. The website slowly gained notoriety for its thousands of puerile field reports and for references by a minority of punters to women who appeared to be reluctant and sometimes very unhappy to be having sex with them.

I've trawled through Punternet more times than I care to think about and have found no references to women being coerced into sex, though it could be argued that the adverse publicity about these reports may have discouraged men from filing anything less than a fun time had by all.

In these last seven years, Punternet's punters have filed just over sixty-two thousand field reports.

Whenever a writer or commentator describes the size of the British sex industry, they invariably refer to an estimate of 80,000 sex workers. This

5. The website URL has been traced to northern California according to the *New Statesman*.

figure was calculated back in 1998 by a researcher called Hilary Kinnell, who used to work for the European Network for HIV and STD Prevention in Prostitution (EUROPAP). Hilary Kinnell collated data from a number of agencies working with sex workers (including men) and then made what she describes as 'an educated guess' about the total UK number. She has now retired and lives in rural Shropshire. I track her down via the Internet, and she's more than happy to talk.

'When I came up with that estimate, up to three-quarters of sex workers were already working off street,' she tells me on the phone. 'But back then, outside of London, most of them were British women. I've read reports about how the industry has expanded massively in this country, and I think the sex industry is probably bigger now than then: but if it's being described as saturated, that strongly implies that though more women may be selling sex, there are not necessarily a lot more men paying for sex.'

For many years Hilary Kinnell tracked aspects of the UK sex industry. In the late 1980s she interviewed sex workers across the country about how many punters they saw and their average daily earnings. She used these two figures to calculate that approximately one in ten men were paying women for sex back then, which could indicate that the men in Helen Ward's study are now more prepared to admit to paying for sex compared with ten years ago, as opposed to there being any major change in the overall number who do so.

Hilary Kinnell has kept track of another set of figures, which provides another insight into the violent realities of the sex industry; since 1990 she has kept a detailed record of the number of sex workers who have been murdered in Britain. During this fifteen-year period almost a hundred women are known to have been killed. In the decade between 1990 and 2000 Hilary traced fifty murder investigations, though she believes this may well be an underestimate. Since 2000, there were at least another forty-seven.

Although the vast majority of these women were working alone on the street at night, Hilary is careful to clarify that not all of them were murdered by punters (some were killed by their partners and one woman by two other females), and that compared with domestic violence figures of two or three women a week being murdered in the UK, the murder rate of sex workers remains low. But these numbers speak for themselves; in the last five years the murder rate of sex workers has apparently doubled. This is an industry in which women do disappear.

When I ask Hilary about trafficking, she, maybe not surprisingly, draws a clear distinction between migrant sex workers and trafficked women.

'The problem is that those of us on the side of the sex workers disagree furiously amongst ourselves—' she starts to explain, but I interrupt her.

'But isn't this one of the underlying problems, this taking of sides?'

Debates over the sex industry are ferocious, and positions entrenched in ideologies that often directly impact on the services being offered to women. Projects such as Praed Street and MASH prioritise the right of women to decide to work in the sex industry and support them in the decisions they make. They view the sex industry as a legitimate choice of work, use models of harm reduction and minimisation, and take their cues directly from what their clients ask of them.

Projects such as Base 75, on the other hand, regard the sex industry as intrinsically violent and damaging to women, and as an industry that women need specific support to get out of. They orient their services specifically towards assisting women in making the decision to exit sex work when they are ready.

This may be a slightly skewed comparison, as the majority of women at Praed Street and MASH work indoors, while Base 75 supports street workers, who earn less, are far more at risk of violence and also struggle with addictions. But it highlights the ideological divides that exist between support services across the country, with both sides believing they best serve women's interests.

Harm-reduction programmes, wherever they operate, offer pragmatic front-line assistance to women who are already involved in sex work, but do not challenge the coercion and trafficking of women into the sex industry, and as the Poppy Project research highlighted, without clear exit strategies in place, women are at risk of having nowhere to go if they do want, or need, to get out. At worst, women may remain in clearly abusive or dangerous situations because they've lost the self-esteem to articulate what they want or need, or they don't believe anyone can help them.

Exit-strategy models also have their critics, who point out the potential risk of alienating sex workers by viewing them primarily as victims of violence.

'It is not realistic to exit every woman from the sex industry,' Tina Threadgold told me bluntly. 'We do not condone violence or coercion in sex work, but if we worked on a specific exit-strategy basis, a lot of our clients simply wouldn't engage with us. We work with them where they are at now.'

Regardless of which models they apply, there are very few resources in Britain for women who want or need to get out of the sex industry. The Poppy Project, with its specific remit of assisting women trafficked into the UK, has been overwhelmed by referrals. There is also a fifteen-bed project in Lambeth for London sex workers. But many other parts of London, and the rest of the country, have no outreach services or exit strategies at all, leaving women isolated and incredibly vulnerable. Base 75 has a total of ten allocated flats for women exiting sex work.

For many of the women who are trafficked into the UK sex industry, the result is potentially disastrous. Even if they do manage to extract themselves from their trafficker, or are fortunate enough to be released after paying off their debt, they may well resort to remaining in the sex industry because they are traumatised, have been physically and sexually brutalised, and have absolutely nowhere to go.

Regarding the contention over migrant sex workers, it strikes me that the voices we never hear are those of the women at the centre of this particular storm. I try to make contact with migrant sex workers. I ask several agencies if they can offer any help, but no women will agree to speak to me. I email a number of independent escorts, then contact several women who advertise on Punternet and receive no responses at all. I even collect a few cards from phone boxes in Central London and call. I am either unlucky or else my phone calls are invasive; three women hang up on me, one after the other.

I'm uncomfortably aware that everything I've heard about the UK sex industry so far has been second-hand information, as opposed to first person. I have never believed that every migrant sex worker is a trafficked woman, but coercion has always been a major component of the sex industry, and the boundaries are now blurring. The industry is being deliberately saturated with young women who owe money to a facilitator, and it is becoming more and more difficult to clearly distinguish between who is being trafficked and who is not.

In a final attempt to talk to a migrant sex worker about what *she* thinks, I call the English Collective of Prostitutes and ask if they can offer any ideas. The Collective have been active for more than thirty years now and, like everyone else in this arena, have their own political agenda; they are veteran campaigners for the complete decriminalisation of sex work.

Nikki Adams is one of their spokeswomen, and just like the other women I've spoken to about sex work, she is also a straight-talker.

'Prostitution is an economic decision that women don't take lightly,' she tells me. 'Women enter prostitution because of deprivation and debt, and in order to gain financial independence. We are against prostitution but for the rights of prostitutes.'

The Collective believe that anti-trafficking legislation is used to target, and remove, migrant sex workers. They claim that trafficked women and girls face disbelief from the authorities, and that a number of women who have managed to flee their trafficker have subsequently been imprisoned for entering the country either without documents or with false documentation.

When I ask Nikki if they've ever had direct contact with trafficked women, she tells me they have supported several women who, having escaped, found themselves completely stranded and destitute.

The Collective have supported these women at their Crossroads Women's Centre office in Kentish Town, including a young African woman who was trafficked here, fled her trafficker and is now fighting to stay in Britain. I tentatively ask if I might be able to speak to her.

Nikki makes it very clear to me that this woman is not a migrant sex worker and says she will ask her whether she would be happy to talk with me. It takes a couple of months, but eventually we arrange a date and time for me to visit the Crossroads Women's Centre and hear her story.

Chapter 14

What Is Not Said

The Crossroads Women's Centre is in North London, a few minutes' walk down the hill from Kentish Town tube station. Italian coffee shops, Kurdish corner shops, Indian and Pakistani grocers, Greek restaurants, English pubs: international and local Kentish Town businesses are slotted in side by side. The high street is congested with pedestrians on the loose, the road choked with traffic crawling home or somewhere else.

When I ring the Crossroads' bell, the door is immediately opened by a tall, dreadlocked woman, who greets me with an outstretched hand and a rather wary smile. She says her name is Cristel. She takes me straight through one room and into another: an office cum kitchen, where a young woman and a much older man are cooking. Cristel says she'll just be a moment: Annette is in the centre somewhere, and she'll go and tell her I'm here. Almost as soon as I sit down and say hello to the man and woman cooking their meal, a young black woman walks quietly into the kitchen. I immediately know this is Annette.

'Hello, Annette. I'm Louisa.'

She looks at me cautiously, says hi and immediately turns half away from me and starts heating a saucepan of milk on the stove.

'I can't stay very long,' she says, avoiding any eye contact. 'I have my night-school class this evening. It starts at seven, so I really need to leave by six o'clock.'

It is already half past five. Before I have time to say anything, Cristel returns and takes us back through into the first room. It's a large, chaotic office full of filing cabinets, computers, desks and a large circle of empty chairs. A suspended naked bulb burns a painfully bright light.

The three of us sit in the circle, a few chairs apart from each other. Annette crosses her legs, then her arms over her chest. She is facing away from me, towards Cristel. She looks very young, and her clenched body language spells out reticence and resignation.

'Do you feel all right about doing this interview?' I ask her, unsure and uneasy myself, because she's looking so uncomfortable, holding herself tightly and staring down at the floor.

'It's OK. It's just that I don't want you to use my real name, and I need to leave soon.' She takes a few shallow sips of her drink.

'Annette has night school this evening,' says Cristel.

'Yes, she told me.'

I hesitate before extracting my notebook from my bag. I feel I should be able to come up with something to lighten the atmosphere and make Annette feel better about talking to me, but I don't know what to say now.

It is Cristel who speaks. She pulls a tape recorder out of a bag and asks if it's all right to record the interview. They need to keep a record, she says, especially as Annette's case is ongoing. I ask Annette if she thinks it's OK. She says yes, but looks up at the clock.

'I know going to college is important, Annette, but it's also important that your story gets out and people find out about what really happens.' Cristel talks to Annette gently. It sounds like she is reassuring rather than persuading her. She glances over at me. 'Annette has done this before.'

I nod and pick up my pen and smile at Annette. 'You OK?' I ask again. It doesn't sound very reassuring even to me.

'Has the interview already started?' she replies, as Cristel turns the tape recorder on.

Annette is not her real name. She is very anxious not to be identified, and doesn't want any personal details, including her nationality, to be revealed.

I ask her once more if she feels all right about talking to me, and once more she replies with a question. 'Where do you want to start?'

'At the beginning,' I say tentatively. 'Before you left home.'

'OK. I was educated abroad until I was fifteen, at a boarding school in Uganda. After I finished school, I went home, and a friend of my family offered to take me away to work for one month. My guardians agreed to his suggestion, and I was not hesitant at all. I thought that I would be back at home before Christmas.'

It was in November 2002 that Annette's guardians agreed she would go abroad with this friend of theirs. Annette's parents had both died through war and illness, and when she wasn't at school, she was under the guardianship of these two adults. They gave Annette no information about where she would be going when she left home with this friend, whom she had never met before. Annette packed her bag, and the friend drove her west into Congo-Brazzaville. Together they travelled through the capital, also called Brazzaville, and out into the countryside. Eventually they arrived at a remote house. Annette has no idea which part of Congo-Brazzaville the house was in.

'It was just a big house,' she says obliquely. 'He locked me in it and went away. Then he came back with a man who raped me.' She looks down at the floor and then up at the posters on the walls and takes another sip of her drink.

Afterwards the man who had locked her up brought other men to the house, and they raped Annette as well. I ask her quietly how long this went on for.

'For about three months. Afterwards we went to DRC [Democratic Republic of Congo], and the same thing happened. He locked me in a big house and brought men round, and they slept with me too.'

Her voice doesn't rise or fall. She talks in a monotone, answering my questions briefly but giving very few additional details. I find myself saying to her, 'And what happened afterwards?' more times than I want to, in an attempt to keep the brittle narrative going. We pass my questions and her answers back and forth between us uneasily. Occasionally Cristel interjects to clarify a time span, or to ask that a detail is not included 'because of the ongoing case'. The recorder hisses slightly as it tapes Annette outlining the history of the violations she has endured.

She thinks that she was held in DRC for about seven months. During that time she was never allowed out of the house.

'I wanted to escape, but I couldn't.' She surprises me, not by her intent but by telling me this in the first place, and I say nothing, hoping she'll open up a little more. 'Here in Britain you can walk out of your bedroom and open the front door,' she says. 'In Africa they padlock the front doors, and even if you get out of the bedroom, you cannot escape.'

'Were there any other girls locked in this house with you?' I ask her.

'There were other girls there, but I don't know how many there were. I never spoke to them,' she replies.

The only people whom Annette did speak to during these seven months were her pimp and his punters. The pimp would go out for the afternoon or sometimes the whole day, and on those occasions he would simply lock Annette in her room. When he was in the house, she was allowed out of the room just to do housework and iron clothes. Her movements were completely confined to the house, and often to just the bedroom. Her world became a small dark place.

'I think it was about the end of December 2003 when we moved again. He didn't tell me where we were going: we always just packed up and left in his car. This time we drove to Kenya. And it was the same.'

'Did any of the men who visited you ever offer to help you?'

Annette shakes her head. Her hair has been scraped back into a short ponytail that hangs stiffly against the nape of her neck. It doesn't move.

'Did you ever ask any of these men for help?'

'No. I did not think they would help me.'

The monotony of being locked up and raped every day continued in Nairobi for about another nine months. Annette had now been away from home for almost two years.

As I sit unravelling the outer layer of her story, it is the things that she does not talk about that become more and more apparent to me, until the air in the room feels heavy. She was still a girl when this horror began and should have been protected from all this, but her guardians bowed out of their responsibility and allowed a man to take her away and do as he wanted with her. Maybe they actually colluded in the whole thing. Whatever the initial circumstances, Annette's experience has been almost unspeakable, and it seems in many ways as though much of it still is: she says nothing about despair, fear or loneliness. She seems completely out of reach, as though she's still confined in a very bleak, faraway place. A clinical psychologist might call this disassociation, a method of coping with extreme trauma that means you remove yourself mentally from what you are recalling. Maybe this is the only way that Annette – or anyone – can describe her experience.

'What happened after Kenya, Annette?'

Annette looks at me and then back up at the clock.

'I'm sorry. Do you need to go?' I ask her, realising it's already past the time she said she needed to leave.

'It's OK for a few minutes. I left Kenya and flew to England with him. We arrived in London at the beginning of September [2004]. I knew it was London because I speak English and the sound system announced, "Welcome to Heathrow Airport." '

Annette had no documents on her at all. Her pimp presumably had a forged passport for her, because they walked together through to the arrivals hall and joined the long queue at passport control. He told Annette not to say anything, explained to the immigration officer that she was his niece and calmly escorted her through the airport. They took the train straight into London.

'It was the same in London. He took me to a house and men came . . .' This time she does not complete the sentence.

Annette's pimp trafficked her into the UK himself, but there is a constant stream of unaccompanied children who arrive at UK ports every day.

Upon arrival in Britain, unaccompanied children are usually granted 'leave to remain in the UK' until they are eighteen years old, when each case is reconsidered by the Home Office. If a child arrives without documents, which many do, as many details as possible are immediately taken from them, and they are subsequently issued a photo ID card. [1] Each child is then assigned a social worker, who tries to match them with a suitable foster family or arrange local authority care. Almost ten thousand foreign children have been privately fostered in the UK, many of whom are originally from West Africa.

Eleven years ago, in 1995, West Sussex social services were disturbed by the disappearance of a young Nigerian girl in their care, who had originally arrived in the UK as an unaccompanied minor. When several other Nigerian girls also disappeared from West Sussex, the police launched Operation Newbridge to tackle child trafficking. Investigations eventually revealed that a small but regular stream of Nigerian girls who had been taken into care were subsequently being trafficked from Britain to Italy for sexual exploitation. Altogether seventy-one girls disappeared in a five-year period. A separate investigation carried out by the *Guardian* revealed that in an eighteen-month period between 1998 and 1999, 180 suspected trafficking victims went missing after they had arrived at Heathrow Airport.[2] By the end of the 1990s the police also became aware of children being trafficked into the UK from Eastern Europe and the newly independent states of the former Soviet Union. It was suspected that at least some of them were being trafficked for sexual exploitation. They were being brought into Britain on the back of lorries, via fraudulent student visas that lied about their age or accompanied by an adult claiming to be a friend or boyfriend, who was in fact a pimp. Sometimes they also arrived in the UK alone.

Since 2000 approximately fifteen thousand unaccompanied children have arrived in Britain, including some as young as five. A majority of these children are from West Africa, often Nigeria, which is the most populous country in Africa and has had migration ties to the UK since being a British colony. But unaccompanied children from all over Africa have arrived at UK ports. Unaccompanied children have also arrived from Vietnam and China. Some child protection workers believe there are 'waves' of trafficking, with children being brought in regularly from one country or region, and the tide then subsiding as traffickers keep a lower profile to avoid detection.

Operation Newbridge was closed in July 2000, and the social services-funded safe house for at-risk unaccompanied children in West Sussex has also been closed. This was the only safe house of its kind in the UK, and now there is no specific housing provision for unaccompanied children considered at risk of being trafficked.

1. Children under five years, however, cannot be either photographed or fingerprinted.
2. Audrey Gillan, *Guardian*, 30 July 2003.

Communication between social services, private fosterers, local and central government has been so cumbersome that the government has just set up the National Register of Unaccompanied Children to monitor what happens after children arrive in the UK. The register is currently monitoring 10,000 'live cases'. The majority of them are sixteen- and seventeen-year-old girls living in small groups in semi-independent local authority accommodation after leaving foster care.

ECPAT (End Child Trafficking, Pornography and Prostitution), a London-based children's rights charity, has documented child trafficking in the UK for years and reports that social services often struggle to identify the age and nationality of unaccompanied children because they frequently arrive in the UK on forged documents.

The vast majority of traffickers are thought to be from the same country as the children they traffic, though there have been several suspected cases of African children being brought into the UK by white men.

There are thousands of other children, like Annette, who enter the UK every year with an adult who claims to be their relative. Many are genuine relatives, and the children are perfectly safe and well looked after within their extended family network; but a legal loophole also permits an adult travelling on an EU passport to escort a child from anywhere in the world into the UK through the EU passport control channel, as long as the child either has his or her own passport or is named on the adult passport. But there is no doubt that some children are brought into the UK specifically to be sexually abused.

Specialist child protection police units, such as the Paladin Team, who work out of Heathrow Airport and track unaccompanied and at-risk children across London, say they cannot estimate the scale of child trafficking into the UK because it is so covert. They believe the vast majority of children are used for fraudulent benefit claims or as domestic slaves, or both.

AFRUCA (Africans Unite Against Child Abuse), a British NGO that campaigns against the abuse of African children in Africa and the UK, was set up after the brutal death of eight-year-old Victoria Climbié in London in February 2000.[3] Its director, Debbie Ariyo, agrees children are usually trafficked for welfare fraud or domestic servitude but argues they are not being well enough protected when they arrive here in the first place. She has documented cases of unaccompanied children found

---

3. Victoria Climbié was trafficked to the UK from the Ivory Coast and died as a direct result of sustained physical abuse. The post-mortem revealed more than a hundred and eighty non-accidental injuries on her body.

wandering along the concourse at Waterloo International, having just cleared customs. She says children are still being regularly picked up at UK airports by adults who claim to be a relative, and the children are being instructed to say they know these adults before being trafficked from their own countries. Immigration officials at Heathrow Airport have been trained in child protection, but Heathrow proved no problem at all for the man who trafficked Annette into London.[4]

'Can I ask you what you thought of him?' I say to Annette.

She frowns at me, and I explain that I mean the man who trafficked her.

'He was an exploiter, and he wanted to use my life and take away my future,' she says.

I ask her if she had a name for him, and she shrugs her narrow shoulders and shakes her head, making it clear she doesn't want to answer this question. Over the last couple of years most of the women I have interviewed have shrugged their shoulders at some point and it is a gesture that I now associate not with nonchalance but resignation and numbness. On this occasion, however, Annette immediately subverts her shrug by telling me, 'As soon as I had the opportunity, I escaped from him.'

The man took Annette out on a number of occasions, to other men's houses, and then afterwards he would drive her back to the house where he kept her locked up as usual. One afternoon, about a month after she had arrived in London, he stopped to buy something while they were en route to another house and briefly left her alone inside his car. The car was unlocked. This may have been a simple error on his part, though he probably assumed he had complete control over Annette by now and would not have expected her to make a run for it. But she did. As soon as he was out of sight, she clambered out of the car and fled in the opposite direction.

She tells me briefly about wandering the streets alone for the next two days, exhausted and bewildered. She had nowhere to go. She resorted to begging a little money from people who passed her on the street and bought some food. She slept rough.

'On the third day I was sitting outside a tube station and I was crying. A woman came up to me and she asked me what was wrong. "Everything is wrong," I told her. I explained what had happened to me, and she telephoned a friend of hers and then asked me to come with her.'

Annette is sitting facing me now, leaning very slightly forward as she describes how she finally got away.

'Did you feel OK about going off with a complete stranger?'

4. 'End Child Exploitation', UNICEF, July 2003, and interview with Debbie Ariyo.

'Yes. She was a woman so I felt OK about going with her.'

'Where did she take you?'

She turns to Cristel, who has slumped a little in her chair and looks less on guard. Cristel smiles at Annette and then over at me. She pats Annette's arm gently.

'It's OK, Annette. You can tell her that the woman brought you here, to the Crossroads Centre.'

The bad times should have ended right there for Annette. After finding this temporary haven, she deserved all the help and support she could get.

Annette had no possessions at all, and was fed, clothed and supported by the women at the Crossroads Centre. They contacted social services, who arranged accommodation for Annette, and they also escorted her to the Lunar House Immigration and Nationality Directorate (IND) in East Croydon, where she made an 'in-country' application for asylum.[5] During her first screening interview at Lunar House, Annette explained her personal circumstances, journey to the UK and the reasons she had no documents and had not been able to make an application for asylum when she first arrived in Britain.

Section 2 of the Asylum and Immigration (Treatment of Claimants, etc.) Act 2004 criminalises any person who enters the UK without appropriate travel or identification documents. However, if the person can 'prove that he/she has a *reasonable excuse* for not being in possession of a document of the kind specified', this constitutes a defence of the charge. Guidelines of reasonable excuses are given in Section 2, but circumstances are examined on a case-by-case basis by the Crown Prosecution Service (CPS).

Annette was called back to Lunar House for several more screening interviews, so officials could clarify her details and identity. At the beginning of February 2005 she returned there for her fourth scheduled screening interview.

'When I arrived, an immigration official told me that the Home Office had found a passport identifying a twenty-three-old Ugandan woman. She claimed it belonged to me. I told her it wasn't my passport. How could it be? I was still seventeen, I didn't have any documents, and I am not Ugandan.'

She was arrested on the spot.

Annette was escorted to a nearby police station and charged with violating British immigration law. 'Not being a British citizen, did seek leave to remain in the UK as a refugee by means which you knew to

5. Claims for asylum are either made 'on arrival' at the border or 'in country' once a person has crossed the border.

include deception by you. Contrary to Section 24a of the Immigration and Nationality Act 1971 as amended' and 'failure to produce an immigration document or passport which is in force and satisfactorily establishes your identity, nationality or citizenship'.[6]

She was taken into custody immediately and allocated a criminal solicitor, who advised her to plead guilty to the charges. But she refused to do so. On 8 February 2005 Annette appeared in Bromley Magistrates' Court, was denied bail and was remanded in Bronzefield Women's Prison, Ashford, Middlesex. If she was found guilty of the charges, she faced up to two years in prison.

'I'm sorry, but we really are going to have to leave now.' Cristel's tone is apologetic: she obviously wants to be able to finish the interview as well, but is more concerned about Annette, who has just checked the clock again.

'No, I'm sorry. I've made you very late . . .'

Annette and Cristel are already standing up to leave as I apologise for delaying them. This is a bad moment to have to finish, so near the end of Annette's story, but we've run well over time.

'I'll take you to night school on the back of my motorbike, that'll be quicker,' Cristel suggests to Annette, who looks slightly startled by this offer. 'Wait a sec and I'll go and get you a jacket and helmet.' She strides out of the room.

'How long did you spend in prison?' I can't help asking her, as we wait for Cristel to come back with the jacket and helmet.

'Eight days,' she says. 'It was very hard.'

The rest of the story will have to wait. I can't pester her for details of prison life just as we're waiting to leave. Instead, I ask her what she's studying at night school this evening.

'German. And I am taking a foundation course in business studies at college. I want to go to university afterwards.' Her voice begins to uncoil and she starts talking, tentatively, about her studies.

'Are you happy here in London?' I ask her afterwards.

'Yes, I am. I don't want to go home. I want to stay here,' she says. 'The days in prison were very bad, but things are better now. They are still not so good, but better.'

Cristel returns with a jacket and helmet for Annette, and they leave straightaway. I thank Annette, and she smiles. When I thank Cristel, she smiles too and says I can call her at the Crossroads Centre if I have any queries.

6. Immigration and Nationality Act 1971; Section 2 of the Asylum and Immigration (Treatment of Claimants, etc.) Act 2004.

Of course, I want to fill in the gap between Annette being remanded in Bronzefield Prison in February and her being free to talk to me now.

It takes a couple of phone calls with Cristel to establish the final sequence of events.

Annette found her eight days on remand at Bronzefield Prison traumatic. She ended up in a hospital wing, depressed, heavily medicated and refusing food. On 16 February the charges against her were dropped and she was released, though she was informed that the charges could be pursued at a later date if additional evidence was forthcoming.

All I know about the man who trafficked Annette across Africa and then to London is that there is an 'ongoing investigation' into who and where he is. Apparently no one has been arrested in connection with the case, except of course for Annette.

After being released from Bronzefield, Annette applied for, and was granted, temporary admission into the UK. The Home Office is now considering her claim for asylum on the grounds of having been trafficked to Britain.

Annette is still liable to detention if she violates the fairly stringent restrictions placed on her life. She may be refused asylum and deported back to the country she was originally trafficked from. Despite her hopes for making a home in Britain and becoming a university business graduate, her future in this country remains tentative and uncertain.

She is now eighteen years old.

Chapter 15

The Downfall of
Luan Plakici

In the newspaper photographs he is quite good-looking, even handsome. He's well dressed and groomed, with a smart haircut and clear, healthy skin. It's only his smile that is off-putting. It is more of a smirk, as though he can't stop congratulating himself on how well business is going whilst he lies back on his living-room couch waving a thick fan of money.

There is another photograph of him sitting in an armchair surrounded by four or five young women. Their faces have been pixilated to obscure their identities. But there he is, poised in the centre, with that same look of self-congratulation.

When the man who calls himself Luan Plakici first arrived in Britain in 1995, he claimed to be an eighteen-year-old Kosovan fleeing from war in the Balkans. He immediately applied for asylum as a refugee and began to set up home in London. His asylum application was successful, and he was then allowed to apply for paid work.

Plakici, who spoke fluent English as well as Albanian, presented himself to various London solicitors' offices and asked for translation work. He was employed by several different firms, including a team of immigration solicitors who transferred him to Lunar House, the Immigration and Nationality Directorate, where he translated during in-depth screening interviews for other asylum applicants.

Plakici also worked as a translator for the BBC. Whilst working at the BBC, he was asked whether he knew a family who would be willing to feature in a documentary series about recent arrivals in the UK. Plakici suggested his own parents, who were living in the UK. Mr and Mrs Islami, as they called themselves, featured in an episode of *Welcome to Britain*, which was an in-house BBC production and broadcast on 22 July 2003. A researcher for the programme said Luan Plakici was recommended to the BBC by the Home Office, as he was on their list of approved translators.

Plakici's work as a translator at Lunar House explains his thorough working knowledge of UK asylum law, but not his lifestyle, or the amount of money that he spent. Plakici lived lavishly. He drove a number of sleek sports cars, including a Mercedes and a black BMW with a personalised number plate. He was also the owner of a Ferrari Spider, which he bought in part exchange for his Mercedes. He paid the remaining £17,000 in cash. He lived on Middleton Road, Golders Green, a fairly run-of-the-mill area of North London, but he frequently travelled abroad. Wherever he travelled, he stayed in plush, expensive hotels.

Plakici was a trafficker. He brought between fifty and sixty people into the UK illegally, though he claims that he merely facilitated their entry for several of his friends. (He later admitted in court that 'All my friends were pimps.') He also claims that twenty to thirty of the people whose entry he facilitated were prostitutes, all of whom came to the UK voluntarily.

Plakici used a number of pseudonyms when he worked: he was also known as Artur Corbajram, Turi and Ilir Raci. He had an accomplice, a younger man who came to the UK in 2000 and also claimed to be a Kosovar refugee. This younger man successfully applied for asylum, and Plakici rented a second flat, in the Palmers Green area of North London, for him to live in.

Although they worked together, Plakici was definitely the master, and his accomplice the acolyte. Plakici had good business connections across Britain, from Brighton to Glasgow, and his European trafficking contacts worked in Italy, the Czech Republic, Serbia, Romania and Moldova. Plakici trafficked a number of young Eastern European women (primarily from Moldova and Romania) into London, and then either sold them on to other traffickers and pimps or confined the women in his own home and forced them to work as prostitutes for him in London flats and massage parlours.

In 2000 Plakici trafficked two sixteen-year-old Moldovan girls to London, Izabela and Mara.[1] Izabela was recruited via a newspaper advertisement for work with elderly people in Italy, and Mara by a neighbour in her apartment building. Plakici's contacts transported both girls overland from Moldova through Romania, Serbia, Montenegro and Albania to Italy, where they met Plakici himself for the first time. This journey took a month, and by the time they arrived in Italy, both girls had already been raped. Izabela had been raped by a man she believed was called Kenar, who had provided them with accommodation en route.

1. The names of all the women in this chapter have been changed.

Mara was raped by more than one man whilst they were travelling covertly by lorry.

Upon arriving in Italy, the sixteen-year-olds had no choice but to put their trust in Plakici, who flew with them from Italy to London. As soon as they arrived in the UK, he sent them both straight to Lunar House to apply for asylum. He instructed them not to speak their own language but to claim to be refugees from Chechnya. They were interviewed at Lunar House and were both issued with identity cards, which had false dates of birth and nationality details on them. Plakici had learned exactly how to manipulate the system.

He forced Izabela into prostitution in a massage parlour almost immediately and also wanted her to have sex with him. Izabela did not want a sexual relationship with Plakici but said she felt compelled to do as he said. She claimed that he beat her 'on a regular basis' and that 'If I brought home £500 one day, he would be happy. If it was only £250, he would get angry and beat and violate me.'[2]

In December 2001, a year after she had arrived in London, Plakici asked Izabela to marry him. This was presumably in order to make her stay in the UK legal, as he had recently become a British citizen. Izabela said that she consented to the marriage 'out of fear'. She and Plakici married three months later, in March 2002. The wedding ceremony was held at 11 a.m. An hour later Plakici forced her back to work, and she was made to have sex with several punters the same day.

Izabela became pregnant twice whilst being pimped by Plakici. He arranged abortions for her and sent her back to the massage parlour almost immediately afterwards. She attempted to leave Plakici on three separate occasions, but he contacted her via her mobile phone, and a combination of promises and threats brought her back. Plakici knew exactly where Izabela's family lived, and she was in no doubt of his ruthlessness.

The other Moldovan girl, Mara, had originally been sold by Plakici to a pimp called Max, who paid £7,000 for her, but Max sent Mara back to Plakici just a few days later, complaining that she had repeatedly asked to return to him and Izabela. Mara had not been violated or forced into sex work by Plakici at this point, and she thought she would be safe if she stayed with him. Instead, Plakici was furious. He coerced Mara into working in a London massage parlour and demanded that she keep a record of how much money she was making for him. Mara worked seven days a week and estimates that she earned between three and four hundred pounds a day for Plakici. If she and Izabela didn't obey him,

2. Izabela, Regina vs Plakici, Wood Green Crown Court, 25 September 2003.

she said that he 'would beat us with a belt, make us shower in cold water'.[3]

Mara was an exception to the women and the girls that Plakici trafficked. Despite his ongoing threats and violence, she escaped from him a year later, and never went back.

He seems to have exerted almost total control over all the others: threatening and manipulating them in order to isolate them from each other and make them psychologically dependent on him. They were young, and most of them had not travelled far from their home town before they were recruited by Plakici and his associates.

Izabela, in particular, had a complex relationship with Plakici, based on her fear of his attraction to her whilst he also relentlessly forced her to work as a prostitute. In the summer of 2002 she attempted to reclaim some control over her own life. She complained to Plakici that he was always travelling whilst she was confined in London. Plakici arranged for Izabela to visit a Moldovan friend of hers called Erika, who was living in Israel and gave Izabela a fake Italian passport for the journey. When she met Izabela and heard her story, Erika immediately wanted to help her escape from her life with Plakici, and they visited the Moldovan Embassy in Tel Aviv together and both asked to be returned home. The embassy gave them no practical assistance and did not offer to return them to Moldova. Izabela was therefore resigned to returning to Plakici in London. She was only eighteen years old but had already been under Plakici's violent control for two years. Erika was worried about Izabela and soon followed her back to London, in a second attempt to help bail her out of her life with Plakici. But Erika was no match for Luan Plakici, who calmly told her she would also have to work for him, as Izabela was recovering from her second abortion and he still needed to recoup the £7,000 that he had spent purchasing her. Erika claims she saw Plakici attack Izabela in the bathroom of his flat. She was extremely frightened of him and did not dare to defy him.

And so Luan Plakici continued to build up his lucrative trafficking empire.

In October 2002 he trafficked two young Romanians: Augustina and her sister, Raluca. They had been living in extreme poverty in a town outside Bucharest. They shared one room with six other members of their family, and both worked full time as cleaners. A woman in their building introduced them to a local man called Lonci, who offered them both work in England. He said they would be cleaning bar tables at first but

3. Mara, Regina vs Plakici, Wood Green Crown Court, 13 October 2003.

could learn English, and afterwards they would be able to work as waitresses.

They both agreed to leave the country with Lonci, who transported them to Prague. Here they met Plakici, who had already arranged the next stage of their journey. He sent the sisters to Italy, where they were collected by two Italian drivers who drove Augustina and Raluca across Europe to Plakici's Middleton Road flat. Plakici moved them into his flat alongside Izabela and Erika. There was an immediate power struggle between the four women, with Izabela and Erika alleging to Plakici that the Romanian sisters were stealing from them. Whether Plakici orchestrated this divide and rule or not, it definitely worked in his favour. He beat the sisters for stealing. According to Augustina, 'He said I was being beaten because he had spent a lot of money on me and my sister, and he said that with this money he could have brought four girls from Romania to London.

The day after they had arrived in London Augustina and Raluca were taken out by the accomplice to be shown to potential clients, and other men came to the flat to bid for them. Plakici ran an extremely efficient business.

A few days later Plakici escorted Augustina from his flat to the Palmers Green flat where his accomplice was staying. Augustina claims that Plakici instructed him to have sex with her and left them alone in the flat. The accomplice then raped her. Afterwards he began to drink alcohol. When he eventually began to vomit from being drunk, Augustina let herself out of the flat and fled outside. She stood outside on the road in the early hours of the morning. She was twenty-three, alone in a strange country in the middle of the night, did not speak a word of English, and she had just been raped. Augustina walked the streets, and a police car on late patrol passed by. She flagged the car down and tried to explain to the officers what had just happened to her.

The trial of Luan Plakici and his accomplice was held in September 2003. They were charged with facilitating the entry of illegal immigrants (seven counts), kidnapping by fraud (three counts), procuring a girl to have unlawful sexual intercourse with a third person (three counts), incitement to rape (two counts) and living on earnings of prostitution (three counts). His accomplice was charged with one count of rape against Augustina.

The seven charges of facilitating the entry of illegal immigrants that Plakici faced were his nemesis. Unfortunately for him, seven of the women he had trafficked courageously agreed to testify against him in court.

After they had picked up Augustina, police raided the Middleton Road flat, where they arrested Plakici, the two Italian drivers (who had just delivered two new women), Izabela and the two women who had just been delivered. Erika was not in the flat at the time. Plakici's accomplice was arrested outside his own flat shortly afterwards.

Raluca had been taken by a pimp to another flat the night before. She told police that inside this flat a group of men had formed a queue to rape her. She was spared from gang rape when the pimp received a phone call from Plakici. During the course of the raid the police had permitted Plakici to make this call in an attempt to locate Raluca, because they were extremely concerned about her whereabouts.

The pimp took Raluca straight out of the flat, put her in his car and dumped her on the North Finchley Road like an unwanted animal.

When uniformed police officers raid private flats and houses, they are not trained to identify trafficked women. Augustina, Izabela and Raluca were immediately arrested as illegal immigrants. It was only after they had been questioned by officers for several hours that the three of them were identified as victims of trafficking. Augustina and her sister, Raluca, were offered accommodation close to Golders Green Police Station, in the exact neighbourhood where they had been held by Plakici.

Both women immediately asked to go home, and were removed to Romania within forty-eight hours. They returned to their crowded one-room house and menial cleaning jobs, and neither sister told their family the truth of what had happened to them in London.

Meanwhile Plakici's unwilling wife, Izabela, agreed to testify against him, as did Erika. They both stayed in the UK as protected witnesses for five months, until March 2003, when they also asked to go home, in their case, to Moldova. They had been told by immigration officials that they couldn't work or study, and neither of them felt safe in London. Their legal-aid applications regarding their asylum claims were rejected. Izabela had told the police she wanted to divorce Plakici, but ending this coerced marriage proved to be very complicated. Izabela had actually married Plakici under a false name, a name he had selected for her. The police were advised by a solicitor that a full investigation into the circumstances of Izabela's marriage and her reasons for requesting a divorce would cost Izabela in excess of a thousand pounds in legal fees. Izabela did not have a thousand pounds: everything she had earned had lined Luan Plakici's pockets.

Both she and Erika said they felt completely let down by the immigration service and were frustrated by the restrictions constantly being imposed on them. They told the Poppy Project, which had just opened, that they felt as though they were 'sitting around collecting dust' in London. The Poppy Project immediately offered them accommodation, but both of them said they had finally given up hope and were resigned to returning home.[4]

Back in Romania, Augustina had started receiving threatening letters at home. Nevertheless, she and Raluca agreed to meet with two British police officers who flew to Romania to interview them, and they both consented to return to the UK to give evidence against Plakici and, in Augustina's case, also against Plakici's accomplice.

Another crucial witness at the trial was a Romanian woman called Nicoletta. She had originally been trafficked to the UK in October 2001 by Plakici and his associates. In London she had been sold to a British pimp and spent a year working in a private flat before it was raided by police.

Nicoletta was immediately removed to Romania. Back at home, she rarely went outside and didn't tell her family she had been sold to a pimp. She was both ashamed of what had happened to her and frightened of the repercussions of confiding in anyone. This was all the leverage that Plakici et al. needed. Nicoletta was warned that her family would be harmed if she did not return to Britain and was also instructed to bring her young cousin, Dragona, to the UK with her. Nicoletta and Dragona were delivered to London in October 2002 by the same two Italian drivers who had trafficked Augustina and Raluca. The four of them arrived at the Middleton Road flat just hours before the police raid.

The police attempted to track down other potential witnesses, with some success. In April 2003 they eventually located Mara, who was still living in London. After escaping Plakici, she had made her own claim for asylum, found accommodation and work. She also agreed to go on the witness stand.

The seven women who testified at the trial each gave their evidence in court from behind a screen. They were offered the opportunity to give evidence via video-link but chose to appear in court and address the jury directly. Each of them could be seen by the jury but not the defendants. They used pseudonyms and were accommodated in pairs in hotels outside London that had already been vetted by the Criminal Justice Protection Unit.[5]

In court each of the women stated that she had been extremely frightened of Plakici, which underlined their courage in agreeing to testify against him.

During her evidence, Augustina described Plakici inciting other men to rape her. Referring to him as Turi (one of his known pseudonyms), she

4. Poppy Project records.
5. CJPU arranges safe accommodation for witnesses and witness protection schemes.

said, 'Turi had been there, and before he left he said that if I didn't do what he [the client] asked me to do, then he would stamp on me and kill me.'[6]

When she was on the stand, Izabela described her attempts to leave Plakici. After she fled the first time, she said that 'He was phoning, screaming, saying that he was going to find me, kill me or my family. He promised not to beat or touch me if I came back and said everything was going to be better. Unfortunately, I did believe him. I was scared, and I went back to him.'[7]

This combination of threats and promises, which included Plakici threatening to kill Izabela's fourteen-year-old sister, was the reason she returned to him on the three occasions she had tried to get away.

Giving evidence in court against a trafficker is a gruelling and frightening experience for any woman who agrees to act as a witness. She will be asked repeated and explicit questions about her experiences of violence and rape, often by a male lawyer and sometimes in an aggressive manner. Whilst she is explaining the details of what has been done to her, and what she has been forced to do, her trafficker will be almost certainly sitting at the other side of the courtroom from her, within earshot of everything she is saying about him.

The prosecutors at Plakici's trial cited the problem of several of the trafficking witnesses going 'off proof', i.e. their evidence in court was not what the prosecutors expected after having read their interviews and statements. Evidence collated by researcher Alice Peycke of the Poppy Project suggests a combination of reasons why the majority of trafficked women often make vulnerable witnesses in court, which can render them liable to being undermined by the defence.

> Trafficked women are victims of serious crime, potentially in grave danger and need to seriously consider their safety and future. Their level of insecurity will vary from day to day and may be exacerbated if they do not feel in control or know what will happen next. The increased dangers and fears of retribution when giving evidence will partly depend on whether, and when, she will return to her home country [. . .] Trauma may affect her recall, she may feel too ashamed to discuss certain things or feel they are irrelevant. She may not have told the police everything: perhaps if the interviews did not sufficiently facilitate her to give full statements, if she did not understand the purpose of the interview or was

6. Poppy Project transcription of Augustina giving evidence at Regina vs Plakici, Wood Green Crown Court, 2003.
7. Izabela, Regina vs Plakici, Wood Green Crown Court, 25 September 2003.

too afraid to disclose information [. . .] Trauma is likely to have a significant effect on witnesses' memory and recall, which, particularly when this has led to inconsistencies in their interviews/statements, can damage their credibility in court.[8]

Alice Peycke also points out that police officers investigating the Luan Plakici case believed it would have been beneficial for all sides if the women had been allowed to remain in the UK throughout the investigation, as it would have enabled officers to be in regular contact with them. If Nicoletta had not been removed from the UK in the first place, she would not have been re-trafficked, and her young cousin, Dragona, would not have been forced to come to London. Finally, Alice Peycke notes, 'Police practice shows that witness protection is taken seriously, but the focus continues to be ensuring their [the witnesses'] physical presence in court, rather than protecting their human rights and ensuring that they receive appropriate support and services.'[9]

One trafficked woman at the Poppy Project, who was not involved in the Luan Plakici trial, stated to project workers that she had judges, solicitors and police officers buy sex from her in the UK, so how could she expect these services to help her?[10]

The Plakici trial lasted almost three months. Luan Plakici pleaded guilty to the seven charges of facilitating the entry of illegal immigrants and not guilty to the rest of the charges. His accomplice pleaded not guilty to rape. The jury spent three weeks deliberating, and finally delivered their verdict on 19 December 2003.

Plakici was convicted of all three kidnapping by fraud charges, one of the procurement charges, one of the incitement to rape charges and all the charges of living on earnings of prostitution. He was sentenced to ten years in prison.

The Italian drivers were released on a technicality. Plakici's accomplice was acquitted of rape. Alice Peycke's report highlighted that defence lawyers utilise poor recall and inconsistency to undermine the credibility of a witness. This does not mean trafficked women make poor witnesses *per se*, but illustrates the difficulty for a woman who has been repeatedly violated to clearly recall one rape or assault *in situ*.

The maximum sentence for trafficking in the UK is fourteen years.

8. 'Prosecuting Human Traffickers: recommendations for good practice: Regina vs Plakici', Alice Peycke, Poppy Project, October 2004. This report was never externally published. Alice Peycke no longer works for the Poppy Project.
9. *Ibid.*
10. *Ibid.*, p.24.

Plakici's conviction was substantial, but it didn't satisfy everyone. An appeal against his sentence was immediately lodged by the Crown Prosecution Service, and a few months later the Attorney General, Lord Goldsmith, took the case to the Court of Appeal. Lord Goldsmith argued that in this particular case the sentence was too lenient and did not reflect either the number or the nature of the crimes committed by Luan Plakici. Lord Justice Latham was obviously persuaded, because on 29 April 2004 he increased the sentence to an unprecedented twenty-three years. Plakici was transferred to a prison in Dover and is scheduled for release in 2026.

The downfall of Luan Plakici made newspaper headlines across the country, and the trial was closely covered by radio, tabloid and broadsheet journalists. He was a ruthless trafficker and brutal pimp who was brought down by his greed and his fatal belief in his own infallibility.

I'm fascinated by this case, partly because Plakici sounds like a model trafficker and pimp: handsome, charismatic and sadistic; and partly because, in spite of all his organisational skills and contacts and those circuitous routes from Eastern Europe to London, his business collapsed the moment one of these women managed to make contact with a police officer. He was completely dependent on the compliance of his victims, which ultimately rendered him totally vulnerable to them.

I wonder if he was a good, as in efficient, trafficker who had a fatal stroke of back luck, or if this is always a trafficker's potential Achilles heel: that one of his 'victims' will blow the whistle because in the end they have nothing left to lose.

The officer who led the investigation into Luan Plakici is Detective Inspector Guy Taylor. His name was in the press when the case went to court, along with his colleague, Detective Inspector Jay Bevan. I contact Guy Taylor fairly swiftly via the Metropolitan Police. I have gradually learned how to pitch these phone enquiries. I explain that I'm writing a book and have been told this particular person 'may be willing to help me, and if they don't work at this office, could you please pass my details on to him or her?'

I never ask them to give me the contact's details, though I am sometimes immediately offered them. Either way, my method seems to work more often than not, and in this particular case Guy Taylor calls me about twenty minutes later. When I ask him if it would be possible to meet him and Jay Bevan to talk about Luan Plakici, he sounds positively enthusiastic.

'I'll call Jay and see if she's available. It will have to be at the end of next week, though,' he says. 'I've got a pretty big job on this week.'

I can't help asking him what the job is, and of course he tells me politely that he cannot say any more.

We arrange to meet on London's South Bank. I have practically moved back to London by now, spreading myself between a few generous friends who have a spare bedroom or a put-up in the lounge and don't mind me wandering in and out of their home at odd hours.

On the afternoon that we meet I am wearing a pink coat. Guy is wearing a brown coat. These are our cues to recognise each other at the café we have decided on. When I arrive, there is a man in a brown coat sitting opposite a woman at a table. She must be Jay Bevan. She immediately reminds me of Maggie from Kosovo: she has the same glinting hair that catches the light. Guy is somewhere in his late thirties, with short, curly hair and an assortment of gentle facial features that somehow make it difficult to describe him in any detail. He's wearing a dark suit and tie.

It is late October but still warm enough to sit outside. We arrange ourselves around a square wooden table, make our introductions and order glasses of wine. Jay tells me she used to be a uniformed police officer, but since the Plakici case she's been working for Operation Maxim, a pan-London police unit that investigates organised immigration crimes, including trafficking and smuggling.

I ask Guy how the big job went last week.

'Oh yeah, good. I've been in court just this morning, hence—' He tugs at the sleeve of his suit.

The waiter brings our wine. We clink glasses, and then I ask them what Luan Plakici was like.

'Sly,' says Jay, without a moment's hesitation. 'Sly and arrogant. During the trial he was constantly making notes and passing them on to his lawyer, like he was giving him instructions or orders. He really thought that he was going to get off lightly.'

'What do you mean, get off lightly? He pleaded guilty to facilitation, didn't he?'

'Yes, but that is a maximum of ten years. I think he was expecting to get less than that. He certainly didn't expect twenty-three.'

'Do you know who lodged the appeal?'

Jay grins at me. 'We did! We didn't think ten years was enough for what he'd done. We immediately made a request to the CPS, and when we got that appeal result, we were absolutely delighted!'

Guy nods. 'We thought he'd get twelve or fifteen years, but twenty-three was unheard of. It was fitting.' He sits back, looking quietly satisfied.

We start to discuss the downfall of Luan Plakici. Jay is animated, talking and gesturing energetically, while Guy mostly sits back, listens and observes. They complement each other, and I see why they make a good team.

They tell me they worked together on this case for almost a year.

'Guy was given the investigation just after Plakici had been arrested, and he brought me on board,' says Jay.

Guy nods, again. 'First thing we did was to go through his flat,' he says. 'There was a lot of evidence there. He used a guidebook to UK massage parlours and saunas to select the places he'd send the girls to work. The fifth edition was in his flat, with a whole series of highlighted pages.'

'What else did you find?'

'Money. He had a lot of money. He had those girls working for him ten hours a day, seven days a week. They didn't get a break. You know, whenever a new girl got to London, the first thing he would do is get her to recite her family details to him while he took notes. Then she knew that he knew exactly where her whole family was: that was one of his methods. After that, he taught them to recite the list of sex acts that they would be doing for punters. These were the first words they learned in English. He used to count the condoms in the morning and then check how many were left when they came back at night. He would tally up how much money they each had to make for him each day.'

Jay leans across the table, shading her eyes from the sun. 'One of the girls wrote the list of sex acts in her diary so she wouldn't forget,' she says. 'We had it translated as evidence. You know, one of the things juries don't understand is the level of control that someone like Plakici exerts over these girls. You get a young, often naïve Eastern European who's been trafficked to London, physically and sexually abused, threatened and sent out to work in a massage parlour. She has to have sex with ten men a day, and at the end of the night she hands over her entire takings because otherwise she'll be raped or beaten with a belt buckle – and they still think she's a prostitute. When that perception changes, then we'll have made some progress.'

'Was it bad luck that he got caught in the end, or are all traffickers vulnerable to women going to the police?' I ask them, testing out my theory.

'The minute Augustina was picked up by police, Plakici was in trouble,' says Guy. 'Up until that moment he was doing very good business. In the cases I've worked on, it's almost always been the victim contacting the police that has kick-started the investigation. So, yes, that's the risk for a trafficker. And that's why they deliberately take down details of the girls' families as soon as they get them to London.'

'And what about all the money that Plakici made from these women?'

'At the end of the case he was ordered to pay the court about ninety-five thousand pounds,' replies Guy. 'But there is a lot of money still unaccounted for. We're still investigating Plakici's assets and finances across Europe and the States. Mind you, we still don't know for sure who Luan Plakici is.'

'What do you mean?'

'The man in prison who claims to be Luan Plakici might well be lying. He claimed asylum under the name Plakici, but we know that's a method that traffickers, and other criminals, use. They apply under a pseudonym, using false documents or claiming they have no documents at all, and assume a brand-new identity. Then they cannot be traced from one country to the next.

'Plakici also knew about passport forgeries. He was used to inserting photos of different girls into passports, and he was obviously very good at it because he brought a lot of people into the UK.'

When he was arrested, Luan Plakici was in the process of changing his name by deed poll to Brandan Moore. The paperwork was in his home; he just didn't have quite enough time to buy this new identity.

Guy and Jay both believe Luan Plakici's real name might well be Artur Corbajram. This was one of several pseudonyms that he used whilst trafficking: the personalised number plate on his black BMW was H1 TUR. And Plakici once met an undercover journalist posing as a Glasgow pimp, and on that occasion, assuming he was amongst fellow traffickers, he referred to himself as Artur Corbajram.[11]

'We've never been completely sure who he really is,' says Guy. 'And despite everything we've tried so far, I don't honestly know if that question will ever be answered. Every now and again I still wonder to myself, Who exactly is Luan Plakici?' He tells me Plakici has now been transferred to a prison in Middlesbrough, near his family.

There is one final strand of justice that might yet weave itself into the conclusion of this complex case. When the man who calls himself Luan Plakici is eventually released from prison, he may find that having gained his freedom, he has just lost possibly the second most important thing to him: the thing that made it far easier for him to abuse both the British legal system and the women that he bought and sold.

A request has been filed at the Home Office for the Secretary of State to consider revoking the British citizenship of Luan Plakici. Under Section 40 of the British Nationality Act 1981, 'The Secretary of State may by order deprive a person of a citizenship status if the Secretary of

11. Derek Alexander, *Mail on Sunday*, 14 October 2001.

State is satisfied that the person has done anything seriously prejudicial to the vital interests of the United Kingdom.'[12]

As Guy Taylor puts it, 'Twenty-three years in prison, a hundred grand confiscated and being stripped of his British citizenship: now that is a deterrent.'

12. I have been advised by the Home Office that this is the appropriate legislation to be used to request that British citizenship be revoked.

Chapter 16

How to Catch Traffickers

Luan Plakici received the longest sentence ever handed down to a trafficker in the UK. His parasitic house of cards collapsed when one of the women he had trafficked managed to flee and contact the police, and because, a year later, she and six others had the courage to testify against him.

Plakici's 'victims' turned on him, threw every violation back at him and nailed him. The meticulous gathering of evidence by Jay Bevan, Guy Taylor and their colleagues facilitated the trial, but I wonder whether Plakici would still be serving twenty-three years if these women had not each climbed into the witness stand, and explained in explicit detail to the jury what he did to them, and how he did it.

Jay Bevan and Guy Taylor both described Plakici's final sentence as 'a huge morale boost'. Certainly, the trial, conviction, appeal and re-sentencing received huge media coverage ('Prison for Sex Slave Gang Leader', 'Slave Trader's Wife Earned Him £144,000 in Two Years', 'Vice Ring Boss's Jail Time Doubled', etc.), and the precedent set by Plakici's conviction has been reflected in heavy sentences being handed down to a number of male and female traffickers over the last eighteen months, aided and abetted by the introduction of specific trafficking offences in the Sexual Offences Act 2003.[1] Across the UK there are now a number of law-enforcement agencies and intelligence services gathering evidence, identifying trafficked women and catching traffickers.

Charing Cross Police Station is on the corner of the Strand and Agar Street, just five minutes' walk from Trafalgar Square. As well as being one

---

[1]. Sections 57, 58 and 59 of the Sexual Offences Act 2003 apply maximum fourteen-year sentences for human trafficking into, within and out of the UK for the purpose of sexual exploitation.

of the busiest police stations in the country, it's also the HQ of Charing Cross Clubs and Vice (CO14), the only major vice squad in the UK.

CO14 was originally set up in 1934. These days the squad's remit is investigating 'organised major vice-related crime'. The emphasis is on street offences (especially child prostitution), trafficking for sexual exploitation, obscene publications, illegal prostitution (i.e. when the sex worker is either an illegal immigrant or a foreign national with no right to work in the UK), brothel-keeping, controlling prostitution for gain, illegal gaming and the supply of Class A drugs and firearms in licensed premises. CO14 also has a counter-terrorism desk and a small Financial Investigations Unit, which initiates seizures and confiscations from vice-related crimes.

The teams within CO14 operate like a series of satellites that relay intelligence to each other whilst orbiting round the central Vice Unit.

When I call CO14, the phone is answered by a cheerful-sounding man.

'Clubs and Vice.'

'Hello, is that the Vice Unit?' I ask him.

'No, I'm Porn,' he replies blithely.

I tell him why I'm calling, and he puts me through to an officer called Julia Roberts who explains CO14 officers have been running London-based operations aimed at identifying under-age prostitutes and women who've been trafficked or coerced into sex work since 1999. Their current operation, Kontiki, has been going since 2003.

Julia and her colleagues make regular visits to saunas, massage parlours and flats across London where sex is sold. They monitor conditions at the premises, identify any new arrivals and arrest any women who are working illegally.

'If I suspect a woman is being coerced in a brothel but her papers are in order and she's entitled to work in the UK, then my hands are tied,' she tells me. 'I've got no grounds to bring her in for questioning. All I can do is return to that particular premise again as soon as possible and try to find out more without putting her at risk.'

Every sauna, massage parlour and flat (bar those where women work alone) has a receptionist, or maid, who oversees the running of the premises and takes entry fees from punters. If Julia wants to identify who actually owns or controls the brothel, or if the premise has been identified as a nuisance brothel, she will often start by bringing the maid in for questioning.

'Before we can question a maid, we have to prove she's committing the offence of "acting and assisting in managing a brothel", so at that point we usually arrange a "test purchase".'

'What's a test purchase?' I ask, wondering if it is what I think it is.

'One of the officers rings the premises, requests a sexual service and the price, of course. The call is taped, then we can bring her in.'

And when the maid is brought in to the station, the cat-and-mouse scenario continues.

'Ninety-nine per cent of the time we bring a maid in for questioning, she'll say she applied for her job via a local paper, was interviewed over the phone and has no clue who her boss is. She'll insist she's never met him and that her salary is either paid straight into her bank account or left for her on the premises every week. She'll keep her mouth shut because she knows in the end all she's going to get is a caution.'

If she has no previous related convictions, the maid will be asked to accept a formal caution by the station duty inspector. The request itself is a legal formality: she doesn't have much choice about accepting it, because otherwise she'll be charged. The caution is logged on the police national computer (PNC) database, and if the maid is questioned again about assisting in brothel management, then she probably will be charged. But even then, according to Julia, she is under no legal obligation to reveal her employer's identity. It's a cumbersome, time-consuming system, and while Kontiki officers are trying to extract information about who actually controls the brothel, the women who may be at risk are still working inside and can easily be moved by their trafficker or pimp.

Operation Kontiki has been going for almost three years. During its first year of operation 300 women were arrested for illegal prostitution, and another twenty women were identified as trafficked. Last year the numbers dropped dramatically: officers arrested fifty illegal prostitutes, and just two women were identified as having been trafficked. So far this year thirty-nine women have been arrested, but no trafficked women have been identified. It's mid-October 2005 now, so barring a major spate of pre-Christmas raids, these figures are unlikely to change substantially.

Julia is surprisingly up front about why she thinks the number of women identified by CO14 as working illegally, or having been trafficked into the sex industry have both dropped so dramatically.

'One factor is that during the first year of Kontiki we visited a huge number of brothels: it was more than four hundred altogether. But even during the three years of this operation things have changed, and we know a lot of brothels have sprung up in residential areas way outside the city centre, like Richmond, Bromley and Hounslow. It's getting much harder to identify these premises and the women working inside them. And even when we do make contact and start talking to the women, it's

always been a small minority of the overall number who will actually
come forward and say they've been trafficked or coerced. Trust is a huge
issue for these women, as you can imagine.'

As the manager of Operation Kontiki, Julia liaises with the Street
Offences and Juvenile Protection Unit within CO14, who carry out
regular impromptu visits to brothels under child-protection legislation.
But if she decides a brothel needs to be thoroughly investigated for
trafficking women or children, then it is the Vice Unit that takes over.

Vice Unit officers specialise in 'lifestyle' investigations: literally track-
ing the lifestyle of suspected pimps and brothel owners, or 'principals'.
Their remit regarding prostitution is to disrupt the illegal sex industry,
and these investigations are based on gathering as much intelligence as
possible before officers raid a brothel.

After talking with Julia, I speak to one of the Vice Unit officers over the
phone. He asks me not to use his name.

'These raids are proactive operations against ponces and pimps,' he
tells me. 'Our priorities are identifying juvenile prostitutes and trafficked
women, but we always go after the principal too because whoever's
controlling the brothel is controlling the women inside it, and that's
controlling prostitution for gain.'

Controlling prostitution for gain has a seven-year maximum penalty.
He points out that whoever is controlling the women may also be the
trafficker.

I ask him whether the Vice Unit are also on the lookout for illegal
workers during these raids. He tells me immigration officers 'normally'
accompany a Vice Unit raid, and if the officers find a woman they suspect
of being in the country illegally and she has no documents to prove
otherwise, she is immediately arrested so that her identity can be verified.

'If she's an asylum seeker, she cannot be removed from Britain and we
release her. But if she's in the UK illegally, she's served with a set of IS91
papers. These inform her she is in breach of her landing conditions. She's
then transferred by immigration to Harmondsworth Holding Centre and
removed from the UK.'

Harmondsworth is an immigration removal centre adjacent to Heathrow Airport. It's a single-sex centre and holds up to 500 men. Women
are actually taken to neighbouring Colnbrook Removal Centre, which
also holds men, but has forty 'short-term holding-facility spaces' where
women can also be held.

'How long does it take to remove a woman?' I ask him.

'We normally remove them within forty-eight hours. But if there is a
plane going four hours later, she'll be on it.'

'What if she says she's been trafficked and wants to stay in the UK?'

There is a slight pause. 'If a woman wants to stay in this country,' he replies, 'then we have major problems.'

One of these major problems is where to accommodate a trafficked woman. The Poppy Project has just twenty-five beds and already receives referrals from all over the country. If they have no spaces, CO14 call social services or certain organisations who may have a refuge space available, albeit sometimes hundreds of miles away at the other end of the country. As a final resort, they will have to book a woman into a Central London hotel room. Before going to the hotel the woman will be questioned by police, who will take a detailed statement from her in order to begin a criminal investigation. This could take a long time: the Poppy project has told me of one instance where a woman was questioned for nine hours.

This is the point at which some women, like Augustina and Raluca who were trafficked by Luan Plakici, may decide to go home anyway. If you've only just got away from a trafficker who has raped you, actively encouraged other men to rape you and regularly threatened to kill your family if you don't shut up and comply, a Central London hotel does not provide much personal security or incentive to stay and testify against him. This scenario does not by any means involve every woman who informs police officers she has been trafficked, but it has happened to some of them, and accommodation for trafficked women is still very ad hoc. The Vice Unit has just fifteen full-time officers to gather proactive intelligence on the illegal vice industry, and identify the most seriously exploited women and girls.

CO14 officers are between a rock and a hard place. Charing Cross Clubs and Vice is not an anti-trafficking unit. It is a squad of eighty-four officers who between them police the entire spectrum of vice across London, tackling everything from hard-core porn to kerb-crawling, illicit gaming to brothel-keeping and drug-dealing.

The officers have no resources of their own to support trafficked women, and apart from referring women to the Poppy Project or emergency services, no other means of directly assisting them.

One of the most insightful commentators on trafficking is Paul Holmes, who used to run CO14. He spent six years there as head of operations, but these days he works as an international law-enforcement consultant. I met him a couple of years ago, at that same London Metropolitan training course where I first met Maggie from Kosovo.

I remember him as a large, charismatic man, with a brooding gaze and hands like boxing gloves. He gave us a presentation on women being trafficked into the UK. Listening to Paul Holmes talk about trafficking left me feeling quite stunned.

'Even when they get to the safety of a shelter, some of these women are never going to recover from what's been done to them. They've been trained to do their job by being raped by their traffickers, and they supply unsafe sexual services which threaten their own lives because they are repeatedly forced to have sex with punters who pay for them. Furthermore, if a woman has been recruited or raped by a police officer, which may well have happened to her en route to the UK, then she's going to have an extremely negative experience of law enforcement by the time she gets here.'

After he'd finished speaking, I cornered Paul Holmes for a moment, introduced myself and asked if I could contact him when I'd done some research of my own. He gave me his email address and said I was welcome to get in touch, though he frequently worked abroad these days, so I'd have to catch him when I could.

To be honest, one of the reasons it's taken me so long to contact him is that until right now I haven't been quite sure what to ask.

After I send him a couple of emails reminding him who I am, he forwards me his office number. I call him the next morning, before he flees the country again, and ask what he thinks about the current policing on trafficking in the UK.

'What is happening here at the moment is a mop-up operation,' he says. 'We are losing the best evidential assets we have, because, to put it bluntly, victims are being removed from brothels and sent straight back home before they have any chance to explain they've been trafficked. Trafficked women have the evidence to put their traffickers behind bars because they know the business. They know the prices because they've been sold. They know where the brothels are because they practically live in them. They spend more time with traffickers and pimps than anyone, and they can even identify the punters. We need them to stay and testify against their traffickers, and we need to make it safe enough for them to do so.'

He tells me he strongly believes that any woman who identifies herself as having been trafficked should be automatically entitled to a period of reflection.

'Giving any victim a safe place to stay for the first few weeks after her escape or release makes total sense. The woman can have her options explained to her, safe in the knowledge that she has a bit of safe, quiet time to get her head together and decide what she wants to do next. Plus, she can give a detailed statement to the police. Unless she is catatonically traumatised, any victim is capable of giving a statement, and every statement is a piece of intelligence. Even if she decides not to testify, you still have the intelligence to go on. You only have to look at Italy to see that if women are given the support they actually need, you'll get better evidence from them and they're more likely to agree to testify.

'If she does decide to cross the Rubicon and become a witness, any trafficked woman is a major asset to a prosecution. A jury will never hear anything more powerful than testimony direct from a woman who has been sold and raped and abused herself. What we have to realise is reflection periods are actually a cost-effective exercise because the testimony of a victim is the best way of securing a conviction against a trafficker, and preventing him from doing any more business.

'Mind you –' he pauses momentarily to inhale '– you also need to tell her damn straight the longer she takes deciding whether to testify, the harder it's going to be to find the evidence to back her allegations. These guys won't be hangin' around for the cops to arrive and turn the place over: they'll just move on and set up shop somewhere else.'

Women who are trafficked to Britain from within the EU are legally entitled to remain here, though their status becomes complicated if they've entered the UK on false or forged documents, as they have, technically, committed a crime.[2] Regardless of whether they agree to testify, there is the chronic problem of where they can be safely and supportively housed, and whether they are entitled to state provisions.

For those who do decide to testify, there's also the crucial issue of ensuring their trafficker(s) can't intimidate or re-traffick them before they get to court.

The women who make it on to the Poppy Project have the unique privilege of four weeks' reflection before they have to make any of these decisions. And because Poppy advises its non-EU clients to consider applying for asylum, and supports them if they do apply, they cannot be removed from the UK until a decision has been made on their asylum status.

Women from non-EU countries who do not make it on to Poppy are in the most vulnerable position of all. Annette, who was trafficked here from East Africa, managed, after being imprisoned, to make an 'in-country' application for asylum and has therefore been granted 'temporary admission' while her claim is being considered.

Temporary admission is granted by the Home Office on the advice of a senior officer from the UK Immigration Service (UKIS). This is the

2. Section 24a of the Immigration Act 1971. Cases are decided on the basis of 'public policy considerations'.

same service that, in a recent independent evaluation of the Poppy Project, expressed 'disappointment' in the project, especially with regard to women who were being allowed to make in-country applications for asylum. 'Whilst acknowledging the victim status of trafficked women, UKIS also has a statutory duty to remove those persons present in the country illegally.'

From the point of view of the Immigration Service, their responsibilities had 'shifted' when the asylum criteria were changed. Or, as one of the immigration officers involved with the Poppy Project put it, 'Being trafficked doesn't mean that they should stay here. We need to give that period of reflection, but eventually they need to be repatriated to their home. [. . .] We are a bit cynical, but if people realise that they can stay here indefinitely by saying they are trafficked, the figures for trafficking will go up.'

One of the recommendations of the Poppy evaluation is that the Immigration Service 'needs to engage more effectively with ministerial strategies on trafficking which do not necessarily culminate in the removal of women who have been trafficked'.[3]

I've been told by police that any woman who is in this country illegally because she's been trafficked here can be granted temporary admission,[4] and have tried to verify how temporary admission is applied. I have contacted the Immigration and Nationality Directorate a number of times in the last few months. So far I've telephoned three times, written to both the IND Policy Unit and the Freedom of Information Team, and emailed the IND Public Enquiry. I've had no replies and am hence none the wiser.

Britain has no specific provision within its immigration legislation that entitles people who have been trafficked to the UK to remain here, either for their own protection or because they want to stay here. Temporary admission is granted to people who have been trafficked on a case-by-case basis; it is not a binding legal standard, and as Paul Holmes reiterates, women are still regularly being removed.

In 2004 the Council of Europe drafted a lengthy Convention on Action Against Trafficking in Human Beings. Article 13 of the convention states that a recovery and reflection period of at least thirty days should be granted:

> When there are reasonable grounds to believe that the person concerned is a victim, such a period shall be sufficient for the person concerned to

3. 'Evaluation of the Victims of Trafficking Pilot Project', Gina Taylor, September 2005.
4. Home Office circular 12/97, or simply HOC 12/97.

recover and escape the influence of traffickers and/or take an informed decision on cooperating with the competent authorities. During this period it shall not be possible to enforce any expulsion order against him or her.[5]

The convention also tackles the issues of renewable resident permits for trafficking victims on the basis of either cooperating with the authorities or personal need, as well as the right to seek political asylum. It has already been signed by more than eighteen European countries. Despite being lobbied by organisations from all sides of the political spectrum, including a substantial number of their own MPs, the government has so far refused to join them.

As an ex-copper, Paul Holmes understands why the government is dragging its feet over these issues.

'I know the British government is concerned about "procedure shopping",' he says briskly. 'They don't want to give the impression of encouraging foreign women to present themselves as victims of trafficking so that they have a period of reflection and then apply for political asylum or indefinite leave to remain. But you can eliminate most of that risk by obtaining a statement from the victim as soon as possible and using police intelligence to verify her information. If she's lying, then I fully support prosecuting her for wasting police time and immediately deporting her. But that's no reason to deny genuine victims a period of reflection.'

I can hear him warming to his subject and visualise him tilting his chair back, or leaning forward with his elbows resting on his desk. I hear a quiet question in the background at his end, the phone is muffled for a moment as he responds, and then he continues gunning down the telephone.

'Once they've gathered themselves together, y'know, most trafficked women want someone to pay for what they've been through, and why wouldn't they? Traffickers are all violent, but some of them, especially some of the Albanians, they're sadists. They treat these women as nothing more than walking ATM machines.

'But if a woman is removed, what does she go back to? Poverty, a debt round her neck and the risk of being re-trafficked.

'One thing a lot of women learn very quickly is how to be a good trafficking victim. It's often how they survive: by being compliant. But that's also why some are immediately re-trafficked.

'When we send a woman straight back, then no one pays for the

5. The rest of this paragraph of the article reads: 'The provision is without prejudice to the activities carried out by the competent authorities in all phases of the relevant national proceedings, and in particular when investigating and prosecuting the offences concerned. During this period, the Parties shall authorise the person to stay in their territory.'

crimes that have been committed, and there's a lot of crimes involved in trafficking: there's rape and coercion, but there's also GBH and money laundering, extortion, falsifying documents and illegal immigration. Traffickers are up to their necks in organised crime. If the victim doesn't become a witness, there's no chance of real twenty-year-jail-sentence justice. Take Plakici. Those women he trafficked set a legal precedent between them, which is one of the best deterrents you can get.'

At this point I can't help smiling to myself. The Plakici precedent: it's a perfect irony that Luan Plakici, who swaggered around London for years buying and selling women like used cars, has become a template for nailing traffickers in the UK. He would cringe if he knew.

The thought of him cringing in his cell distracts me for a moment, and when I switch back to listening to Paul, he's still going at full speed. '. . . because that's what they are . . . successful traffickers are good businessmen. And like the managers of any corporation, they make risk assessments. Going to prison for a few years is a risk they build into their business plan. But if you get fifteen years and you have to serve the whole sentence, plus all your cash is seized and the Mercedes and the swanky house, then you're gonna start wondering whether the UK is really the place to do business.'

I hear him smile down the phone as he adds, 'You know what, when you do arrest a pimp or a trafficker who's made himself rich by absolute bloody cruelty, there is something quite beautiful about putting the cuffs on and asking him if he wants to take a last look at his Mercedes. Because, you tell him, my colleague's just about to drive it round the corner and you're never going to see it again. I tell you, their faces fall. They can't quite believe it's finally happened and the game is over.'

Human trafficking is considered to be the fastest-growing form of organised crime in the world. The annual profit made by traffickers bringing women into Western Europe is estimated at $5–7 billion. This refers to the money that traffickers make selling women into the European sex industry: it does not include profits extracted from the women afterwards.

The CO14 Financial Investigation Unit (FIU) has just three investigating officers at the moment. There used to be five. During the last financial year (April 2004–5) these three officers seized, confiscated and restrained cash and assets worth more than £5.25 million between them. Since April 2005 they've already taken another £1.325 million, including one confiscation order for £600,000 from a brothel keeper. Their investigations are not all trafficking-related; the FIU officers work alongside both the Vice and Obscene Publications Units. But the amounts involved underline how cash and asset-rich vice crimes are.

The Proceeds of Crime Act 2002 gave police additional powers to seize, restrain and confiscate criminal money and assets, and also allows them to claw back a substantial proportion of the value of monies and assets they recover. The crime of money laundering now carries a maximum fourteen-year penalty.

When I recently visited the unit, Lawrie Day and his colleague Shaun Galloway showed me examples of brothel timesheets. Each sheet consisted of hand-drawn columns and figures, with exact calculations of how much each sex worker had earned during her shift, plus the business expenses of renting the premises, paying for the maid, security, advertising and even sundries. Brothel keepers are renowned for keeping paper records: they regard computers as a liability. These records, seized during a recently completed investigation, exposed the whole economic crime, including the use of thirty separate bank accounts to launder funds. In other FIU cases, brothels' timesheets have illustrated that some sex workers are charged up to £100 a day for being sick or unable to work. It is all there, in black and white.

'Compared with drugs, which can only be sold once, women continue to produce revenue,' Lawrie stated baldly. 'It's not a sufficient deterrent to arrest and convict those on the bottom or middle tiers. By seizing assets, you can severely damage the infrastructure of these organisations and reduce their capacity to traffic women. But we are the only financial investigators in the country working inside a specialist vice squad, we're two staff down, and our work is a slow, intense burn.'

The FIU officers are financial beachcombers; using 'forensic-accounting' methods, they sift through databases, financial records, files, mounds of paperwork and the contents of many a safety-deposit box until they find strands of evidence from which gradually to build the foundations of a case.

This is exactly the approach Paul Holmes advocates with regard to gathering intelligence on all human traffickers, including those whose business is outside the sex industry.

'You've got to start these investigations with low-level intelligence-gathering: monitor the local press, check out Internet sites, talk to local union activists about workers being laid off because cheap labour's just arrived from elsewhere, talk to people in the medical profession about who has been turning up at A&E with work-related injuries. There's a huge stack of stuff to go through and monitor, and it takes time and resources, but it's not expensive, and it will pay off.

'You can't do quick and dirty trafficking investigations. But, remember, all traffickers trade people for cash: they're hyper vulnerable to intelligence. The evidence is all around you . . . if you are looking carefully.'

Paul Holmes makes it clear he has no criticisms of his police colleagues, but underlines the limited resources with which they have to work. He believes the way forward is for the Home Secretary to add human trafficking to the existing list of police 'performance indicators'. These 'police authorities (best value) performance indicators' are yardsticks by which the performance of every police authority in England and Wales is measured.[6] There are currently thirteen performance indicators, ranging from public fear of crime and risk of personal and household crime to the percentage of police-officer time spent on front-line duties and the number and percentage of offences brought to justice.

According to Paul, if human trafficking became a performance indicator, the chief constable of every force would be compelled to review how his officers deal with trafficking and it would become a national policing priority.

'Then we could start making some serious inroads,' he says, his voice sounding slightly hoarse. We've been on the phone for nearly an hour and a half. 'At the moment, convictions for human trafficking are not measured in national crime statistics. That's partly because of recent changes in legislation, but we need to know exactly how many traffickers are being convicted. We also need to know how many women they're trafficking, which is why we shouldn't be removing them in the first place. It effectively renders trafficking a victimless crime.

'Look, we both know trafficking is ultimately about economic disparities and poverty and gender politics, but while we're waiting for international poverty alleviation, the criminal justice response is the best short- and medium-term answer we've got.

'This is an economically driven crime. Britain has some of the best asset-seizure laws in the world, and our police have a sound record of intelligence-gathering. It's about resources and priorities, plus having a bloody good judicial deterrent in this country. Give 'em Plakici-style prison sentences and make sure they come out of prison absolutely skint.'

In the eighteen months since Luan Plakici had his sentence increased on appeal, there have been a number of other high-profile convictions of traffickers in the UK. Many of these have involved operations funded by Reflex: the UK-wide multi-agency law-enforcement partnership approach that was set up in May 2000 in order to disrupt and dismantle

6. This jurisdiction does not apply to Scotland.

organised immigration crime. Reflex has three priorities: tackling 'volume facilitation' (aka smuggling), combating human trafficking, and dismantling the infrastructures that support organised immigration crime, including smuggling and trafficking routes and forged documentation.[7]

A substantial number of police forces across the UK have secured funding from Reflex in order to focus on organised immigration crime. In South Yorkshire, officers whose anti-trafficking work has been funded by Reflex have been particularly successful in prosecuting a number of traffickers.

In December 2004 Taulant Merdinaj and Elidon Bregu were convicted of trafficking two Lithuanian women who were imprisoned in a flat in Sheffield and forced to work in a massage parlour. The two women, who were personally thanked by Judge Walker for their courage in testifying in court, were housed by the Poppy Project in the months before the trial. Merdinaj was sentenced to eighteen years, and Bregu got nine.

Another operation, code-named Operation Return, involved a fifteen-year-old Lithuanian, 'Elena', who had also been trafficked to South Yorkshire. Elena was initially recruited in the Lithuanian capital Vilnius by a local trafficker. She flew to Heathrow with him in July 2004, where they were met by two Albanians, Shaban Maka and Ilir Barjami, and a woman called Lina, who was Maka's girlfriend.

Elena was taken into London and immediately sold to a pimp. Over the next two months she was trafficked to Birmingham, London, Leicester and Coventry, and finally purchased by Ilir Barjami, who took her to Sheffield, where he raped her repeatedly and paraded her as his trophy in a local nightclub. Elena was bought and sold seven times.

While in the nightclub with Barjami, Elena managed to escape by claiming she needed the toilet. She ran outside, asked for directions and fled to a nearby police station. Her statement led to the arrest of Maka, Barjami and Lina. Their trial was held in February 2005, and Elena gave live evidence in court, facing the defendants. Darren Booth, one of the Reflex officers directly involved in the case, described her courage as 'astounding'. Maka was sentenced to eighteen years, Barjami got fifteen years, and another Albanian, Xhevahir Pisha, who was charged with trafficking Elena within the UK, got seven years. Lina was acquitted on the grounds of duress. She was then accepted on to the Poppy Project as she had been trafficked into the sex industry herself

7. Reflex partners include the National Criminal Intelligence Service, the National Crime Squad, the Foreign and Commonwealth Office, the UK Immigration Service, the intelligence agencies and the Association of Chief Police Officers.

and also needed support. Elena, who later chose to return to Lithuania, spent the five months prior to the trial living with a foster family in Sheffield.

Not all women who are trafficked to the UK want to remain here. Two Lithuanian teenagers who were publicly auctioned for £3,000 each by their traffickers at a Costa Coffee outlet in Gatwick Airport in November 2004 both wanted to return home after extricating themselves from their traffickers and contacting the police.

They also both agreed to return to the UK and testify against their traffickers. Whilst in Lithuania, they were visited by Sheffield Reflex officers who kept them fully informed of proceedings, liaised with the local organisation that was supporting them and talked them through what to expect at the trial. Their traffickers were sentenced at Sheffield Crown Court in October 2005. Tasim Axhami, a Serb, received twenty-one years. His accomplice, Emiljan Beqirat, a Lithuanian, got sixteen years. Vilma Kizlaite, also Lithuanian, was sentenced to eleven years. She claimed duress, but was considered an active member of the trafficking network.

These three cases have several factors in common, including the nationality of the females. Since Lithuania joined the EU in May 2004, there has been a surge of trafficking cases involving young Lithuanian women. Some commentators point to poverty being an obvious factor 'pulling' young Lithuanian women to the UK, and to Lithuania being targeted by traffickers as a new market, especially now that Lithuanian women can travel to and remain within the UK legally. However, this doesn't explain why Lithuanian women and girls have been especially targeted, as opposed to Latvians or Estonians. It is thought that large groups of both Russians and Belarusians have moved over the border to Lithuania in the run up to Lithuania joining the EU, creating an apparently flourishing industry in forged Lithuanian and other A8 passports. It is also known that traffickers who bring Lithuanian women into the UK confiscate their passports, insert false photographs and use them to bring women from outside the EU into the UK.

There were, however, no doubts expressed about the genuine nationality of the Lithuanian women who were brave enough to testify.

In the last few months I've read through a number of reports of trafficking trials and have yet to come across a case in which a trafficker has been convicted in the UK without the testimony of one of the women he, or she, has trafficked. In most cases, the investigation itself has been sparked by a woman managing to escape and contact the police. There have also been a handful of cases in which investigations have been intelligence-led from the outset, but these have been the exceptions not the rule. Under current British legislation, trafficked women are vital prosecution witnesses in the trials of their traffickers.

To date, eleven women from the Poppy Project have testified in court. Six trials involving women from the project have been completed, and twelve traffickers have been convicted.

Neil Brown, head of the Reflex Secretariat, acknowledges that at the moment it is very unlikely a trafficker would be convicted in the UK without the testimony of a woman he trafficked. He explains to me that the Interception of Communications Act 1985 prevents the use of interception evidence in court.

'As the law prevents the use of such material, it would be difficult to support a victimless prosecution in such an environment.' Though he adds the proviso that 'It may be possible.'

Simon Jeal of the Crown Prosecution Service recently confirmed that in terms of prosecuting traffickers, 'the difficulty to date has been that there have been few, if any trafficking cases where the weight of non-victim testimony would satisfy the requirements of the Code for Crown Prosecutors. Therefore, I think it is highly likely that many trafficking prosecutions will rely on first hand victim testimony in the foreseeable future.' However, he added that he believes the formation of the Serious Organised Crime Agency (SOCA) will in time alter the situation.

Following on from Paul Holmes's comment that trafficking convictions are not included in national crime statistics, I ask Neil Brown how many traffickers have been convicted since the introduction of the Sexual Offences Act 2003.

He says he will get back to me. When he does, he explains the data has been 'more difficult to obtain than I expected, and I'm unable to give you the exact figures at the moment.'

If we do not know how many traffickers have been convicted in the UK, there is no way of assessing how many women they have trafficked into or within this country. More women are now being identified as victims of trafficking, but UK intelligence on trafficking is limited.

The National Criminal Intelligence Service (NCIS) drafts an annual UK 'threat assessment', which assesses threats to the UK from serious organised crime and how organised crime is likely to develop. In its most recent assessment, NCIS points out that compared with the number of people being smuggled into the UK, the number being trafficked is small. It also draws attention to the 'unsafe assumption' that all foreign women working in brothels are trafficking victims. Regarding the increase in numbers of women being identified as trafficking victims, it states:

It is not clear to what extent this represents a growth in the vice trade, a new trend in the recruitment of prostitutes or simply better intelligence. [. . .] Most trafficked women come from the Balkans and the former Soviet Union or from the Far East, especially China and Thailand. The latter appear much more costly to procure, and this may explain the relatively rapid growth in the former.

The NCIS threat assessment also describes the dynamic regarding traffickers and how ethnic Albanians are apparently attempting to wrest control from other organised crime gangs:

> There are signs that criminals from the Balkans, especially ethnic Albanians, where there is a large vice trade, are seeking to gain control of the trade in the UK. They are doing so [. . .] by taking over ownership of brothels and saunas. [. . .] While there have been some law-enforcement successes in targeting the traffickers, it appears that prostitutes who are arrested or deported can be replaced within days.[8]

One interpretation of this intelligence picture is that the triads who were first identified by CO14 back in the late 1980s, when they began trafficking South-East Asian women into UK brothels, are now being undercut by gangs from the Balkans, who have a plentiful supply of cheap sexual labour to exploit, with women from a dozen nearby Eastern European countries to target. It is a perfect application of modern globalisation. Other intelligence sources believe the triads, Albanians and other groups of traffickers have divided the market between themselves, with Albanians dominating the cheaper end of the sex industry.

The final point, about women being rapidly replaced, is crucial. If the police are either identifying trafficked women or the women are identifying themselves to the police but being removed and almost immediately replaced by others, then the underlying trafficking dynamic is not changing at all. In 2001 ECPAT published a report called 'What the Professionals Know' which included an analysis of the UK sex industry. The report claimed migrant women were being trafficked straight into Soho, and when they left the area were immediately replaced by new women. This strongly indicates the trafficking status quo in London has not changed in the last five years.

One of the reasons South Yorkshire police have made such breakthroughs in convicting traffickers is that in 2004 they managed to secure a £2.5 million grant from Reflex to dedicate time and resources to

---

8. NCIS UK Threat Assessment 2004/5, 2005/6, p.34.

policing trafficking locally. Working alongside colleagues from West Yorkshire and Humberside, they have made a substantial impact on trafficking in their region. They also lobbied for government and private funds to set up a local refuge for trafficked women and have spent the last two years developing what they describe as 'a victim-centred human rights approach to policing trafficking'. Detective Sergeant Steve Titterton who works for Reflex in South Yorkshire says the force have spent time gathering effective low-level intelligence, such as scouring local classified ads. They make regular visits to brothels, saunas and flats, and have slowly seen a reduction in the number of migrant sex workers in the area. But he acknowledges not all migrant sex workers are trafficked women, and that the reduction itself could be the result of women who are at risk being dispersed to areas less rigorously policed. 'We have no way of knowing for sure, but this is how criminals operate per se: so it's an educated guess that trafficked women may simply have been moved elsewhere.'

NCIS is one of the Reflex partners that will soon become part of the government's latest initiative to fight organised crime. In April 2006 it moved to the new Serious Organised Crime Agency.

SOCA will employ at least five thousand investigators, plus support staff, in order to target 'the top tier of criminality' in the UK. It has already been allocated a £340 million annual budget from central government, with additional start-up costs of £28 million.[9]

Though the agency will apparently dedicate 'significant' time and resources to investigating organised immigration crime, including human trafficking, SOCA will not have either a specialist human-trafficking unit, or any dedicated human-trafficking investigators. The NCIS Threat Assessment spells out that the vast majority of organised immigration crimes committed in the UK are smuggling offences. Although there are international trafficking networks, many traffickers, especially from the Balkans, are known to operate in small groups and to traffic relatively small numbers of women, like the traffickers convicted in Sheffield. These small groups, that sometimes trade women amongst themselves and usually have a connection to London, do not represent the top tier of criminality in the UK. Therefore they will not be a priority for SOCA.

Britain does not have a specialist human-trafficking unit. The Metropolitan Police quietly announced recently that they intend to set up a small human-trafficking unit in London. No dates or other details have

9. Serious Organised Crime and Police Bill Final Regulatory Impact Assessment, November 2004.

been confirmed, but this will apparently be a team of around eight people and confined to London.

Human trafficking is a tripartite crime, involving organised immigration crimes, economic and violent crimes. The policing of trafficking has so far been dominated by a government emphasis on prosecuting traffickers and particularly on the immigration status of the trafficked migrants. Nationwide provision and protection for these same women has not been a priority.

In direct contrast with the funds being allocated to policing nationwide organised immigration crime, the Poppy Project are now 'hoping' to raise the money to open a house in London where another five women can take refuge, which would take the project capacity up to thirty.

We ask a great deal of women and girls who are trafficked into Britain. We ask them to trust the police despite the experiences they may have had with police officers before they arrived here; we ask them to identify themselves immediately as having been trafficked, or else they may be removed at once from the UK. Trafficked women are migrants, and as such are subject to the rigours of our immigration laws and restrictions. We ask them to testify in court and describe their experiences of physical and sexual violence in explicit detail. For some women, testifying in court is an immense risk in terms of their ability to ever be able to return home.

But we do not give these women any explicit legal rights to stay here even for a short period of time unless they are from our part of the world, and we do not provide for them adequately.

Chapter 17

Mr He, Lan and Keung

'When I came to the UK, I knew I would have to work very hard to pay them back for bringing me into this country. But I did not mind, because I had to leave China, and this was the only way out for me.

'Five of us left together. It was 1996. We travelled from Fujian province to Yunnan province in the south-west of China, and from there we crossed the border to Thailand and flew to Malaysia. The snakeheads had already given us passports, and they escorted us to the airport at Kuala Lumpur and came to the passport control with us. Then they took our passports away. They left us at the airport, and we flew to the UK. We landed in Heathrow Airport, terminal three, and then I made my application for political asylum.'

Mr He used to work in Fujian as a primary-school sports teacher. He had wanted to leave China for a long time because 'The poverty is one thing, but the political repression is worse.' While working in the primary school, he made the mistake of openly criticising several local government officials to his teaching colleagues, and says this small act of defiance was the reason he had to leave quickly.

'I was worried that I would be sent to prison. It was impossible for me to leave my country legally, but I knew the snakeheads could organise to smuggle me to the UK. They did not advertise publicly, but everyone in Fujian knows they can bring you here for a price.'

The price was Chinese RMB 190,000, the equivalent of about £12,000. Mr He didn't have any money to pay the snakeheads in advance, and they said that was fine as long as he adhered to the arrangement they made with him before he left Fujian.

As soon as he had applied for political asylum in Britain, Mr He started working to pay back his debt. The snakeheads had given him a bank account number, with instructions to pay £100 a week in to the account. It took him almost five years to pay the whole thing off. Mr He could speak only very basic English, so he had to take whatever work he could find. The snakeheads charged a hefty interest on his debt, and the money had to be paid on time each week.

'In London, I worked in a kitchen for twelve hours a day for a whole year. Afterwards I worked in other cities, like Windsor and Liverpool and then Leeds. I had to keep working, and if someone offered me a job in another city, then I took it. In some places the wages were OK, but sometimes they were very low, but I had to accept whatever they gave me.'

The rate of Chinese migrants having their claims for UK asylum rejected in 2000 was estimated to be as high as 95 per cent by some commentators. But the snakeheads still had plenty of business smuggling people across Asia. People who needed to get out of China for political reasons usually had to go to the snakeheads, who have 'facilitated' the smuggling of Chinese migrants, especially from Fujian, for decades. The name 'snakehead' (or *Ren She*) refers to the head of the snake leading the body (of migrants) on their route. It is a generic name for the networks that started business smuggling mainland Chinese south to Hong Kong and now have well-established routes and connections across Asia and into Europe. Mr He had no choice but to go to the snakeheads: he was afraid of being imprisoned, could not get permission to leave his country legally and couldn't apply for political asylum in Britain unless he managed to get here himself.

For other people living in Fujian, stories of how much money could be made in Britain were already legion, and families talked with pride about relatives who were living in the UK and regularly sending cash back home. These migrants had all invariably come to Britain on the snakehead route.

The reality, however, was often harshly different. Chinese migrants who did make it here were desperate to make money immediately, and therefore often willing to be overworked and underpaid.

Mr He joined the ranks of hundreds of thousands of migrants – legal and undocumented – who work across Britain in agriculture, construction, food processing, restaurants and takeaways, and as cocklers on stretches of unpredictable coastline, like Morecambe Bay, at dawn.

On 18 June 2000 Mr He was working back in London when the news broke that fifty-eight Chinese migrants had been found suffocated to death in the back of a tomato lorry in Dover. They were all reported to be from Fujian.[1] He immediately called his family in Fujian to reassure himself that none of his brothers was involved. Before China instigated

---

1. Fifty-four men and four women died in the tomato lorry at Dover. Two other men survived.

its 'one child' policy in 1979, larger families had been the norm, especially in rural communities, and Mr He had five brothers back at home. When he spoke to his mother, she was extremely anxious. She told Mr He that his second oldest brother, Ming, was somewhere en route to the UK, but she didn't know where he was or whether he was safe.

'I tried to call the police in Dover, but it was impossible to get through, so I took the train to Dover with my friend. We went to the police station there, and they had photographs of the dead people in the station. The photo of Ming was there on the wall amongst them, and then I knew he was dead.'

The narrow street outside continues its noisy, congested-traffic-filled day. We sit in complete silence for several moments, absorbing what has just been said. It is Mr He who breaks the silence.

'I didn't know he was coming to Britain. I didn't know anything about it until my mother told me.'

It took three months for the fifty-eight bodies to be formally identified. The Chinese government initially denied the dead men and women were even Chinese citizens, and many Chinese living in the UK were reluctant to come forward, as they were worried about being identified by the authorities themselves. The police eventually resorted to a televised appeal for Chinese people to assist them in their enquiries, assuring them they wouldn't be questioned about their own immigration status. It was another four months before the bodies of the 'Dover 58', as they have collectively come to be remembered, were transported home to Fujian for burial. The Dutch driver of the lorry, Perry Wacker, is serving fourteen years for manslaughter. He apparently closed the air vents so the Chinese wouldn't be heard talking.

Mr He and I are sitting in the lobby of a London hotel, opposite the Central London Law Centre, which still represents Mr He because his attempts to obtain asylum and then afterwards leave to remain in the UK have dragged on for almost ten years now.

The centre is always busy, and today it's so crowded we've decamped across the road to the far corner of this lobby. There are two other people sitting with us: a Chinese community activist called Jabez Lam, who arranged this meeting, and a woman called Iris, who is translating between me and Mr He.

Jabez Lam is from Hong Kong and has lived in London for almost thirty years. He's one of the founders of Min Quan, a political and human rights organisation that advocates on behalf of the ethnic Chinese community in the UK.[2] Jabez travels the length of Britain

2. Min Quan translates as 'Civil Rights'.

troubleshooting for people who have lived here for generations, students, recently arrived migrants and anyone else who asks for help. He is a wiry, energetic political animal, and a walking archive of the British Chinese community.

I contacted Jabez Lam, via Min Quan, because I wanted to look outside the sex trade, at the experiences migrants have working in other UK industries. The term 'human trafficking' has become completely synonymous with sexual exploitation. But, especially since the tragedies of Dover and Morecambe Bay, there's acknowledgement of widespread exploitation in other industries, particularly where migrants have no documents because their entry into the UK has also been facilitated. Jabez Lam offered to meet me to talk about Chinese migrants who arrange to have themselves smuggled to the UK, and he also offered to introduce me to Mr He.

Jabez sits impassively while Mr He tells his story. Afterwards, Mr He sits, hands folded in his lap, as Jabez talks.

'We Chinese have been living here in this country since the beginning of the nineteenth century. The first big wave of immigrants was during the 1950s and 1960s, when people moved south from the mainland to Hong Kong and then began to emigrate over here because of the ties between our two countries. Now we are well established! How many of us are there? Well . . . that depends on whether you use the British government's figure or our estimate. The 2002 UK Census stated there were 250,000 ethnic Chinese in Britain, and a quarter of them had been born here. I would say it is between 400,000 and 450,000 people, including students.'

'What about the number of undocumented migrants?'

'I would say 70,000.'

'Are they mostly men?'

'Yes, with families to support back at home. The majority come from Fujian province. That is where the Dover 58 and most of the Morecambe Bay cockle pickers came from.'

The nineteen Chinese cockle pickers who died on 6 February 2004 drowned because they didn't know about the treacherous local tides and no one had told them. The bodies of two other Chinese cocklers have never been recovered, and both are presumed dead.

Jabez Lam describes the Morecambe Bay tragedy as a repeat of what happened in Dover four years earlier.

'The British government and industry have created this situation between them. Their obsession with deregulated labour and profit margins has led to this underclass of exploited undocumented migrants. These migrants have no value in this country apart from being cheap labour, and they're regarded as disposable and replaceable. The More-cambe Bay cockle pickers were replaced immediately, because there are plenty of other Chinese still desperate enough to go out on to those sands.

'Chinese migrants are still being smuggled into this country by snake-heads because people still want to leave provinces like Fujian; many of the villages are incredibly poor, people are exploited by the Chinese govern-ment, and they just want the opportunity to work and improve their lives. And when they eventually arrive here, the government exploits them too, even though they need us. This country relies on migrants to do the rotten jobs: the cleaning, the work in the fields and factories, and producing cheap food. The gangmasters are ruthless, and many of them are migrants themselves. But gangmasters are also used as a justification for the government to crack down on undocumented migrants rather than the conditions migrants have to endure.'

One of the government responses to the Dover and Morecambe Bay tragedies was an immediate public vow to crack down on 'illegal gangs of people traffickers'. Jabez believes this response feeds the networks that already control migrant-smuggling routes from East Asia.

'For most Chinese migrants, the snakeheads are the only passport they have.'

The UN Protocol Against the Smuggling of Migrants defines smuggling as 'the procurement, in order to obtain, directly, or indirectly, a financial or other material benefit, of the illegal entry of a person into a State Party of which the person is not a national or a permanent resident'.

In principle, the difference between smuggling and trafficking is the relationship between the migrant and their facilitator. A smuggler inserts a migrant into a third country for an agreed price, then leaves them to their own devices; a trafficker uses deception, threats or physical violence to move a person from one destination to another and then coerces them into work in order to extract profit from them.

But many migrants, like Mr He, arrive with a debt around their neck or desperate to work in order to send money back home, both of which render them especially vulnerable to being abused by employers who deliberately seek out cheap, compliant labour.

In February 2005 two migration researchers, Bridget Anderson and Ben Rogaly, published 'Forced Labour and Migration to the UK'. This investigative report was jointly commissioned by the Trades Union Congress and the International Labour Organisation (ILO), a United

Nations agency that specialises in promoting social justice and international human and labour rights.

The report highlighted widespread exploitation of both legal and illegal migrants working across the UK and investigated how flexibility and deregulation of the British labour market have directly impacted on pay and conditions. It received widespread media attention, especially because the government did its best to have publication delayed until after the general election on 5 May 2005.

The report was originally scheduled to be published in September 2004, but the government threatened to cut its funding to the ILO unless publication was postponed for another eight months. After 'some very sensitive discussions' between the government and the ILO, certain unspecified revisions were made to the report's contents, and it finally saw the light of day in February 2005.[3]

Bridget Anderson's only comment about the delay was 'The publicity around it meant that what actually attracted attention was the government's alleged concern, rather than what matters, which is the structural reason behind the many examples of abuse and exploitation of migrant workers.'

As the *Guardian*'s consumer affairs editor, Felicity Lawrence, recently commented, 'The UK has Europe's most flexible labour force; it lives in squalor, is paid a pittance and is bussed around the country to work in the shadows of the night shift.'

Bridget Anderson and Ben Rogaly examined levels of coercion in the recruitment and employment of migrant workers, and assessed how focusing on forced-labour conditions (as opposed to immigration status) could lead to better protection of migrants and better law enforcement against abusive employers. They identified abuses by state and private employers in four key industries: construction, contract cleaning, agriculture and residential-care work. These included migrants being forced to work through physical, psychological and sexual violence, wages being withheld or being far less than the legal minimum, employees being prevented from obtaining help or assistance and even being threatened at gunpoint. As the report says:

> The practices used by a minority of [UK] employers fall under the internationally agreed definitions of forced labour [. . .] Far from being restricted to the extreme fringes of the economy, forced labour can be found at the base of key industries, and goes far beyond the agricultural and sex work with which it is normally associated.

3. Hsiao-Hung Pai, *Guardian*, 3 February 2005.

They describe instances of Chinese factory workers working sixteen-hour shifts for three weeks and being immediately deported afterwards without pay, a group of African care workers being forced to work long night shifts on threat of deportation, Eastern European factory workers being told upon arrival in the UK that they had to work seven days a week for a year without pay to reimburse their travelling and living 'expenses', and it goes on. Much of the report makes for grim reading. Just one week after the Morecambe Bay tragedy, forty migrant workers were once again stranded on the bay's sands, caught by the tides. They were lucky.

The May 2004 expansion of the EU, which offered people from ten new countries the right to live and work in the UK, also provided an informal amnesty for thousands who were already working here without documents. But Anderson and Rogaly point out that being legally registered to work offers in itself no guaranteed protection from abusive employers. Some employers deliberately use chains of subcontractors to do their recruiting, making liability difficult to prove. UK-registered companies and recruitment agencies have also charged substantial, sometimes extortionate fees to migrants to arrange UK work contracts, which is illegal. One UK company charged a group of Chinese nurses £9,000 each to work at a British hospital; they ended up working in Tyneside as low-paid cleaners and dishwashers.

Migrants employed on work permits are tied to their employer because the permit is obtained by the employer not the worker. If the employer decides they don't need or want the migrant, that person immediately loses his or her job and right to remain in the UK. Nurses, for instance, usually enter the UK on work permits.

Other industries where migrants are most in demand are those where work is usually badly paid, often seasonal and sometimes downright dangerous. Construction is Britain's biggest industry, and also one of the most dangerous to work in. Between March 2004 and 2005, seventy-one construction workers were killed at work, and another 4,000 seriously injured. The industry employs increasing numbers of migrants who, according to this report, say they are regularly either underpaid or not paid at all for their labour.

Anderson and Rogaly acknowledge that some progress has been made. The crime of 'trafficking people for exploitation' was included in the Asylum and Immigration (Treatment of Claimants, etc.) Act 2004. Like trafficking for sexual exploitation, this also carries a maximum fourteen-year sentence and applies to people who are trafficked into the UK for other forms of forced labour. However, Anderson and Rogaly also question the application of the term 'trafficking', arguing that:

It is significant that the above provision is to be found in an asylum and immigration bill, suggesting that the primary concern is with the movement and its facilitation as constituting the kernel of the [trafficking] crime, rather than the forced-labour aspects or abusive employment relations [. . .] Moreover, one does not have to be 'illegal' or be working without state permission to be 'trafficked' [. . .] migrants who are working with permits may [also] be subject to forced labour and illegal deductions.

They argue that the government has reacted to abuses of migrant workers by tightening legislation and cracking down on illegal immigration rather than questioning whether the immigration status of certain migrants leaves them more vulnerable to being exploited by employers in the first place. 'Perversely, this means that immigration controls can be presented as a solution to human rights abuses.' Or, to put it another way, immigration controls can be used to remove the symptoms rather than addressing the cause.

The London-based Immigration Law Practitioners Association (ILPA), a group of leading UK immigration practitioners, claims that the crimes of smuggling and trafficking both raise complex questions about perpetrators and 'victims'. 'Where the victim is the state, as in the case of smuggling, its protection is by way of criminal prosecutions. The smuggled person will always be complicit with the smuggler and depending on the member state may be criminally liable either as an accomplice or separately for incitement of the crime (whether or not the crime took place).'

But with regard to people who enter the UK in order to seek asylum, ILPA point out that, 'refugees may be forced to seek the services of smugglers in order to get out of their country of origin and into another country . . . Sometimes it is those persons with the greatest incentive to use smugglers and traffickers who are most at risk of persecution and torture in their country of origin. As visas and border controls are increasingly directed at preventing exactly this group from arriving in EU states, so their recourse to smugglers and traffickers to cross the border may increase.'

Organisations set up by migrant activists in the UK have been fighting their corner for specific rights for years. Kalayaan, which takes its name from the Filipino word for freedom, was set up by a small group of women almost twenty years ago to support migrant domestic workers (MDWs) of all nationalities living in the UK. Kalayaan spent ten years campaigning for MDWs to be able to leave an abusive employer without facing deportation. In 1998 the UK law was finally amended, giving MDWs the right to change employer and still remain working in the

UK. Every year Kalayaan register around four hundred and fifty new, mostly Asian clients and provide services to around three thousand MDWs. Ten per cent of the workers are male.

More than three-quarters of Kalayaan's newly registered MDWs report they have suffered psychological abuse from their employers, and 40 per cent have also endured physical abuse. Half the workers have had their passports illegally retained by their employer. And almost seventy per cent of them work fifteen hours a day, seven days a week, for less than £200 a month. This means that they earn just under 47p per hour.

These employers are both foreign nationals living in the UK and British families. The migrant domestic workers are all living and working legally in the UK.

I email Jabez Lam to thank him for arranging the interview with Mr He. He replies a couple of weeks later and asks if I would like to meet another Chinese migrant, a woman called Lan.

> I think you will find her story very interesting: she came here to pay off her husband's debt to the snakeheads. He was very sick after his journey and couldn't work, so she was forced to come here and work instead of him.
>
> If you like, we can meet you at the Law Centre on Friday.

A dozen Chinese sit around the perimeter of the small reception area in the Law Centre; all silently waiting their turn to be seen.

Jabez is already there when I arrive, and waves his greeting. He has dark circles beneath his eyes, and his skin looks so pallid it's almost grey this morning. He introduces me to Lan, who smiles and shakes my outstretched hand but says nothing. Iris is also here, and says she'll do the translation, as soon as she can find an office that's free.

We crowd into a small upstairs room and sort out our seats. Lan has not said a word to me or anyone else. She has thick black hair cut short, pale skin and large, very white teeth that protrude slightly against her upper lip. I forget to ask her how old she is, but I guess she's in her mid-thirties, which would make her the same age as her husband, Keung. They live in Hackney, North London, now, but like Mr He, they both come from Fujian.

As Lan originally came to London because of her husband, and because he's not here himself, I ask her about Keung's journey to the UK.

She is reticent at first, shrugging her shoulders and staring down at the carpet as she clutches her handbag against her stomach. I recognise this body language by now: it's the stance of someone deciding whether she is in fact willing to confide in a stranger who will write down every detail and publish this extract of her life.

Iris persists with the translated question, and Lan begins to make eye contact with her, and slowly she starts to gesture and talk.

'We lived in Fujian. There was no work for my husband in the village, and the cities were overcrowded with peasants who had migrated from the countryside. Keung had already talked about wanting to leave so he could earn money. Then we had our child and we had to make something for her. The snakeheads were telling Fujianese people how wonderful it was to live in Britain, with its democracy and human rights. They said you could pay them for the journey after you arrived in the UK by working for a while, and then you would be free to enjoy life in the UK. They could arrange everything.'

The price was the same as Mr He paid: £12,000. And just like him, Keung couldn't afford to pay anything up front, so he knew he would have to work as soon as he got to the UK. He and Lan agreed he should go. Keung would send money home and return a couple of years later with enough for them to set up a small private business.

Like most people who put their life in a smuggler's hands, Keung had never been abroad before. In June 1998 he boarded a flight from Beijing to a city in former Yugoslavia. Lan doesn't know which city it was. Her husband has only ever told her sketchy details of the journey. She knows he was smuggled alongside nineteen others; there were fifteen men, including him, and five women. After the flight they were divided into small groups of four or five, so they could travel more discreetly. They met up as a large group occasionally and were immediately re-divided into other small groups with different people. The snakeheads never told them which country they were in, even when they had to cross a range of mountains on foot for two or three weeks in order to avoid an official border.

In one place – he thought it was Italy but couldn't be sure – Keung's group was instructed to clamber into a wardrobe on the back of a horse-drawn cart. They were then dragged along for hours, in hot, claustrophobic darkness. When they arrived at their destination for that night, they found the rest of their large group crammed into a room.

All evening more Chinese people kept arriving, until he counted fifty of them altogether in the one room. They were given a large basket of bread to share between them for supper, and people fought each other for the dry bread.

Keung eventually crossed over to Britain in the back of a lorry, stowed away with four others. He didn't know he was in the UK until the driver banged on the side of the lorry and told them to get out and scarper. The snakeheads, who had taken their passports and any other documents that could identify them, had long gone. Keung and the others clambered down on to a deserted street three months after they had left Fujian province.

'That is all he told me about his journey,' says Lan. 'I don't know what else might have happened, but he did not find it easy to be in London.'

Keung immediately claimed political asylum and began to look for work to start repaying his debt. But the stress of being slowly shunted like cargo across Asia and Europe had disturbed him. Within a couple of months of his arrival in the UK he began to display symptoms of mental health problems.

He became withdrawn, agitated and uncooperative. He struggled to find regular work and resorted to street trading, hawking CDs around the Charing Cross Road area of Central London. But he was sacked for not always turning up for work, and not selling enough stock even when he did. After that, finding any kind of regular work was a strain for Keung, and in the meantime the snakeheads were expecting to be paid £100 a week. Keung had also been instructed to pay the money into a bank account. When he failed to pay, the snakeheads tracked him down to his room in Hackney.

'They threatened him,' says Lan. 'They said they would beat him badly if he didn't pay. But they could also see that he was not well. It was the stress of the journey and also having to find the money every week. They made him work as a machinist in a factory in Hackney, stitching clothes. But he couldn't cope. That was how he ended up in hospital.'

At the end of 1999 Keung tried to kill himself. A Chinese friend of his called an ambulance and Keung was admitted to Homerton Hospital, where he was diagnosed with schizophrenia. He had no previous history of mental health problems, and Lan knew nothing of her husband's situation until the snakeheads visited her at home.

'Five of them came to my house. They all came inside and said to me, "Your husband has become sick in the head and can't pay back his debt. So you have to pay for him now, or we are going to take your daughter." '

'What did you say?'

'I said we need to negotiate. We can find some way to resolve this.'

'And what happened?'

Lan shrugs. 'They said, "There is no negotiation. We are taking your daughter because your husband can't pay his debt." So I was thinking very quickly, and I told them, "I have worked as a machinist here, and I'm a good, quick machinist. I can go to the UK and work to pay his debt." '

The snakeheads agreed that Lan could go to the UK and pay off her husband's debt, in order to keep their daughter. But they reminded her that the only way she could get there was by being smuggled by them, and that was going to cost her another £12,000.

Like her husband, Lan also flew from Beijing to the former Yugoslavia and then trekked through the mountains. From what she says, it sounds as though she took a similar route to Keung, though it was certainly a lot quicker. She was in the UK six weeks later.

I ask her if she can describe the journey a little, and she nods.

'Sometimes there were just a few of us, sometimes a large group. Sometimes when we were in a lorry they blindfolded us. I don't know what they were trying to stop us looking at, but then I was scared. We also walked across mountains like Keung did. Long walks, to avoid the guards on the other side.'

There is not a shred of self-pity in her voice.

'Once we took a long train journey. It was a freight train, and a lot of us, maybe sixty people, had to crawl inside, in the space between the freight and the walls of the train. I had to lie very still, and there was no room even to turn over. Several people fainted from the heat and lack of air and had to be revived by the snakeheads. But the worst thing of all is that they give you no information about where you are, or even when you will arrive. They don't tell you anything. You just have to follow them and do whatever they say. There were several pretty girls in the group with us. I have heard what happens to them, and I was worried for them.'

Jabez suddenly interrupts. 'Young women are often taken to one side and raped on the way,' he says grimly. 'I know of several cases of women who wanted to be smuggled to the UK. They knew there was a big risk that they would be raped, so they arranged to be sterilised before they left. That way, when they were raped, they would not become pregnant.'

In March 2005, three Chinese teenagers who had been in the UK for just a few days went missing. Lin Xiu King and He Yun Jin were both sixteen years old, their friend Weng Miu Fang was just fifteen. The three girls had arrived at Newcastle Airport together, on a flight from Paris. They were apparently travelling on fake Japanese passports. They were detained by immigration officials upon arrival, and all said they wanted to claim asylum. They were placed in the care of social services and given temporary accommodation at a local project for young homeless people, Elswick Lodge. Three days later, on 30 March, they vanished together.

Despite extensive media coverage, and appeals to the public for any sightings to be reported to the police, they have never been found. There is no trace of them, or what has happened to them, although there are suspicions they may well have been trafficked into the sex industry. As they arrived in the UK on false passports, the police have not been able to contact their families in China.

Almost everywhere I visited in the Balkans I heard rumours about Chinese migrants being smuggled overland and Chinese women being trafficked into sex work. I heard the same in Italy: rumours about women being confined in apartments that used to be visited only by Chinese punters, but the pimps were expanding their business and now touting for business elsewhere. And I've heard these same rumours in London. I asked Jabez about it; he wasn't evasive, just said he really doesn't know. These networks that traffic Chinese women, either alongside smuggled migrants or on their own, are particularly impenetrable. Even the small China Unit team of police based at Charing Cross Station say they cannot confirm whether Chinese women are trafficked into London, and they have been policing the Chinatown community for nearly twenty years.

PC Peter Clark has worked at the Chinatown unit since 1990 and is considered an authority on both the snakeheads and the triads. He believes the snakeheads exist 'in order to make money by smuggling people out of China and into other countries'.

Whilst the triads have founded many legitimate businesses in the catering industry, they also operate lucrative loanshark businesses, continue to smuggle South-East Asians into Britain, especially Malaysians – and to traffick women from Thailand, which they have done for decades now.

Paul Holmes believes the main reason police didn't become aware of women being trafficked into London earlier was simply because trafficking was not recognised as a phenomenon, not because it wasn't happening. Throughout the 1970s and 1980s the sex industry was much smaller, and the South-East Asian community less integrated and fairly impenetrable.

In the UK, the triads are now more financially powerful than the snakeheads, but the snakeheads are also less predictable, and operate as criminal wild cards. There are power struggles between the two networks, with, for instance, the triads deliberately recruiting Fujianese migrants in order to swell the number of 'soldiers' at their disposal. Meanwhile, the snakeheads have diversified into other forms of organised crime, especially counterfeit DVDs, which Peter Clark describes as a 'multi-billion dollar industry'.

Fujianese migrants often join or form gangs for protection and status once they have inserted themselves into London. Many undocumented Chinese arrive by aeroplane now, though people still apparently take the risk of stowing away in trucks: others, like Lan, arrive overland by train.

I remember my conversation with Ruth Rosenberg at the Tirana IOM office and her information about the small number of Chinese migrants being detected on the borders between Greece and Macedonia, which implies they might have travelled from Skopje. I ask Lan if she recognises the name Skopje, but she shakes her head and shrugs, because it obviously doesn't matter to her any more which place it was.

'And at the end, I arrived in the UK on the Eurostar. And I was arrested.' Lan suddenly grins and gives a thumbs-up.

I've lost the sequence of events somewhere and look to Iris to explain.

'What does she mean? Why was she so happy to be arrested? How did she get on to Eurostar?'

Lan begins to talk rapidly. She breaks into smiles and then several peals of laughter. I wish I could understand what she's saying. Iris listens to her intently, frowning.

'They travelled through northern Europe, and then Lan boarded a Eurostar train with a small group. The snakeheads took their passports away once they were on the train and told them to claim asylum as soon as they arrived in the UK.'

Without any documents identifying them, Lan and her group, just like Keung and his, were far less likely to be 'removed' and sent back to China. The UK Immigration Service are obliged to positively identify each person, including where they are from in China, before he or she can be removed, and it's in the migrant's interests not to give this information. The Chinese government is not always very cooperative, to say the least, which leaves migrants effectively stateless – in legal and immigration limbo.

Lan told the immigration officer at Waterloo International that she was claiming asylum. She says she was questioned briefly and then released, with instructions to find a solicitor and to attend a screening interview.

I don't honestly understand how this happened – how it was so easy for her to enter Britain without a passport. But I take her word for what occurred at Waterloo International because I believe her whole story. She adds that the snakeheads had instructed her group to meet someone at a designated point. They were met as arranged, escorted to a solicitor's office, where they filled out paperwork and forms, and then told they were all free to go. Everything had gone according to plan. Afterwards, the snakeheads even offered her a lift to Homerton Hospital.

'I was very happy to see my husband,' she says, smiling broadly.

I notice she's sitting upright now and has let go of her handbag, which sits loosely in her lap. She is relaxed and enjoying this moment of her own story. I ask her how Keung was feeling when she arrived, and she makes a fluttering gesture with her small hands.

'They put him on medication and he was more stable. When he saw me, he knew everything would be OK. I could work and pay the debt to the snakeheads and then there would be no trouble.'

'Were you daunted by having to pay back so much money?' She owed the snakeheads £24,000 for the two debts.

She purses her lips together for a second. 'It was a lot of money, and I knew I would have to work very hard. But I knew before I even left China that I would have to pay them all this money back. I signed a contract to say I would do this.'

Her tone is completely matter of fact.

'Did they make any threats about what would happen if you didn't pay them on time?'

I know this is a loaded question, but can't think of another way to put it. I want to know if the snakeheads use the same brutal methods as traffickers in the Balkans.

She shakes her head. 'No. They did not say anything. But they always know where you are, and it was clear what would happen. It would be my daughter. They would take her. So they knew I would pay money into the account.'

'What sort of account was it?' I am pressing her for details because I am trying to pin down a few of the snakeheads' work tools.

I expect her to say the name of a Chinese or at least Asian bank, but she refers slowly in heavily accented English to a UK building society.

Lan had been given an account number and instructed to pay the money in to the building society every week. She immediately looked for work amongst the London Chinese community and at the same time moved into a room that had just been allocated to her husband by social services. While Keung concentrated on maintaining his mental health, Lan took on three separate jobs in order to pay off their debt. She describes her daily routine.

'I got up at five o'clock in the morning and started my first job at six. I was cleaning toilets in a bar and a Chinese restaurant. Then I went to my job in a factory in Hackney, where I worked as a clothes machinist. After that work finished at six o'clock, I worked as a dishwasher in another Chinese restaurant in the east of London. I finished work at about half past ten and went home to see my husband and to sleep.'

Lan was working illegally and knew she was being paid less than the other machinists at the factory, but she was in no position to negotiate.

She estimates that she worked about eighty-five hours a week. She earned £270 a week, of which £200 went straight into the account. She sent half of the rest of the money home to her daughter and family.

I am trying to work out the repayment figures in my head, but give up and instead ask her how long she had to do this in order to pay the snakeheads back in full.

'Four and a half years,' she says.

'Bloody hell!'

Jabez laughs throatily. 'The problem is not just the debt,' he explains. 'It is also the interest. The snakeheads charge a very high interest rate on the debt.'

He confers briefly with Lan, and they agree the interest rate is about twenty per cent a year.

I ask Jabez if he has a calculator. Using his mobile phone, we work out between us that Lan paid almost ten thousand pounds a year into the building society account. In four and a half years she paid the snakeheads £43,200. She tells me with no apparent irony that she was exempt from payments during the official Chinese holidays, like New Year, when the snakeheads gave her the week off.

I ponder the thin blue line between choice and coercion, smuggling and trafficking, for a moment, then ask Lan how she would describe what has happened to her. She looks at me quizzically, not understanding the question.

'I mean,' I say awkwardly, 'were you forced to come here, or do you think you had any choice?' It's a clumsy way of asking her to define her experience.

'I chose to come,' she says, 'but I also had to come, or else I would have lost both my daughter and my husband.'

Lan made her final debt payment just over a year ago. Keung has now been granted asylum. Ironically, his mental health problems speeded up his application, and, as his spouse, Lan has been granted indefinite leave to remain and now lives in the UK legally. Their daughter, who is now seven, has also been allowed to join them in London.

But, best of all, Lan tells me, beaming, 'I have been able to have another baby!'

Lan and Keung live with their daughter and new son in Hackney. Lan grows vegetables in the back garden.

'Life is very good, except for the British food,' she quips, visibly relaxed and comfortable now that we have moved on to the better part of her life.

I ask her how Keung is doing these days. Her expression tightens at the question, and her voice when she replies has suddenly lost its buoyancy.

'He is still fragile,' she says. 'As long as he takes his medication, he is

OK. But if he forgets, which he does sometimes, then he can be difficult. He has beaten me.'

Keung paid a heavy price for being smuggled to the UK, and Lan has had to pay it too. All I can say is how sorry I am, and she acknowledges the comment with a slight nod.

'I have one last question,' I proffer, hoping I haven't worn her out. 'What do you think of the snakeheads?'

'They are very good businessmen,' she says, almost without hesitation. 'They do what they say they will do. They brought me here, just as they said they would, and they are very reliable.'

'What about the threats, and the interest on the debts they charge people?'

'They are businessmen. If people want to come here and they ask the snakeheads to help them, they have to pay them for this service. I would have felt bad if I could not pay the money back every week. They brought us over here, and I am very thankful to them.'

Mr He does not feel so grateful to the snakeheads. After his brother died in Dover, he was interviewed on BBC TV and also talked to Chinese journalists.

He criticised the Chinese government for being repressive and forcing people to go to the snakeheads. He also claimed there were links between the government and the snakeheads. He knew he was jeopardising his own chances of ever being able to go home, but felt he had to speak out. When his comments were published, the Chinese police informed his family in Fujian that if he ever did go back, he would immediately be arrested.

In spite of this, Mr He was refused asylum in Britain and also lost his appeal. In 2002, with the help of the Central London Law Centre, he applied for leave to remain under the Human Rights Act 1998. He is hoping to be granted five years' Humanitarian Protection, after which he would be eligible to apply for Indefinite Leave to Remain. The application is based on Mr He's belief that his right to life and security will be at risk if he is returned to China. Another Chinese man who lost his brother in Dover, Mr Li, has already won his case to stay in the UK. However, three and a half years later, Mr He is still waiting for the outcome of his application. If it fails, he is liable to be returned and imprisoned. In the meantime, he has no entitlement to state benefits and is no longer allowed to work or to study for more than a few hours a week. He lives outside London, in the spare room of a friend's house, and has to depend on others for almost everything.

When I met Mr He, there was something almost childlike about him;

he seemed bewildered about what was happening, as though he had no control over his own life. Because he hasn't been allowed to work for the last few years, his development has been stunted. He has spent the last ten years of his life waiting. All the money he earned while he was working went towards paying off his debt to the snakeheads.

Chapter 18

UNMIKISTAN

I am somewhere between Austria and Kosovo. We have just been told that we're cruising at an altitude of 39,000 feet. I wish they wouldn't announce these details or show that TV screen map of Europe, with the tiny red plane nudging towards its destination. Flying has always made me jittery.

I am en route to Pristina. I guess it was inevitable, really. The one thing I learned from that first trip in April 2003 was how little I knew about trafficking, and in that way it was, perversely, useful. I didn't find out much else, though.

In May 2004 Amnesty International published a report on trafficking in Kosovo. 'Does That Mean I Have Rights?' was a rigorous investigation into women and girls being trafficked across the territory. The Amnesty report claimed that within months of the UN and KFOR arriving in July 1999, women and girls from Kosovo and other Eastern European countries were being confined in bars and nightclubs frequented by soldiers and UN staff, and that 'Kosovo has become a major destination country for women and girls trafficked into forced prostitution.'

Citing numerous case studies of women and girls, some thought to be under twelve years old, who had been forced to sell sex to local and foreign men, Amnesty claimed that during the UN Mission in Kosovo's first year of administration, internationals comprised 80 per cent of the clients of trafficked women, and that UNMIK 'in failing to prosecute international personnel suspected of involvement in trafficking or of knowingly using the services of trafficked women, has created a climate of impunity for abuses and violations against trafficked women'.

Within twenty-four hours UNMIK fired off a press release in which it claimed the Amnesty report was 'Highly unbalanced [. . .] contains many generalisations but misses these essential points: criminal gangs are exploiting vulnerable people, law-enforcement authorities in Kosovo are addressing the problem, and making some progress and much greater regional cooperation is needed.' The mission also alleged that:

> The report draws heavily on conditions existing in 1999–2001, when the UN mission was at the incipient stage and when scarce resources were available to address serious crime. Outdated information from that period is extrapolated on and presented as current, giving the impression that problems which existed in 2001 remain at the same level in 2004. The true facts tell a different story.

UNMIK reiterated it had taken 'significant action against trafficking and prostitution in Kosovo over the last four years' and cited that TPIU (Trafficking and Prostitution Investigation Unit) had conducted more than two thousand raids in 2003 and had found only one international police officer and three international civilian staff in off-limits establishments.

It's worth mentioning again that UN and KFOR personnel are all subject to the 'exclusive criminal jurisdiction of their nation of origin', which means they are liable to be repatriated and investigated back at home, as opposed to the country where any alleged offence takes place.

I have the Amnesty report with me now. I've already read through it once, quickly, but there's almost an hour left before we land, so I have another look at it. As I turn over the contents page, it strikes me that this is the first difference between these two trips. I wouldn't have read a human rights report on the plane the first time I came to Pristina. I'd have felt too exposed. But now I know that no one's going to pay much attention: as the report itself illustrates, plenty of other people have researched trafficking in Kosovo.

Halfway down page fourteen, I take a sharp breath, staring at the black type in front of me. Then I turn and gaze at the unruly clouds drifting across the languid blue and white universe outside. 'Shelters working with trafficked women in Kosovo report that around forty per cent of women bore signs of physical abuse on entering the shelters; they were predominantly bruised, but some also had broken bones. One woman had been beaten so severely that she was immediately repatriated for surgery to save her eyesight.'

Olga, I think, staring out of the window. That was Olga.

We land on time, at 4 p.m. The wind is dry as we straggle towards the arrivals hall and form sprawling queues at the half-dozen passport control counters. I stand waiting my turn, hoping they will let me in.

In a perfect illustration of how I presume there are no travel restrictions to worry about wherever I go, I didn't even bother checking the FCO

(Foreign and Commonwealth Office) travel advice website until late last night. I found out at the eleventh hour that a new travel regulation was introduced in Kosovo six months ago. Visitors may now be asked to produce documents to clarify they have a 'valid reason' to enter the territory, and are granted a ninety-day entry visa. If you want to stay any longer than that, you have to apply for a work permit. These are the first visa regulations introduced by the UN since they started administering the territory in 1999. UNMIK is scheduled to hand over to an EU-monitored mission at the end of 2006, though Kosovo's permanent status has yet to be decided. In the meantime many local people refer to their homeland as UNMIKISTAN.

It is Monday afternoon, and I'm only staying until Friday, but I don't have any documents to suggest a valid reason for being here. I fret about this in the queue and, when it's my turn, smile passively at the immigration official, who appraises me coolly. He spends a minute leafing through my passport, stamps it and hands it back over the counter.

'Welcome to Kosovo,' he says.

Maggie works at the airport now. We have kept in touch, and I know she resigned from the police a couple of years ago and now has a job in the airport in the human resources department. She sent me an email explaining where the department is, and I finally locate her office, up on the second floor of a separate building. It's lovely to see her again.

I perch on Maggie's desk.

'Why aren't you staying with me?' she demands.

'I'm sorry. I'm only here for a few days, and I need to be in the city. I'll come and visit Obilic.'

'So, where are you staying, then?'

'At the Grand Hotel.'

Maggie laughs. 'That place has not changed since you were here! OK, come on, my friend is waiting for us outside in his car. He will take us to your grand hotel.'

As we drive into Pristina, I ask her how life is in Kosovo these days.

She shrugs. 'Not so much has changed. We have more buildings and cars, but I think everything is very similar. Although I was just in Italy for two weeks, visiting my brother, so at least that is different! It's easier for me to travel there.'

They drop me off at the Grand, and I arrange to meet Maggie later at the expat pub, which is just round the corner. She tells me it's not called the Kukri any more; these days it's the Phoenix.

The Grand Hotel is huge and ugly. My room on the third floor is spacious, but as overheated and anonymous as the rest of the building.

When I wake the next morning, groggy-eyed from the zealous central heating, the view from my window is the rooftop of one of the lower-floor wings. This roof is obviously accessible from the street because there are several stray dogs roaming around. It also has a large concrete bunker on one side, and someone has created a sublime act of graffiti art on the bunker wall facing my room: a man in his middle years, wearing a blue-and-white checked cap is smoking a roll-up and exhaling a luxurious cloud of smoke. He has a pencil moustache, strands of wispy hair brushing the nape of his narrow neck and the droll hint of a smile. The artist, MC*, has captioned his work in beautiful cursive English, *'Another dedication to the gray city . . .'*

I still have Brian Wilson's old business card, with the number for TPIU. When I call the unit, I'm put through to an UNMIK receptionist, who tells me the unit has been renamed the Trafficking in Human Beings Section, or THBS. She puts me through, and the phone is answered by a brisk-sounding Englishwoman, who introduces herself as Jill Norwood.

'Fine, no problem,' she says, when I ask if I can come and talk to her. 'How about two o'clock this afternoon?'

The THBS is not in the UN compound but up the hill, about fifteen minutes' walk from the Grand Hotel. I set off early and wander through Pristina a little on the way. The city looks exactly the same as before to me, which seems odd but also feels quite reassuring.

I hand my passport in at the station reception and clamber upstairs to meet Jill Norwood. She is a stout, blonde woman who shakes my hand energetically and immediately offers me a cup of tea. 'Tetley,' she says. 'Milk and sugar?'

When we have our mugs of tea, Jill tells me she is deputy of the department and has been in Kosovo for three years 'on and off'.

Like Brian Wilson before her, she also used to work for the Ministry of Defence and was hired partly because of her firearms expertise. She likes her work and likes Kosovo, 'even though the weather is Baltic all winter'.

I tell her I was here in April 2003 and ask her what she thinks of the trafficking situation now as compared to then.

Jill tilts her head slightly to one side, as though mentally weighing up the evidence for a moment. 'Some things have definitely improved. The border police are now better trained to look for signs of human trafficking, and they're actively on the lookout for foreign women who are either being escorted overland or turning up at one of the borders alone, apparently to work here. Since the introduction of the work-permit regulation any woman who arrives at the border saying she's come to work in Kosovo has to be in possession of a formal employment contract. First thing the police do is ask to see the contract, read through it and check whether the woman knows where she'll be working and exactly what she'll be doing. The contracts are usually vague, saying she'll be employed as a waitress or a barmaid in some bar. The police can't do anything else about the contract, but they can check she's got valid travel documents, that she knows she has to register with the police when she arrives. And, if she wants to stay here for longer than ninety days, she also has to register for a work permit at the UNMIK Office of Registration of Foreigners. As soon as she registers there, the Office of Registration takes a photocopy of her contract, and they pass a second copy on to us. When she gets a work permit, the woman is also issued with a local photo ID card, and we get a copy of that too. So we already know her identity and whereabouts when we do our bar checks.'

'Bar checks? Are these instead of the bar raids?'

Jill nods. 'Yes. We've changed our system because the traffickers have changed their *modus operandi*. When TPIU first opened, the officers had a hard approach because it was a hard, unpredictable situation. So they raided bars to get the women out. But we've found out what works now is making regular checks of bars, which the owners consent to; mind you, they probably know we're on our way before we do.'

This last comment sounds almost like an unintended aside, and I frown at her, puzzled.

'What do you mean, they probably know before you do?'

'Well . . . you know, they have their own ways of finding out.' Her facial expression hasn't changed, but Jill's language is suddenly vague, confirming or denying as little as possible. I think about it for a moment, decide she probably isn't going to tell me any more about bar owners knowing about their bars being checked in advance, and change tack.

I want her to tell me more about what the THBS police are doing, but if she feels backed into a corner I don't think she's going to tell me anything.

'Do you identify many women who may have been trafficked when you do these bar checks?' I ask her.

'The checks have not been particularly fruitful in identifying women. They're more of a disruptive measure, to make sure the bar and club owners know we're keeping an eye on them and what's going on in their establishments. But the whole trafficking trend has changed; the number of international women being trafficked into Kosovo is definitely dropping. Trouble is, we're seeing a lot more local women being, shall I say, "persuaded" by their boyfriends and husbands to work as prostitutes.'

At the same time as identifying fewer foreign women being trafficked into Kosovo, the police have become aware of more local women being involved in the sex industry. THBS are now regularly seeing cases of young women being introduced, persuaded and coerced into selling sex within their own communities.

'Because more local women are involved and a lot of them are married to the men who are pimping them, the problem is becoming less visible and much harder to identify and tackle,' says Jill.

She tells me that because of this changing trend THBS officers now rely more on intelligence-led investigations than bar checks per se. This year the section have identified a total of fifty-five trafficked women. Thirty-one of the women requested assistance from the police; the others declined help. More than half the women who did want assistance were Kosovan, and fewer foreign women now seem prepared to accept help from the authorities.

If women don't want their assistance, there is nothing the police can do once they have removed them from the premises. The THBS victim assistance coordinator is a Ukrainian woman called Mila. While we're talking, Mila walks into the office, her eyes bright with anger.

'Six Moldovans!' she exclaims. 'Just one hour ago they were sitting downstairs. He brings them in himself, their boss, so they can register with the police. All six of them are working in his bar! I just interviewed them all separately, and each one of them told me that everything is fine in Pristina, and she is just a barmaid. When I put them all together, then I started to get angry with them. "Don't you realise we are trying to help you?" I told them. "We are not prostitutes," they told me back. So I asked them why they said this – I am not accusing them of anything. They said because prostitution is a crime here and they are not committing any crime. So, what can I do?' She sits down heavily.

'Does this happen very often?' I ask her.

'Sometimes. I think they are worried because prostitution is against the law, but they forget we are actually trying to assist them. All I can do is tell them what options they have, where they can get help; nothing more.' She shrugs, wearily frustrated.

Prostitution is classified as a minor offence in Kosovo and carries a maximum two-month prison sentence or a fine of between a hundred and fifty and two hundred euros. But a woman convicted of prostitution can also be deported.

'It all sounds very complicated,' I say to Mila and Jill. 'What about the international men working here? How much are they involved in all this now?'

'Very little international involvement,' says Jill. 'We check the bars regularly and rarely find any internationals in them. Every new inter-national officer who arrives now gets a bumph-load of awareness-raising material to read, which includes information on trafficking, and they have to sit through a presentation about trafficking during their induction. They all know about the UNMIK off-limits list, so there's no excuse for them to be in any of these places anyway.'

'What happens if you do find someone off limits?'

'First thing we ask is what the hell they're doing in one of these places! Ignorance is no excuse, though we know genuine mistakes are made. But we always inform the UN, and if someone turns up in the same place two or three times, they're going to have to answer some serious questions.'

I ask Jill how many venues are still on the off-limits list, which has been circulated every month for almost five years now, and am surprised when she tells me there are still more than two hundred banned premises. The first off-limits list, issued in January 2001, had seventy-five, but for the last three years there have consistently been more than two hundred premises listed. The UN says this is a precautionary measure. (Amnesty noted in their report that by the end of 2002 at least eleven UNMIK police officers had apparently been repatriated in connection with trafficking offences.)

I ask Jill whether I can have a copy of the list, and she nods. 'Don't see why not.'

The list has just been updated. Two hundred and thirty names and locations slowly chug out of the office printer.

As I'm putting my coat back on, I remember one last question.

'Are you still carrying out "entry and extraction" raids?'

'We still do raids,' she says. 'When we have grounded suspicions of trafficking in a particular premise, we organise a raid, but we don't use entry and extraction tactics any more.'

UNMIK first started registering foreign women who were working in bars and nightclubs back in 2001, though the women didn't need work permits at that point. By the end of 2001 TPIU (as it was then called) had registered just over a thousand foreign women working in Kosovo: one thousand seven hundred were registered in 2002, though the number dropped back to a thousand in 2003 and has stabilised at around four hundred and fifty women since then. In January 2001 UNMIK also issued Regulation 2001/4, prohibiting trafficking of persons in Kosovo.[1]

1. UNMIK Regulation 2001/4 is based on the UN Trafficking Protocol. Quoted in 'Does This Mean I Have Rights?', Amnesty International, p.21.

It applies a maximum twenty-year sentence for organising human trafficking in the territory.

In October 2003 the UN Secretary-General, Kofi Annan, issued a bulletin of 'Special Measures For Protection from Sexual Exploitation and Abuse' which outlined codes of conduct for all UN staff. This was the first clearly articulated policy on sexual abuse and exploitation by the UN. It was also a clear acknowledgement that UN civilian and military personnel has been directly implicated in sexually abusing and exploiting women and girls.

Women who are identified as having been trafficked into Kosovo and do want help from the authorities are referred to the UN Victim Advocacy and Assistance Unit. The coordinator is Tihana Leko. Her office is stashed with papers; they stand in precarious towers on her desk and are spread across tables, chairs and every other available surface in the room. Even the floor is lined with boxes of files.

As I look around, Tihana follows my gaze and laughs casually. 'I know! This is what happens after five years working for the UN in Kosovo. What can I do?' I presumed she was local, but she tells me she's Croatian.

Tihana agrees with Jill Norwood that fewer foreign women are being identified as victims of trafficking, and the recruitment trend has changed.

'Three years ago women were being trafficked into Kosovo and immediately exploited. We had no idea where they were being held. Now they are being brought over with contracts and incrementally introduced into sex work.'

'So basically the situation has become more insidious?'

'Yes. These work contracts allow police to keep track of foreign workers, but they haven't stopped traffickers bringing women into Kosovo. If she has a contract and travel documents, then the border police have to let her in, and we prefer they do so, because then at least we can register her whereabouts.'

She also agrees that fewer women are willing to accept assistance from the UN and the international organisations that provide services, including the IOM, who arrange voluntary repatriation. Tihana's unit has supported just three foreign trafficking victims this year. They were all Moldovan, and she says the vast majority of foreign women being trafficked here are still Moldovan.

'They are turning down assistance services because they don't want to go home afterwards. Once they are out of their trafficking situation, they want to remain in Kosovo, but we don't have anywhere to put them. One of our forthcoming priorities is to establish provision for women who want to stay here.'

This is a novel approach. Assistance programmes for trafficked women across the Balkans, such as IOM programmes, are very much geared towards 'voluntary repatriation'.

Although women are trafficked from their own countries because in the vast majority of cases they are desperate to migrate, regional anti-trafficking programmes have overwhelmingly responded by sending as many of them as possible back home again afterwards. The small minority of women who are abducted and taken abroad against their will may well want to go home, but the available evidence suggests that more and more women who have been trafficked are turning down services focused on voluntary repatriation.

Women who want assistance here in Kosovo are interviewed by trained victim advocates and temporarily housed in the ISF (interim security facility), while police verify the information they have given and assess their trafficking status. Security is tight at the ISF. Tihana insists this is essential for the welfare of the women; female traffickers are known to have infiltrated the facility in the past.

Women stay at the ISF for just a few days. After being interviewed and having their options explained, they have a brief window to decide what they want to do next. In order to stay in Kosovo, they have to be involved in an official assistance programme but are not obliged to cooperate with the police, or to testify in court. It's a very similar provision to Article 18 in Italy, and Tihana says that most of the women, once they have had a space to decide what they want for themselves, do either cooperate or agree to testify against their trafficker.

There are several refuges where foreign women can be housed. For local women, there is no UN-funded refuge, but there is a semi-independent-living project where they can stay, and several local organisations also run refuges for local women and girls. A national trafficking hotline opened in November 2005; calls are free twenty-four hours a day, seven days a week.

I tell Tihana I recently spoke to a human rights lawyer in Bosnia who said provisions for trafficked women are now in many ways better in the Balkans than in the UK. What Madeline Rees actually told me, after the recent fiasco of the Birmingham 'Cuddles' massage parlour being raided, was 'As a woman, you'd be better off being trafficked to Bosnia than the UK.'

The Cuddles raid, which national media were invited to film, was part of a local anti-prostitution crackdown. TV footage showed a number of young women being led out of the parlour (nineteen were released), and the BBC later confirmed that six of these women were handed straight over to immigration officers. The massage parlour had an electric-fence perimeter, and police used battering rams on several of the internally locked doors. Workers from the Poppy Project re-interviewed the women who'd been handed over to immigration, and two of the women were transferred to the Poppy Project as they had in fact been trafficked to the UK.

'After hearing about assistance provision here,' I tell Tihana, 'I think you would be better off trafficked to Kosovo than to the UK.'

Except that the UK doesn't have thousands of foreign troops barracked across the country. There are still 16,400 KFOR soldiers in Kosovo. Amnesty International was particularly critical of KFOR in its trafficking report. 'Evidence of KFOR's use of trafficked women comes from the testimonies of trafficked women, from reports and sightings of KFOR soldiers in bars known to have been involved in trafficking and from a small number of cases in which disciplinary procedures against members of KFOR have been reported.'

The report mentions examples of the repatriation of three Royal Marine commandos and a British Army lieutenant colonel for misconduct,[2] and notes that between January 2002 and July 2003 up to twenty-seven KFOR troops were suspected of trafficking-related offences, although Amnesty International had been unable to obtain any further information about disciplinary or criminal proceedings.

As a NATO-led multinational task force in Kosovo, KFOR troops enjoy local immunity from prosecution, although this can be lifted at the request of commanders of national contingents or the provost marshal, who coordinates all military police functional support for KFOR operations. It is the multinational military police brigades who monitor the conduct of KFOR soldiers.

NATO itself has no powers of enforcement over the peacekeeping troops and civilian workers it deploys. Each NATO member or partner contributing forces determines the law and policy for its own personnel and is solely responsible for enforcing these laws and prosecuting offenders back at home.

In 2003, after years of criticism that repatriated offenders were rarely investigated or prosecuted back at home, NATO drafted Resolution 323 on Trafficking in Human Beings.

Amnesty's response to Resolution 323 is that although it does develop policy on combating human trafficking, it fails 'to address the issues of demand and accountability'.

A year later, in 2004, NATO adopted a zero-tolerance policy

---

2. 'Colonel Caught in Brothel', *The Times*, July 2002. The repatriation of the Royal Marine commandos was reported by AFP in January 2001.

prohibiting personnel from engaging in, or facilitating, human trafficking. The policy addressed issues including appropriate training modules for NATO personnel, assistance to authorities in host countries to combat trafficking and does also mention imposing penalties on contractors who work for NATO-led operations. It was seen by many human rights advocates as a major step forward, though they pointed out that the policy was driven by the US and Norway and its success will rest on the adherence to, and accountability of all NATO members.

I telephone KFOR, ask to speak to a spokesman, and am informed I need to email any questions I have. In response to my email about KFOR regulations regarding the off-limits list, and what happens if a soldier is found in violation of these regulations, I receive this reply:

> Dear Ms Louisa Waugh
> This is the answer to your question:
>   Related to the subject which interests you, KFOR applies its proper regulation, which is also reinforced by each nation policy.
>   There is a NATO-wide policy that commits each nation to ensure that appropriate mechanisms are in place.
>   Best regards,
> Maj. Valerie-Claire Bermond
> Deputy Spokesperson
> PIO HQ KFOR

Someone gives me the number of a UN staff member who liaises between UNMIK and KFOR. When I call him, he agrees to meet me for coffee.

At the café, he tells me his mission will be over one week later, and he's looking forward to returning to France. I ask if it would be possible for me to meet a KFOR representative, and he shrugs.

'I don't think so; but let me try.' He calls someone, talks rapidly and snaps his mobile shut. 'No chance, I'm afraid. You don't have official accreditation, so they are not going to meet you. Look, I am official UN liaison personnel, and I applied for leave to go into one of the bases three months ago, and I'm still waiting. OK – tell me what you want to know, and I will ask these questions on your behalf.'

I write down several questions about the off-limits list and KFOR Code of Conduct, and he pockets them. He asks about my book, and when I mention Sarajevo, he interrupts me.

'I was on mission in Bosnia too. That place; the trafficking situation was desperate when I was there. They moved the women up and down the country like cattle.'

'Did you ever hear of a Ukrainian woman called Olena Popik?'

'Yes! I saw Olena many times. Professionally, you understand! I was based in Zenica, and she was always there, working on that road from Sarajevo to Zenica.' He exhales slowly. 'She was there all day, and at night, you know, her pimp rented some small cabin set back from the road, and she had sex with clients in this shack. She never stopped working.' He tells me the police could do nothing, because Olena was always with her pimp and would deny she was a sex worker or a trafficked woman.' He knows she is dead now. 'Look, I don't know what was happening with her. I don't know her story. But her life, it was a complete waste,' he says. 'Even when she was in Zenica, she was sick, but it never stopped her pimp from renting her out to truck drivers. Those fucking pimps, they kill the women. They treat them worse than dogs.'

Olena was sold and pimped across four countries before she even reached Bosnia and the road to Zenica. When she was healthy, she worked in nightclubs, but once she started getting sick, she had to stand at the side of the road every day and tout for punters.

It was relentless unprotected sex that killed her. She had unprotected sex with strangers at the side of the road, more unprotected sex in a draughty wooden cabin near a lay-by, where trucks could stop easily, and then, when she was sold to a pimp in Mostar, she was rented out as a trophy to birthday parties of drunken men who would push each other aside so they could see her having sex with their friends while they waited for their turn. This is what killed Olena Popik; and whenever I think of her, I wonder how she lasted as long as she did.

Four Bosnian men have stood trial in connection with the trafficking of Olena Popik: Djenan Golic, Zdravko Vidovic, Edin Kreso and Milan Galic. A fifth, Danijel Rague, is apparently on the run, and an international warrant has been issued for his arrest. The EU Police Mission reported that the trial concluded on 16 September 2005. Edin Kreso was apparently allowed to plea bargain and given a one-year sentence; Milan Galic received a two-year suspended sentence with five years' probation; Zdravko Vidovic was sentenced to eighteen months in prison; and Djenan Golic, widely considered to be the main culprit, received two years. However, the seven months he spent in custody prior to the trial will be deducted from the time he will now serve behind bars. There was no mention of the Ukrainian woman who apparently sold Olena to the pimp in Mostar.[3]

3. Email from Monja Koluder, EUPM (European Union Police Mission) spokeswoman, Mostar, 17 August 2005 and 21 April 2006.

I tell the Frenchman about the trial.

'She was just a poor Ukrainian prostitute,' he says with deliberately heavy irony. 'Why would they want to make an example of her pimps?'

I've always assumed there was no trafficking here until the UN and the troops arrived, but a local man who's employed by one of the international organisations that works with trafficked women tells me otherwise. 'You know, it is easy to say that in our country there was no trafficking until the internationals arrived, but it is not completely true.' I look at him in surprise, and he continues, 'Women were being trafficked into Kosovo before the war. For sure not so many, but it was happening. There were these houses – what do you call them? – bordellos, where men went to buy sex. The houses were organised by Serbs; at that time there was no way a Kosovar Albanian could have run one of these places as a business. The Serbs were ruling us. And the women inside the houses were not locals. Some of them came from Moldova . . . the others, I am not so sure, but maybe from Bulgaria and Romania. But they were not Kosovar or Serb women: that I can tell you.'

I call Igo Rogova, the activist who told me what was going on the first time I came to Pristina. We've also kept in touch, sporadically, and she invites me round for dinner.

We eat at her flat, in a suburb called Sunny Hill. Igo looks older and tired, and tells me she's weary of campaigning but so much still needs changing she might actually go into politics. She has run out of patience with the UN dragging its feet over Kosovo's 'final status' and despairs of the Kosovan interim government.

'They are stealing from us,' she says angrily. 'We have mass unemployment, people are really struggling, and they blatantly line their own pockets.'

Igo is sometimes contacted by international organisations who presume she's married to the President, because his surname is Rugova, and they can't distinguish the difference in the spelling.

After dinner she offers me a cigarette. I've just given up, again, but the Balkans will always get the better of me and nicotine.

I ask Igo about the trafficking situation. She says she thinks it's reduced here, but that troops and UN staff still go south to Macedonia for weekends. Macedonia still has a reputation for being a human-trafficking junction.

I tell her that just last week the *Sunday Telegraph* ran a front-page exposé on 'The Plight of the Cellar Girls' – a graphic account, complete with pitiful grainy photographs, of scores of Romanian, Moldovan and Ukrainian women being trafficked into western Macedonia and locked in unlit, unheated cellars, while their traffickers negotiated prices with pimps and punters. The journalist, David Harrison, said police had raided bunkers in several Macedonian towns, including Gostivar. This is where Anna, the second Moldovan woman I interviewed, was held when she was trafficked.

Harrison claimed the women in the cellars were en route to Western Europe, including Britain.[4]

The Amnesty International report refers to its 'concerns' that KFOR personnel visiting Macedonia and German KFOR troops stationed there may be using trafficked women. It also refers to women being trafficked from Kosovo to Macedonia and to several testimonies of women who were confined inside cellars in Kosovo. Igo says stories about trafficking in Macedonia have been circulating for several years now. For a while we smoke and drink our wine quietly.

Later, Igo calls a taxi for me and gives me a packet of cigarettes on my way out.

'Make it your last,' she says, 'and good luck, Louisa.'

'You too,' I say, hugging her.

On the way back to the hotel, I think about our conversation and how, two and a half years after my first trip to research trafficking, I still feel like I've only just scratched the surface. Fragmented details of the Balkans have just started to align: Olga and the Amnesty International report, Gostivar and Anna, Olena Popik and Zenica. Somewhere along the line all the stories that I've heard are linked together, by place, or date, or experience.

You could spend your life investigating these crimes. The breaking up of the former Soviet Union, the collapse of civil society in the Balkans and the breakdown of communist regimes in Eastern Europe have between them created a vast supply of cheap and disposable migrant labour that has been ruthlessly exploited from Eastern to Western Europe, by traffickers, smugglers, employers, pimps and punters.

It is my last evening in Kosovo, and Maggie is taking me out for dinner. A friend of hers has kindly offered to drive us south from Pristina to Prizren, where there are good restaurants overlooking the river, and we can spend the evening in the beautiful old town centre for which Prizren is nationally famous. I meet Maggie and her friend, Dehin, in the hotel lobby. Dehin is six foot something, with swept-back black hair and

4. David Harrison, *Sunday Telegraph*, 27 November 2005.

slender, regal features. He is quite stunning; a Balkan prince in a long, dark winter coat. He and I don't speak each other's language, but we both speak German, although Maggie doesn't, so between us we use a tri-partite of languages; Maggie and I speak English, she and Dehin talk in Albanian, he and I in German. It works remarkably well.

'Where did you meet him?' I ask Maggie, wondering if they are an item.

'We work together,' she tells me, grinning. 'But that is all we do!'

We leave Pristina just after 5.30 p.m., but it is already night outside, and as we gradually climb up into the hills, snow begins to fall gently from the dark sky. The drive takes an hour and a half. I sit on the back seat, talking and listening, waiting for the right moment to ask Maggie for one more favour; I can't do this last thing without her.

Finally, as we approach the outskirts of Prizren, I say, 'Maggie, I have something to ask you. There's something I need to do this evening.'

'What is it?'

I pull the off-limits list out of my bag and hand it over to her. 'These are all the bars and clubs that are off limits. You know, the places where the UN, the police and the internationals can't go. But we can, because you don't work for the police any more. Can we visit one of these this evening, please?'

Maggie takes the list from me, switches on the car light and looks through it. There are sixty-six off-limits venues listed in Prizren.

'Louisa, we have come for dinner! Why do we have to do this?'

She confers with Dehin, who says that he doesn't mind but can we eat first?

'Let's see,' says Maggie, giving me back the list.

The old town centre of Prizren is lamp-lit and atmospheric. We wander slowly along the riverside, ask a local couple if they can recommend a restaurant, and eat good Italian food in a large bar cum trattoria overlooking the river.

We finish our meal and order one more round of drinks.

'This is the end of my last research trip,' I tell them both. '*Gezuar!*'

It's one of the few local words I know. We clink glasses.

'Are you glad to finish this research?' says Maggie.

'Yes, I'm very glad. It's been very intense, and I'm weary. I'm ready to stay at home for a while.'

She smiles at me. 'You pick a difficult subject like this, and your work will swallow you up. OK, this is your last evening of work in Kosovo.

Next time you come to see me, come on holiday, and we will drive down to Skopje for the weekend. So, where is this list?'

I give her the list. She and Dehin study it, and when the waiter comes to take our plates away, they show him the list, and he points and gives directions and marks out several places with his pen. He doesn't seem the slightest bit curious about why we want to visit a list of dubious Prizren bars.

'He says these bars are all outside the centre,' says Maggie. 'A lot of them are near the bus station. He says it is a rough area, and that these bars' – she points to the venues the waiter has highlighted – 'these places have very bad reputations. So I suppose this is where we should go.'

'Yes, I suppose it is.'

'We are not going to stay very long,' says Dehin. 'Just to see what is happening.'

'OK. Thank you. I can't do this without the two of you.'

'So, let's go.'

We wander back along the cobbled riverside street to Dehin's car and drive towards the bus station. It takes quite a while because Prizren has a complicated one-way road system and we keep coming back on ourselves.

Eventually, after driving through a semi-industrial district, we arrive at the dark, empty bus station on De Rada Street. Everything appears to be closed, and there are very few people around. Even the street lights are sparse.

Maggie and Dehin check the list again. We are in the right place but can't see anywhere that appears to be open. Dehin turns the engine off, and then the lights, and we sit in the dark car looking for signs of life outside.

I see a car turn down a side street, and tap him on the shoulder. 'Look.'

We follow it down the side street, which is less of a street and more of a rough track around the back of the bus station. There are several flimsy-looking travel agencies, and as we turn the corner, there are a couple of open restaurants, a large, low building that could be a warehouse, some sort of a trailer park and an illuminated sign that says, 'Te Nazja'.

This is one of the bars on the off-limits list.

We crawl past Te Nazja and immediately know that we've found what we are looking for. The bar has red curtains, which are parted. A woman in a tight, revealing sweater is doing something inside. Behind her, I catch a glimpse of several other young women and a group of men.

'It's a brothel,' I say to Maggie.

'Yes, of course it is,' she replies.

Dehin parks just beyond Te Nazja, on the same side of the street. I am suddenly very glad of his size. We clamber out of the car, and Maggie strides fearlessly towards the bar. Dehin walks between the two of us. I am the one lagging behind. I wonder what we'll find, and whether they'll even let us in. I don't look like a Kosovan, and feel very exposed, even with my friends on either side.

The bar is almost completely red inside. It's a caricature of a cheap brothel: red curtains hang over the windows, the carpet is red, and a string of red fairy lights has been nailed around the red walls. There are two narrow interconnecting rooms, with no doorway between them, just long, red drapes on either side that have been tied back loosely, so we can see almost from one end to the other.

We sit at an empty table, opposite a table occupied by seven or eight men and women. They stare at us, and their conversations stall as they look each of us up and down. Maggie smiles a greeting over to them, Dehin nods, and they slowly resume their cigarettes and drinks and banter.

The cloth on our table is red, pocked with cigarette burns. I fumble in my bag for the cigarettes Igo gave me last night. Dehin offers me a light, I offer him a cigarette, and as we begin to smoke, a young blonde woman walks over to our table and asks if we want something to drink. I can't understand what she's saying, but her tone is neither interested nor hostile. Dehin and I ask for red wine; Maggie asks for juice.

I sit back and look at the people at the opposite table. There are three women and five men. The women are all young, and two of them look particularly haggard, though the third is visibly plumper and better dressed. One of the haggard women is wearing a very tight grey sweater and starts to thrust her breasts in time to the arabesque music playing in the background. The man sitting next to her moves closer, leering. His eyes look bloodshot.

Another woman brings our drinks to our table: two large tumblers of cold red wine and a small bottle of juice. As she puts the drinks down, Maggie smiles and starts talking to her. I hear her ask a few questions casually, and the woman's brief replies.

'She's Albanian,' Maggie tells me afterwards. 'She is from Durres and has been here for just one month. I think the other girls are all Albanian too: their dialects are not Kosovan.' She is listening to the conversations on the other side of the room. She leans forward and says to me quietly, 'You look, and I will listen.'

I take a sip of the wine, wince at its cold acidity and look slowly around the rest of the brothel. There are half a dozen oriental fans pinned to the walls, with kitsch serene illustrations of gardens and flowers, reeds and ponds. In the room on the other side of the drapes are another three tables and two other women sitting amongst several men. The group in this room are getting drunk and steadily louder. The blonde woman who took our order joins them, as the plump, well-dressed woman leaves the table and walks to the bar. The three women left at the table all have a man on either side of them, and they laugh shrilly as the men begin to touch them up. One of them is scrawny as a fledgling. She rests her elbows on the shoulders of the men sitting beside her, looking from one to the other, a nervous panicky expression flickering across her tight, smiling face.

A large television has been mounted on one of the walls, next to a couple of posters of women in bikinis promoting cans of beer. The TV is on, with the sound turned down. A balding man wearing a shiny shirt and a wide, green tie is being interviewed in some sort of chat show. He gestures to his audience and leans forward slightly, inviting them to laugh at his joke or anecdote. I stare at him for a few minutes, blankly watching his silent performance before bringing myself unwillingly back into the bar. I glance over at Dehin, who is talking to Maggie but looking round every minute or so, his eyes vigilant.

A new woman walks through; she is small and dark-haired, and walks with a pronounced limp. Her face is completely devoid of expression, blank as a board. She brings over a clean ashtray. Maggie does the same smiling and casual small talk, and the woman tells her that she's from Kukes.

Kukes is in north-eastern Albania, near the Kosovan border. During the Serbian war many Kosovans fled straight over the border to Kukes, which became one of the main refugee camps. Like the rest of northern Albania, Kukes is dirt poor, and now Albanians regularly cross over to Kosovo to find work. It's an easy border to cross. If you don't have a passport, a driving licence will often suffice. The people of Burrell, where I visited Natasha, also use this route to come to Kosovo, and Prizren is the first town after the border; an obvious stopping-off point to look for work.

This is the route Aldon's mother would have taken from Burrell to Kosovo. And this is the sort of place some of these women end up scraping a living; a brothel on a dark street at the back of Prizren bus station, because how else are they going to survive?

I carry on looking around, carefully filing away details, taking mental snapshots, feeling very remote from what is right in front of me. I don't know whether these women have been trafficked. All I know is they are poor and drunk, and they will have sex with some, maybe all of these men later, and someone will get paid for it.

The atmosphere is charged with alcohol but doesn't actually feel volatile. I feel quite safe, especially with Dehin here. The men from the other table are still glancing over, and the one with the bloodshot eyes stares at me from time to time, but I don't think he's going to do anything. Only the women come to our table.

The plump woman walks over from the bar, greets us and offers us all cigarettes from a fresh pack. She looks at me quizzically. Maggie immediately says something, and the woman nods, apparently satisfied with the response. We are obviously not police. She tells Maggie this is her bar, and business is not so bad. She's from Albania too but has been living in Prizren for a long time now. She returns to the large table, joins in with the shrill laughter and starts pouring more drinks.

So she's the owner; that explains why she is the smartly dressed and well-fed one, the cat amongst the pigeons. Pimps thrive on a diet of poverty and desperation.

Maggie, Dehin and I look at each other in turn. It is time to go. It's getting late, it's a long drive back to Pristina, and we have seen enough of this bar. Maggie gestures to one of the women, the blonde woman who first took our order.

As she collects our glasses, Maggie asks her something, and though I don't understand the language, the tone of her response is utterly clear.

Maggie says to her, 'So, how did you come to be working here in Prizren?'

The woman stares at her for a second or two, picks up the empty bottle of juice and replies curtly, 'What do you mean, why am I here? Why do you think I'm here? I have to eat.'

Chapter 19

The Impunity of Peace

It was late when we left Prizren. Maggie slept on the back seat, and Dehin and I said very little on the way back towards Pristina. He dropped Maggie off first, at her home in Obilic, and she went inside, yawning and sleepy. We drove back to the city past one of the power stations that squat either side of Obilic; it was lit up like an oil rig, belching a chemical haze of luminous smoke that stank even though the car windows were shut.

When we got into Pristina, Dehin and I went to a late-night drinking den called the Depot and spent the next couple of hours listening to a band and drinking beer, blurring the edges of the evening.

On my way to the airport, someone tips me off about a group of French KFOR soldiers who were apparently apprehended at a brothel in Mitrovica, northern Kosovo, at the beginning of the year. I reply to Major Bermond's email, asking if there's been any investigation into this allegation. This time I receive an email from a Major Christian Shultz, who tells me he has just replaced Major Bermond and KFOR has no further information for me, 'as you have already received a reply through my predecessor'.

So far as I know, there has been no investigation into what did or did not take place at a brothel in Mitrovica.

In Kosovo, UNMIK police cannot sanction KFOR troops, even if they do find them in off-limits premises. Jill Norwood's boss at the UNMIK Trafficking in Human Beings Section is Robert Gordon Bruce. He's a Scotsman. He was working in Macedonia while I was in Kosovo, and I speak to him on the phone when I'm back at home and he's returned to Pristina. I ask if he knows anything about the allegations against the French soldiers.

'That report was unconfirmed,' he replies. 'Look, we all know soldiers use prostitutes. But we have no jurisdiction over KFOR troops. They are all under the jurisdiction of their own multinational military police brigade. We do joint operations with the military police; in fact, we'll be doing one next week. But it's the military police who monitor KFOR troops.'

When I ask him about other internationals being involved in trafficking, he tells me, 'Less than one per cent of the people we find in off-limits venues are internationals, and sometimes they genuinely don't know it's off limits. Many of these bars open, close down and then quickly reopen under a different name. Even the names of streets aren't clearly marked in many parts of Kosovo, and people make mistakes.'

Robert Bruce describes the Amnesty report as a 'slur, which set back progress in Kosovo and took no account of the changes that have been introduced in the last few years'. He says things have improved considerably during the eighteen months he's been in Kosovo, though one of the ongoing problems for his department is that when they arrest someone, even if the police have done their own investigation, the state prosecutors usually redo the investigation themselves, and information is rarely relayed back to the police.

'They hardly ever tell us even if they've secured a conviction; we have to rely on reports in the local press, which makes it very hard to keep track of progress.'

If NATO is unaccountable to the United Nations, why are their troops on peacekeeping missions? Paul Ingram, senior analyst at the British American Security Information Council (or BASIC), tells me NATO has had an identity crisis since 1990, which it has yet to overcome – i.e. now that the Cold War is over, it has no clearly defined role. Although NATO has, as he puts it, 'extended its competency to include peacekeeping, at its core it's still an organisation designed to tie the US into European defence, using the threat of overwhelming force against any aggressor'. To put it crudely, NATO doesn't want the UN affecting the leverage that it still has. Paul Ingram believes NATO is keen to keep troops in peacekeeping operations because the organisation is dominated by the US, who would otherwise have to cede peacekeeping power to the UN Secretary-General.

UN peacekeepers, on the other hand, have been an integral part of the United Nations almost from its inception. Originally employed as unarmed observers to monitor ceasefires and peace agreements, the first major peacekeeping operation was set up in the Congo in 1960. This drained UN resources and full-scale peacekeeping operations didn't fully resume until 1989, when the UN established the UN Transition Assistance Group (UNTAG) in Namibia.

The UN Department of Peacekeeping Operations (UN DPKO) was set up in 1992 to 'plan, prepare, manage and direct UN peacekeeping operations'. Allegations of sexual violence committed by peacekeepers began to surface a couple of years later and have tainted UN peacekeeping missions across the world ever since: from the former Yugoslavia in the mid-1990s to South-East Asia, Somalia and East Timor, followed by damning reports from Liberia, Eritrea, Sierra Leone, Kosovo, Burundi and the Democratic Republic of the Congo (DRC).

There are currently eighteen UN peacekeeping operations around the world, employing just under ninety thousand personnel. Half of the peacekeeping operations are in Africa;[1] the others are in Haiti, India, Pakistan, Cyprus, Georgia, Kosovo, the Golan Heights and Lebanon.[2] The approved DPKO budget for June 2005–6 was $5.3 billion, which represents approximately half a per cent of global military spending. Allegations against peacekeepers in many of these operations have been ongoing, especially in DRC, where the United Nations has faced a torrent of ugly accusations, many of them substantiated.

In July 2004 the UN Secretary-General, Kofi Annan, announced that 'a fundamental change in approach was needed' in order to tackle the peacekeeping crisis. This was widely seen as a response to the revelations of sexual exploitation and abuse by a significant number of United Nations peacekeeping personnel in the Democratic Republic of the Congo. He asked Prince Zeid Ra'ad Zeid Al-Hussein, permanent representative of Jordan (and a former civilian peacekeeper himself), to write a comprehensive report on sexual exploitation and abuse by UN peacekeeping personnel, complete with a list of recommendations of what to do about it.

During his research Zeid visited DRC, where he met local women who described their experiences with UN peacekeepers as 'rape disguised as prostitution'. After a woman had been raped, she would often be given a little money or a portion of food, to present the illusion of consent. Peacekeepers were offering girls of twelve and thirteen a dollar for sex.

The UN's attempt to investigate more than a hundred and fifty allegations of rape and forced prostitution against peacekeepers in DRC led to further accusations of the same peacekeepers threatening the UN investigators and offering bribes to witnesses to change their testimonies. The UN Chief of Mission in Congo, William Lacy Swing, said he was 'sickened' by what was happening around him. Annette, who was trafficked from East Africa to London via several other countries, spent much of 2003 imprisoned in DRC.

1. Sudan, Burundi, Ivory Coast, Liberia, Democratic Republic of the Congo, Ethiopia/Eritrea, Sierra Leone and Western Sahara.
2. The additional two operations are the UN Truce Supervision Organisation (UNTSO) based in Jerusalem and the UN Mine Action Coordination Centre.

Zeid presented his report to the UN in March 2005. It underlined the scale of abuse by peacekeepers and acknowledged that though many efforts are now underway to address these issues, they are 'ad hoc and inadequate', and potential whistle-blowers are frightened they won't be protected if they break rank and speak out. It's a lengthy, detailed report containing a host of recommendations, all written in formal UN language.

Briefly, Zeid recommended that all personnel appointed or contracted by the UN be bound by the same 'uniform and binding standards', as set out in the 2003 Secretary-General's Bulletin, regardless of rank or appointment; he suggested the General Assembly establish a professional investigative capacity to tackle sexual exploitation, which would be staffed by experts and work independently of UN missions and the Department of Peacekeeping Operations. This could be made up of regionally based teams. He advocated more women be deployed in peacekeeping and that nations contributing peacekeeping troops conduct on-site courts martial for serious criminal offences. All peacekeepers should undergo intensive training to deal with sexual-abuse issues, and effective whistle-blowing mechanisms should be introduced. Military police should, if possible, be from a different country than the troops they monitor.

He stated that all UN missions must institute measures to deal with allegations and provide assistance to victims, that UN staff guilty of serious misconduct be subject to disciplinary action, or immediately resign and never be re-employed by the UN, and that any contingent commander who fails to cooperate with, or obstructs, a DPKO investigation be immediately repatriated.

Zeid also tackled the legacy of the Convention on the Privileges and Immunities of the UN (1946), which grants immunity from local jurisdiction to UN staff while they're working. He recommends a serious effort be made to address 'shortcomings in accountability because the [UN] charter envisaged that immunity would be functional, and sexual exploitation and abuse are not within the functions of any staff member or expert on mission'. He proposed the UN Secretary-General appoint a group of legal experts to ensure that 'UN staff and experts on mission would never be excepted from the consequences of criminal acts that they committed at their duty station'.

He proposed that if allegations against a UN soldier are well founded, his country be obliged to forward the case to its national authorities to be considered for prosecution, and the outcome be reported direct to the UN Secretary-General.

There's a great deal more than this in Zeid's report, and the range of reforms it calls for represents a breakthrough for human rights campaigners. Amnesty International called it 'the first comprehensive analysis of the problem of sexual exploitation and abuse by UN peacekeeping personnel'. The UN Special Committee on Peacekeeping Operations, who met in April to consider Zeid's report, formally stated they were committed to fundamental changes as a matter of urgency, but that implementing these changes, which would draw on Zeid's recommendations, would take time. The majority of these changes are expected to be implemented by UN DPKO by June 2007.

Though Zeid's report laid out the scale of abuses committed by peacekeepers, it never, however, attempted to address the question of why sexual violations, including trafficking into forced prostitution, have become such an ingrained part of UN peacekeeping missions.

Peacekeeping involves sending large contingents of (mostly) men abroad, often to violent and unstable countries, where they wield a disproportionate amount of power over the local population and are not bound by local law. Peacekeeping has from the onset been a very macho culture. Even now, women represent just 4 per cent of civilian UN police and 1 per cent of military personnel in peacekeeping operations. Although UN standards of conduct prohibit sex with prostitutes, soldiers are routinely issued with condoms, which are also easily available to soldiers through the United Nations Programme on HIV/AIDS. And when crimes, including sexual violence, have been committed by peacekeepers, they have very often got away with it. The Department of Peacekeeping Operations itself recently admitted:

> Human trafficking is a form of serious exploitation and abuse that is increasingly present in UN peacekeeping environments [. . .] This perception of a large-scale use of the services of [trafficking] victims by peacekeepers is exacerbated by an equally strong perception that peacekeeping institutions do not take the issue seriously. This latter perception is extremely damaging and has been compounded by 'boys will be boys' attitudes of the past.

For some peacekeepers and UN personnel, immunity has created a culture of impunity.

Sarah Mendelson works for the Washington DC-based Center for Strategic and International Studies, a non-profit public policy organisation that researches and analyses global security policy. In February 2005 they published 'Barracks and Brothels: peacekeepers and human trafficking in the Balkans', a sixty-page report that meticulously documents the links between a number of UN personnel, NATO peacekeepers and the trafficking of women and girls in both Bosnia and Kosovo. Sarah Mendelson wrote the report.

From the outset she acknowledges the vast majority of peacekeepers are not complicit in trafficking. But she also reiterates that peacekeeping as a whole has been tainted by the abuses committed by a minority of personnel who are rarely held accountable for their crimes. She points out that in stark contrast to the vast resources devoted to documenting the phenomenon of trafficking in the Balkans and providing for its survivors, 'the numerous studies on peacekeeping and post-conflict reconstruction have almost entirely neglected the nexus of trafficking and peacekeepers.' Although there is obviously no definitive figure of how many people have been trafficked in the Balkans, UNICEF has estimated that up to fifteen thousand females were trafficked through the region between January 2000 and June 2003.

Sarah Mendelson hones in on the national and international security implications of peacekeeping complicity in trafficking. 'In peacekeeping missions, corruption inside deployments undermines efforts at establishing the rule of law and thus prolongs the deployments.' Also, when peacekeepers pay traffickers to have sex with women and girls, they are handing money straight over to criminals. 'Peacekeepers – including military personnel and civilian contractors – who exploit trafficked women and girls not only break local and international laws but also unwittingly support precisely the people who do not want a safe, stable and secure environment.'

The UN Office on Drugs and Crime (UNDOC) has also identified links between surges in criminality and post-conflict areas, claiming that organised criminal groups take advantage of weak state control mechanisms and engage in large-scale human trafficking operations. And the IOM has published compelling evidence of criminals thriving on the proceeds of trafficking. In a report published in 2004, IOM researchers documented numerous links between trafficking in the Balkans and other forms of organised crime, including drug and weapons trafficking. They described how human trafficking has 'modernised' into an incredibly sophisticated sequence of crimes which have adapted 'very efficiently' to regional anti-trafficking programmes, and drew attention to the emergence of 'new and younger criminal managerial figures who invest large sums of money into the sector, especially in Moldova and Bosnia'. They also cited evidence of 'several transnational groups of organised criminals composed of members of both Albanian and Italian Mafia which are working together on drugs and weapons deals. There is also cooperation in trafficking of persons with organised crime groups in Kosovo.'

According to the IOM, several 'protective rings' have been conceived and established by Balkan criminals in order to obtain maximum economic return from trafficking.

The first, and most effective of these rings is the protection provided by the corruption of state functionaries and officers in police forces and armed services, of politicians, or even personnel in foreign embassies and consulates. This allows trafficking to survive without obliging criminal groups to modify the form or method of their operations.

The report adds that one of the most effective methods of intimidating a 'victim of trafficking' is when a trafficker demonstrates that he (or she) has a friendly relationship with a member of the police in the destination country.

If a peacekeeper pays money to a criminal in order to have sex with a trafficked woman, he breaks the law, violates and damages the woman and also directly contributes to organised crime. Traffickers have become so wealthy and established in the Balkans that they are increasingly trafficking people directly to Western Europe, Turkey and the Middle East, as opposed to taking circuitous overland routes through the region. They often use either very sophisticated forged documents or else legitimate identity papers, all of which make detection of the crimes harder.

Sarah Mendelson claims that human rights abuses committed inside a post-conflict zone should be treated as threats to stability. She quotes the Norwegian Ambassador to NATO, Kai Eide, as saying that when peacekeepers are involved in trafficking, 'not only do we destroy the reputation of our country and our organisation and the operation, we violate fundamentally [the] human rights of women and children. And we do harm to the objectives of our mission, which is to establish rule of law, establish the foundation for democracy and for a decent economy. Not to tear down the rule of law, not to create grey economies [and] stimulate corruption.'

In May 2005, two months after Zeid's report was presented to the UN, the Head of DPKO, Jean-Marie Guehenno, informed the Security Council that since the end of December 2004 there had been 152 investigations into allegations of sexual abuse involving UN peacekeeping personnel. Seventy-seven military personnel, including six military commanders, had been repatriated or 'rotated home on disciplinary grounds'. He informed the Security Council that more allegations were now being reported, which could mean staff were now more prepared to break rank and speak out. He also admitted that 'The problem of sexual exploitation and abuse is likely to look worse before it looks better.'

'I believe NATO is now far more professional in its peacekeeping than the UN, as a consequence of funding and training,' says Sarah

Mendelson. 'One of the issues seriously hampering the department of peacekeeping operations is its institutionalised impunity regarding trafficking in prostitution and sex-abuse issues. There has not yet been effective training and allocation of resources in this particular arena, in order to field the surveys, create messages and mount effective awareness-raising campaigns. There is a well-documented pattern of sexual abuse by peacekeepers. The concern my colleagues and I have is that, given this well-established pattern, we fear trafficking for forced prostitution is ongoing in peacekeeping operations.'

Lisa Kurbiel works for UN DPKO at the United Nations head-quarters and is one of the pivotal figures inside the department working on these peacekeeping reforms. She says that progress is being made, although there is still a long way to go.

'The problem is that ten years ago we were not asking the right questions,' she says. 'The standards of conduct have now been drawn up and every peacekeeper is made aware of them. The problem is of peacekeepers adhering to these standards. Adherence needs to start at commander level, and include every single member of personnel.'

She tells me that approximately half the allegations made against peacekeepers involve individuals paying women or girls for sex, and the DPKO reforms will be incorporating an anti-prostitution strategy, on the grounds that paying for sex is also an abuse of the very unequal power relationship between peacekeepers and local populations. However, there has been 'some resistance' from some peacekeepers to being told they cannot pay for sex whilst on mission.

Lisa Kurbiel believes it is essential that peacekeepers do not hide behind the draper of national sovereignty, and that the international community demands effective follow up where malfeasance has occurred. 'Whilst blame is easily laid at the door of the UN, we have to remember that the UN is made up of its member states,' she says. 'All members, especially troop-contributing countries, have responsibility for dealing with allegations and incidents of sexual abuse and exploitation.' The three largest troop-contributing countries are India, Bangladesh and Pakistan.

The immunity of UN staff is occasionally lifted to allow a criminal investigation in the host country. On 31 October 2005 Rashidoon Khan, a Pakistani national employed by the UN High Commission for Refugees in Kosovo, was charged with 'sexual abuse of persons under the age of sixteen years, trafficking in persons, unauthorised purchase, possession, distribution and sale of dangerous narcotic drugs and psychotropic substances'. The trafficking charges were dropped because of insubstantial evidence, and Khan was convicted of the other charges. He's now serving three years in prison in Kosovo.

Whilst his prosecution and sentence demonstrate the UN is occasionally prepared to tackle serious accusations head on, it's a very rare occurrence for a trial to take place under local jurisdiction. Commentators like Sarah Mendelson believe that in order for UN and NATO peacekeeping to survive with any real credibility, adherence to these reforms will have to go much further. If anti-trafficking policies are rigorously implemented, Sarah Mendelson questions what effect this will have on the ability of organisations to recruit peacekeepers in future. 'Do some [peacekeepers] see access to women and girls as a perk of the job?'

Women and girls have always been one of the main spoils of war.

Throughout the history of conflict they have been enslaved as trophies, used as prostitutes to boost 'troop morale' and abused for sport or humiliation or retribution.

Rape was used systematically against women in conflicts throughout the last century. The most recent revelations of mass organised rape were reported during the wars in the Balkans, Rwanda, Sierra Leone and the Democratic Republic of the Congo. In Bosnia thousands of women and girls were detained in camps in the north-west of the country and raped by Serbian forces and police. According to the Institute of War and Peace Reporting (IWPR), an EU Commission in Brussels calculated that as many as 50,000 women and girls were raped during the war. Many of them were repeatedly raped for weeks, even months on end. The Hague Tribunal recognised that rape was used as a systematic weapon of ethnic cleansing in Bosnia, making it indictable as a war crime. Women and girls were also targeted for rape and sexual abuse during the war in Kosovo.

Since 1992, UN and NATO peacekeepers have been entrusted to protect women and children and men who are frightened and traumatised and often already violated. For women and girls in the Democratic Republic of the Congo, Bosnia, and during the first two or three years of the UN Mission in Kosovo, a minority of the peacekeepers became the predators.

When I was in Bosnia I met a local poet called Ferida Durakovic. She lived in Sarajevo throughout the war and told me about having heard a rumour that young girls were going to the UNPROFOR (UN Protection Force) headquarters in Sarajevo and prostituting themselves for food. A week or so after hearing this rumour, Ferida met an UNPROFOR soldier, a Frenchman, who was visiting a friend of hers, offering food to the woman's family. When Ferida asked this French soldier about this rumour, he did not deny it.

'I am very sorry Madam: I believe it is happening, and it is wrong,' he said. 'The best thing we can do to prevent this is to have some foreign whores brought here instead.'

Epilogue

Chronic poverty, violence against women and girls, lack of decent work opportunities, coupled with restrictive migration and immigration policies have all played their role in creating multinational trafficking industries. However, people have been trafficked since at least as far back as the seventh-century Muslim slave trade, when millions were enslaved and trafficked, seven hundred years before the Transatlantic Slave Trade began its mass plunder. The context was radically different during both those trades: slavery was legally sanctioned and funded by governments back then. Slavery is now illegal in every country of the world. The year 2007 will mark the bicentenary of the Slave Trade Act 1807, which eventually abolished slavery throughout the former British Empire. But the legacy of trafficking has continued.

Contemporary human trafficking also operates on a global scale, involving the trade of several million people at a time. The most recent figures produced by the International Labour Office estimate that some two and a half million people worldwide are caught in the cycle of trafficking. Millions of others are trapped in other forced labour situations that fall outside the scope of this book.

Globalisation is often cited as a trafficking catalyst. In its first global report on forced labour, published in 2001, the ILO described trafficking into forced labour as 'the underside of globalisation'. Its most recent forced labour report goes further, stating, 'The forced labour associated with trafficking represents one of the most blatant failures of labour markets, and even global governance, to address the needs of arguably the most vulnerable and least protected human beings in the world.'

Human trafficking encapsulates the most extreme ethos of globalisation: movement of economic units for profit regardless of human cost. Traffickers do not regard their cargo as human. Former head of the London vice squad Paul Holmes' bleak metaphor of trafficked women being 'walking ATM machines' slices through the rhetoric. People are trafficked for the profits that can be extracted from them in the destination market. Traffickers prey on their needs, aspirations and lack of opportunity to alleviate their situations independently.

The ILO are clear that trafficking networks extend well beyond the commercial sex industry. At least a third of the people trafficked are exploited in other industries, agriculture and construction work being two of the biggest known culprits. There's also a huge international market for migrant domestic workers, who are often, though not always, forced to work long hours in appalling conditions. The ILO believes responses to trafficking need to address forced labour issues outside of the commercial sex industry.

It's a salient point, and I wish I had spent more time researching trafficking into other industries. I did try to investigate the trafficking of men early on in my research but found very little information, and realised that I'd have to start almost from scratch, which would have taken a long time. The IOM has documented increasing evidence of Eastern European men being trafficked into forced manual labour within the region itself, and also to Israel. The organisation has also reported evidence of Albanians, usually boys, being trafficked to Western Europe for homosexual exploitation. In Italy there are several local organisations, particularly in the north-west, who now support severely exploited male migrants.

But within the context of this book, which has focused on adults being trafficked through south-eastern Europe, Italy and the UK, the vast majority of those being trafficked are women and the majority of them are trafficked into the sex industry.

I've spent just over three years researching and writing this book. Towards the end I contacted some of the people I'd met on the way, sourced recent UNICEF and IOM reports, and tried to assess the current situation in the countries I previously visited.

In Moldova trafficking is still chronic, though UNICEF recently reported that the number of trafficked women returning home is slowly declining. The routes and destinations also seem to be changing, with more women being trafficked to Turkey, the Middle East and directly to EU countries rather than via the western Balkans.

The IOM reports that Moldovan women are still being deported from EU countries, and describe re-trafficking as 'a common phenomenon'. In 2004 there was anecdotal evidence of several 'recruiting centres' in Chisinau, where batches of women were being trained before being trafficked: though there has been no further confirmation of this disturbing report.

More than three quarters of Moldovans still live in relative poverty, and the country is heavily dependent on remittances from migrants working abroad. Steady numbers continue to leave. Moldova has also emerged as a major hub for Asians making the long trek towards Western Europe. Migrants from Afghanistan, Pakistan and China have all been identified at the border. The UN High Commission for Refugees now has a reception centre in Chisinau.

I recently contacted the Moldova IOM, and asked whether they could give me any news of Olga and Anna. The medical officer at the counter-trafficking unit, Viorel Gorceag, kindly said she'd try to find some information for me. A few weeks ago she sent me an email. Olga is living in Chisinau with her son and close family. She is still unable to work because of her near blindness, and receives a small disability allowance. Anna has married a local from her village and they have left Moldova together to work as seasonal migrants in Russia. Her children are being cared for by her mother and she visits them as often as she is able. Viorel knew no more.

In Bosnia, the number of foreign women being trafficked into the country seems to have reduced substantially. But more Bosnian women are now being recruited and coerced into the sex industry, and both local and foreign women are frequently confined in private apartments, where it's harder to identify them. Women who have been identified have consistently reported physical and sexual violence. Because of the increased use of private apartments, the number of bars and nightclubs suspected of trafficking women has plummeted; UNICEF reports that thirty 'venues' are currently under suspicion. But this is a double-edged sword; the women working in these bars and clubs are apparently more resigned to their situation, because they are being better paid by their pimps. Bosnia issues temporary resident permits for trafficked women who do not want to return home; but fewer women are asking for assistance, or refuge or to go home. The IOM has also highlighted that when the International Police Task Force (IPTF) left Bosnia at the beginning of 2003, they did not hand over intelligence or relevant databases to the local Bosnian police. Thousands of vital records of enquiries, investigations and details about trafficked women, and traffickers, were not passed on. This has created an information vacuum that seriously hinders their work.

In December 2004, the NATO-led task force SFOR handed over to the EU Force in Bosnia – EUFOR. There are still around seven thousand troops in Bosnia. Under a bilateral agreement between Bosnia and the United States, a small contingent of US soldiers remains in Tuzla. In November the Mlin bar on the road to Tuzla was finally raided. Six foreign women were taken to a refuge, the bar was closed and the owner, Tasim Kucevic, faced a criminal investigation. I called Mara Radovanovic's office in Bijeljina, to ask her what was happening, and whether the Mlin was closed for good.

It took a few days to get hold of Mara herself; and by that time the Mlin had already reopened under a new name. According to Mara, and reports in the Bosnian newspaper *Nezavisne Novine*, Kucevic was charged with prostitution offences, and sentenced to thirty days' imprisonment, which he served at the end of 2005. The newspaper stated that whilst he was serving this brief sentence, the BiH Prosecutor's Office believes he continued running an illegal prostitution business. In the meantime the Mlin was renamed the Millennium. Mara believes trafficking in Bosnia is ruled by a handful of criminals who no one, including the police and judiciary, has been prepared to take on. She says these men are now targeting Bosnian girls, and she has recently sheltered several girls who were just twelve years old.

'A small group of big criminals is running this business,' she says over a clear, distant phone line. 'We recently had to move our shelter because one gang broke into it. This is why the victims are too frightened to testify and why I sometimes advise them not to.'

Milorad Milakovic may be in prison, but a few criminal kingpins seem to have assumed they can do as they want, and treat the law with contemptuous disregard. However, Kucevic is perhaps not quite as invincible as he thinks. The Bosnian media has reported that he has been rearrested and, alongside a second defendant, Meliha Pjevic, has been indicted on a new series of human trafficking, prostitution, money laundering and tax evasion charges. Eight other defendants are involved, making this one of the biggest trafficking cases ever investigated in Bosnia. The tide may just be starting to turn.

There are also fewer reports of foreign women being trafficked into Albania, or detected en route to Italy or Greece. This is partly because the waters between Albania and southern Italy are now so well policed, and traffickers are known to have altered their routes. Albanian women are still regularly deported home from Western Europe with no assistance at all. A third of the women being currently assisted back in Albania say they have been trafficked more than once.

The IOM reports that 'a significant number' agreed to work in the sex industry before they were initially trafficked. This implies that, as in Kosovo, Bosnia and Moldova, more local women are being recruited and coerced into prostitution because of poverty and lack of other opportunities. UNICEF also reports a growing sex industry within Albania.

Migrant women used to be transited through Albania en route to Italy, and often exploited on the way. Now more local females are involved in the Albanian sex industry. Some are subjected to violence from the outset, others are paid by male and female pimps who know their monetary worth and exactly how much psychological pressure to apply.

The rise in female traffickers has also been recently documented across this region, especially those doing the initial recruiting. In Moldova the majority of recruiters now appear to be women. Many are thought to have been trafficked themselves; the implication being that they secure benefits, status or even their own freedom by ensuring a replacement.

This is one of the control mechanisms used so successfully by Nigerian traffickers in Italy, where victims eventually become recruiters and then pimps, and are deliberately made complicit in coercing other women and girls. It is also the mechanism employed by some Thai women in London. For some women this is the only way they can get out of the industry themselves. Others are coerced into recruiting new women to make their own lives more bearable, and some simply become hardened by what they endure. Several police officers I've spoken to have referred to Stockholm Syndrome, where a hostage exhibits seeming loyalty to their captor in spite of the danger and abuse they have been subjected to. The term was first used to describe the startling reaction of several Swedes who were held hostage during a Stockholm bank robbery, but applies to a situation where a person is isolated, unable to escape and eventually develops an apparent dependence on their abuser. However, though it's tempting to believe all female traffickers have previously been trafficked themselves, as it provides a clear explanation for why one woman would resort to selling another, there is no evidence to support this. Some female traffickers, including several women who have been recently convicted of trafficking offences in Britain, appear to be ruthless businesswomen who trade women simply because it is very lucrative.

There is an ongoing debate amongst organisations in south-eastern Europe about the current trafficking status quo. Data from the last three years shows a general reduction in the number of victims being assisted in the region; but there have been different interpretations about what this actually means. Some organisations, like the IOM, believe traffickers have changed their *modus operandi* and people are being trafficked even more clandestinely, as opposed to there being any real decline in numbers. In its most recent research on trafficking, south-eastern Europe, the organisation states that information from a number of sources 'makes it clear that the actual number of trafficking victims is significantly higher than the number of assisted victims'. IOM researchers are considered to be reliable and well informed.

The organisation also acknowledges that in south-eastern Europe there are barely any programmes for trafficked women who do not want to return home, and that women have sometimes declined assistance for several different reasons. Some women want to remain abroad in order to earn money, others do not necessarily identify themselves as trafficking 'victims' (but maybe as sex workers, domestic workers or simply undocumented migrants); and some are frightened of being seen as collaborators if they are known to have cooperated with the police.

In its most recent report, 'Trafficking in Human Beings in Southeastern Europe' UNICEF makes the point that if trafficking has not reduced in the region, then the anti-trafficking strategies in place have not been particularly effective. Over the last six years there have been a myriad of awareness-raising campaigns featuring leaflets, radio and TV broadcasts, telephone hotlines and billboards. But UNICEF says few of these campaigns have been properly evaluated to see how effective they really are, and what lessons could be learned.

The UNICEF report draws a clear distinction between anti-trafficking campaigns which aim to inform people of the risks involved in migrating, and those which equate migration with trafficking per se. 'Repressive campaigns focused only on the risks and dangers of trafficking and migration should be regarded as anti-migration propaganda rather than anti-trafficking information.'

The report was written by a Polish researcher called Barbara Limanowska, who has studied trafficking trends in the region for a number of years. She highlights the fact that 'Women judged to be victims are refusing the assistance being offered to them,' and says there needs to be a serious examination of anti-trafficking measures in light of this new information. The issue of women turning down assistance is controversial, because it challenges the assumption that most women do want to return home, and that it's in their best interest to do so. Barbara Limanowska also discusses the root causes of trafficking; honing in on violence against women as a major factor, particularly domestic violence. She questions why refuges for battered women are struggling for resources and funding in spite of constant high demand, whilst well-funded shelters for victims of trafficking are now increasingly empty in the western Balkans. Shelters are vital: but so are refuges for battered women, and other local projects that offer sanctuary and space from the violence that can precede trafficking. A local women's organisation I previously visited in Montenegro told me they had assisted fifty-eight trafficked women and girls in the last four years. During the same period they had received more than nine hundred requests for assistance and refuge from local women enduring domestic violence, yet were struggling to fund their domestic violence work.[1]

I met Barbara Limanowska when I briefly returned to Bosnia last autumn. She is a quietly spoken woman, and a well-respected researcher who is not afraid to put her head above the parapet. 'The shelters in the western Balkans are almost empty,' she told me. 'But international donors love to support shelters for trafficking victims even if they are almost empty.' She believes the governments of south-eastern Europe are now showing a stronger political commitment to tackling this issue, and have for instance drafted detailed National Plans of Action to combat trafficking. But she also believes that more needs to be done to address the issues of migrant labour and the human rights of migrant workers. 'After all these years we still do not have human rights-based solutions to the problem of trafficking,' she said. 'We still have immigration-based solutions.'

In Britain, the government also recently drafted a proposed 'UK Action Plan on Trafficking in Human Beings', which outlines how it intends to combat trafficking. The action plan, which is currently at consultation stage, has some sound proposals. The Ministry of Defence has committed itself to zero tolerance of sexual abuse in conflict areas, in line with NATO and UN policies. The Crown Prosecution Service has developed materials to assist prosecutors working on trafficking cases, and witness protection programmes are being extended to protect vulnerable witnesses. The proposal confirms that to date there have been fourteen convictions for human trafficking under the 2003 Sexual Offences Act.

But in spite of the government's dependence on women to testify in order to secure convictions, and its stated determination to 'tackle this terrible crime', its immigration position has not shifted. The government has still not signed the 2004 Council of Europe trafficking convention, which has now been signed by 24 other nations. People trafficked to the UK still have no specific right to remain here, and there is no stated commitment from the government to provide one. The consultation states, 'All cases are dealt with on their individual merits,' that leave to remain may be granted in appropriate cases, and that people from outside the EU have the right to claim asylum.

The Poppy Project and the London-based Refugee Women's Resource Project have recently published an analysis of claims for asylum made by a number of women who were trafficked to the UK and

1. This was the Women's Safe House, Podgorica, Montenegro.

subsequently supported by Poppy. The report concludes that women supported by Poppy are 'six times as likely as any other asylum seeker to succeed at appeal'.[2] It reiterates that the absence of specific legislative measures means the protections afforded by the 1951 Refugee Convention and Human Rights Act are currently the only means by which women can ensure they won't be returned to their country of origin once police proceedings against their traffickers have been completed.

Albania and Moldova are both on the UK government 'safe country list', which means that women from these countries who apply for asylum and have their claims rejected have no automatic right of appeal, and are in most cases expected to leave the UK and lodge any appeal from back home, or a safe 'third country'. The list is drawn up on the basis of a large number of factors, but seems particularly draconian as Albania and Moldova both report high rates of re-trafficking.

We do not know how many women and girls are re-trafficked to the UK. Research into re-trafficking would be extremely useful material for both the government and police, especially if it involved women and girls being asked what *they* want and need in order to be safe.

To date the Poppy Project has received more than 400 referrals from across the UK, and has been able to house 83 women, which is less than 25 per cent of those referred. Many women have stayed at the project for longer than expected because there has been nowhere else for them to go. However, the project has just received confirmation of increased Home Office funding for the next two years, which will enable them to open a new five-bed house and establish an outreach service. The Poppy team say they are 'absolutely delighted'.

A seven-bed refuge for trafficked women in South Yorkshire has been open for several months now, and has also received referrals from across the country. It's worth noting that in the last two years just forty-four trafficked women have been referred to the London IOM for assistance or voluntary repatriation.

In addition to the proposed UK action plan, there have also been recent reforms of the sex industry, with an emphasis on assisting women to exit commercial sex work and amending legislation so that women who remain in the industry can work more safely together. This is in many ways a courageous prostitution strategy. Some people would like to see the government go much further and adopt the 'Swedish Model' approach. In 1999 Sweden became the first country in the world to outlaw men purchasing sexual services, whilst decriminalising the selling

2. 'Hopes Betrayed: an analysis of women victims of trafficking and their claims for asylum', February 2006.

of sex by women. The law garnered fierce responses on both sides. Those in favour apparently include 80 per cent of the Swedish electorate, plus many police and social services who claim prostitution and trafficking have reduced in Sweden as a direct result of the law being changed. Considerable resources were also put in place to assist women to exit the sex industry. Critics include sex workers in Sweden who say they were not consulted about the law and are now far more apprehensive about asking police for assistance. The Norwegian media have reported women being trafficked over the border to Norway, and there have been claims that more Swedish men are now purchasing sex in Norway. The Norwegian government decided not to enact similar legislation.

Paul Holmes believes the Swedish model was, in principle, completely sound. But he thinks sex workers should definitely have been consulted about what they thought beforehand, and that the law itself 'was based on the naïve assumption that any pimp would take a cut in earnings because there are less punters around. These pimps in Sweden are actually working the women harder now, to make damn sure they keep the money rolling in,' he told me. 'You've got more women being advertised on the Internet in Sweden, and the sex industry has been driven under-ground, where the most vunerable women are even harder to reach. You could apply the Swedish law in Britain, and really make it work: but not without bringing all sides on board beforehand.'

As the debate on how best to regulate the UK sex industry, and protect the women within it, rages on, the British police recently launched their own nationwide anti-trafficking campaign, Operation Pentameter. Funded by Reflex, this rolling campaign aims to assess the scale of the illegal sex industry, and the number of females being trafficked into it. The police are attempting to detect women and girls at UK borders, as well as inside brothels, and offer them information, assistance and protection. The original idea for Pentameter came from former NCIS Deputy Director, Nick Kinsella. 'This is the first nationwide police operation of its kind,' he explained to me. 'In terms of identifying people who've been trafficked in the UK, the vice industry is a very good place to start. Our emphasis is on rescuing victims from the sex trade.'

Front-line officers have been given training materials on trafficking, and women and girls are not being taken to police stations for question-ing, but being escorted to 'reception centres', and offered assistance if they want it. Every police force has been briefed on 'victim care issues'. The police have also honed in on the responsibility of punters to ensure the women they are paying for sex are willing to be having sex with them. Grahame Maxwell, who is Pentameter's programme director, was quoted in the *Guardian*: 'Trafficked women are being forced to work through fear and intimidation. Men who act as their clients risk being charged with rape.'[3] A media campaign is scheduled to highlight this issue, and challenge the male demand for young female sex workers that has fuelled trafficking across Europe and into the UK. If the campaign has real teeth, and violent punters are actually penalised, it could make a vital difference.

These changes under Operation Pentameter represent a tangible shift in attitudes towards trafficking: combining pragmatism with compassion and justice. A number of women, and several girls, have already been given refuge, suspected traffickers and pimps have been arrrested, and the numbers look set to increase. But the police's stated emphasis on 'rescuing victims' doesn't address the issue of giving trafficked migrants legal rights. Although immigration officers are not apparently accompanying the police during brothel raids, they are very much part of Operation Pentameter – and a number of illegal migrant sex workers have already been identified, and swiftly removed from the UK.

The police claim thay have to comply with immigration officers, and that their hands are effectively tied. But these removals give massive credence to claims that migrant sex workers are 'soft' immigration targets, and are used to boost official removal figures. The recent, breathtaking scale of chaos and incompetence at the Home Office has left convicted criminals who should have been considered for deportation free to roam the country, whilst migrant sex workers are still being arrested, shunted onto aeroplanes, and removed from the UK as fast as possible.

No one knows for sure whether any of these women were in fact trafficked but too frightened to speak out.

'You could argue that, by removing women, we're actually doing the punters a favour,' one police officer told me quietly. 'We remove them, and the traffickers bring the fresh meat straight in.'

Immigration-based solutions to human trafficking do not confront the reasons people are trafficked in the first place. We've used an immigration-based response to trafficking in the UK for the last ten years, and it has clearly not worked. The government has acknowledged that trafficking and severe exploitation extend well beyond the sex industry in this country, and we could start examining migration-based solutions; how legal avenues to migration could be extended, clearly regulated, and how we could match national skill and labour shortages. Our health services, hospitality industry, construction, food processing,

3. *Guardian*, 25 April 2006.

agriculture and service industries are all increasingly dependent on migrant labour. Last year the GMB Union passed a resolution calling for 'employers who seek to circumvent their obligations by hiring contractors to be made jointly and severally liable for the conduct of the contractor', which would be one practical step forward, though activists and some human rights lawyers have called for far more radical reforms to ensure migrant workers are protected from unscrupulous employers. There are at least 450,000 undocumented migrants living in the UK, and they are not going to leave in the short term, or be removed. Most of them are not criminals and the vast majority want to work and contribute. We can ignore them, neglect them, or continue the tentative debate about how to live alongside them.

If human trafficking becomes a police performance indicator (which many of the police I've spoken to think it should) then the police should be able to sustain long-term operations against traffickers, pimps and punters. The Serious Organised Crime Agency (SOCA) will undoubtedly have a major capacity to gather intelligence, and initiate asset seizures, and may also be able to move the emphasis from women having to testify against their traffickers in court. With dedicated teams of human trafficking investigators, SOCA could also make inroads into the numerous small groups trafficking women and girls into the UK, and dispersing them around the country. Some of the monies and assets seized by SOCA financial investigators could be used to extend services for people who have been trafficked, and to compensate the women and girls who earned the money in the first place.

When trafficking is being debated and national policies and laws being drafted, it is sometimes easy to forget that it is people who are being legislated for and against. The 'victims' of trafficking are individuals with aspirations and desires, who usually make active decisions to migrate in order to work and improve their own lives. They are often angry about what has happened to them, and want justice. Anti-Slavery International, which is the world's oldest human rights organisation, has campaigned for years for the introduction of binding legal standards to protect those who have been trafficked. The organisation warns against regarding trafficked people only as 'victims' who need 'rescuing' by the authorities, and emphasises that 'trafficked persons do not always behave in the way in which officials would like them to, but this should not affect their ability to exercise their basic rights'.

The pressure on the British Government to sign the Council of Europe Convention on Action Against Trafficking in Human Beings is intense, and signature looks imminent. Signing this convention will not stop people being trafficked into this country. There is still a long way to go to combat human trafficking, particularly in terms of gathering intelligence on, and building profiles of, the traffickers themselves. Far less is known about traffickers than the people they traffic.

There is also the very real issue of ensuring that, alongside services supporting migrant sex workers and trafficked women and girls, UK sex workers are also supported to work either as safely as possible, or to exit and stay out of sex work, once they have made that choice for themselves. UK sex workers are some of the most marginalised constituents in our country.

But signing the Council of Europe Convention will evoke real change: it will provide physical and legal sanctuary for people who are being trafficked into Britain: it will undermine the ability of traffickers to re-traffick women and girls into sex work – and control other severely exploited migrants – and it will give 'victims' human rights: the kind of rights that give a person some control over their own life once more. In other words, this will also be a good place to start.

Sources of Information

Trafficking of Women for Sexual Exploitation: IOM Moldova, 2002.

Trafficking in Human Beings in South-eastern Europe: UNICEF, 2002.

Trafficking in Human Beings in South-eastern Europe: UNICEF, March 2005.

End Child Exploitation: UNICEF report, July 2003.

'Does That Mean I Have Rights?': Amnesty International report on women and girls trafficked for forced prostitution in Kosovo, May 2004.

'Hopes Betrayed': Trafficking of women and girls to post-conflict Bosnia & Herzegovina for forced prostitution: Human Rights Watch, November 2002.

The Natashas: the New Global Sex Trade: Victor Malarek, Vision Paperbacks, 2004.

Safe for Whom? Women's human rights abuses and protection in 'safe list' countries: Asylumaid, June 2004.

Child Trafficking in Albania: a report by Daniel Renton for Save the Children, 2001.

Human Traffic Human Rights: Elaine Pearson, Anti-Slavery International, 2002.

International Peace Research Institute, Oslo.

Stopping Traffic: Liz Kelly & Linda Regan, Police Research Series Paper 125, May 2000.

Sex in the City: Sandra Dickson, the Poppy Project, July 2004.

Prosecuting Human Traffickers: Recommendations for Good Practice: Alice Peycke, the Poppy Project, October 2004. This report was never externally published.

Evaluation of the Victims of Trafficking Pilot Project: Gina Taylor, Home Office Research, Development and Statistics (RDS), September 2005.

National Criminal Intelligence Service (NCIS) UK Threat Assessment 2004/5, 2005/6.

'Forced Labour and Migration to the UK': Bridget Anderson and Ben Rogaly, February 2005.

UN Department of Peacekeeping Operations (UN DPKO) Policy paper, March 2004.

A Global Alliance Against Forced Labour: International Labour Office (ILO), 2005.

Consultation on a proposed UK Action Plan on Trafficking in Human Beings: Home Office & Scottish Executive, January 2006.

Hopes Betrayed: an analysis of women victims of trafficking and their claims for asylum: the Poppy Project & the Asylum Aid Refugee Women's Resource Project, February 2006.

The following organisations can be contacted for advice, information or donations:

The Poppy Project
Eaves Housing for Women
1-3 Brixton Road
London SW9 6DE
tel: 0207 735 2062

Kalayaan: Justice for Migrant Domestic Workers
St Francis Centre
Pottery Lane
London W11 4NQ
tel: 0207 243 2942

Useful to Albanian Women
Naim Frasheri no. 8
Tirana
Albania
Tel/fax +355 42 223001/247 502
email: uaw@icc-al.org

Acknowledgements

I have many people to thank for their advice, assistance, information, stories and generosity.

Thank you to Olga and 'Anna', for agreeing to speak to me in Moldova: to 'Bright' for talking me through your story in Sicily; thank you Annette, for meeting with me in London, and to Mr He, and to Lan, for being so honest about how and why you both came to Britain.

My thanks to Julie Bindel, for inviting me to the 'trafficking in the Balkans' workshop at the beginning of my research; to 'Maggie' Kelmendi for inviting me to Kosovo, and to her family for their welcome; to Igo Rogova in Pristina for her encouragement, and her Gauloises; to Jill Norwood and Robert Bruce of THB Section, Tihana Leko of UNMIK, and Tomara at the IOM for guiding me to Moldova.

Thank you to everyone at the Moldova IOM, especially Doru, Liuba, Liliana Gorceag, Natasha and Natalia. Thanks also to Liliana Sorrentino, and especially to Viorel Gorceag, for poignant news from Moldova.

In Bosnia, Madeleine Rees and Mara Radovanovic were both stellar with their information and assistance, whilst Barbara Limanowska offered a radical critique of trafficking. Thanks to Ferida Durakovic, to Jonathan Ratel; and to Fadila Hadzic at La Strada in Mostar, for sharing her story of meeting Olena Popik.

Thank you to all the 'Useful to Albania' women in Tirana, especially Sevim Arbana, for arranging my visit to Burrell – and Fabiola for getting me on the boat in Durres! Thank you to Klodi and Revena, for taking me under your wings; to Natasha and her daughter, Albina, in Burrell; and to Julie Vullnetari and her family in Cangonj, near Korca, who were fantastically hospitable.

Carla Corso and Hermine Gbedo talked me through Article 18 in Italy. Terese Albano offered valuable insights. My friend Alessia and her family revived me in Vicenza. Thank you, Franco, for taking us on to the streets with you. And thank you, Vivian Wiwoloku, for all your help in Palermo. The good sisters of Buon Pastore convent, and the young women staying there, were both a fierce inspiration. These research trips were supported by generous grants from The Scottish Arts Council and the Society of Authors K Blundell Trust.

In Britain I've had a huge amount of help with my research: Gemma Thompson agreed to be my temporary researcher and was invaluable. Jay Bevan and Guy Taylor talked me through trials and error; Steve Kupis, Nick Kinsella, Neil Brown,

Chris Bradford, Julia Roberts and Gary Young each offered information and clarification. Thank you to Lawrie Day and Shawn Galloway for aiding and abetting me; and to Peter Clark at the Chinatown Unit.

Special thanks to Paul Holmes for responding to persistent questions with humour and candour, Sian Jones at AI for her encouragement; to Louise Hinchcliffe at the Poppy Project for her graciousness, to Sarah Mendelson, Lisa Kurbiel, Bobby Chang, and to Jabez Lam, for his generosity of heart.

Jane Ayers, Tina Threadgold, Hilary Kinnell and Ying Zhang all offered vital insights into the UK sex industry. Natalia Dawkins talked me through the Poppy Project, Mel Steel of Asylum Aid offered clarification on immigration law. Thanks to Debbie Ariyo at Afruca, Bridget Anderson at Compas, Rita Gava at Kalayaan, Mike Kaye and Klara Skrivankova at Anti-Slavery International, Richard Danziger at the Geneva IOM and Alex Sklan at the Medical Foundation.

I also want to thank Niki Adams at the English Collective of Prostitutes and Cristel Amiss at the Black Women's Rape Action Project.

Thank you to Alan Samson for his faith in this book, and absolute patience with it, to Lucinda McNeile for her astute editorial comments, and to David Grossman for being an insightful and supportive literary agent.

Love and thanks to my friends Kate Balfour, Tam, Dylan, Jo Hodges, Kyna, Mike Stewart, Gica, Carmella Rose, Ali, Trish, Alma, Brian and Catherine, Nick Thorpe, Rahul and Bev, Sonia, Tina, Pat Rogers, Katie, Bertie and family, Derek Wheeler, Tuesday, Sue B, Alice Francis, Siri, Liz Law. To Lynn, for coming to Bosnia, and being my ally through the wilderness months; to Rob Gilliat for reading the best and worst of it all; to Debbie for truth and laughter; to Adam for being your wonderful self.

Thank you, Mark Richelieu, for being my port throughout my storms.

To Ma, and to Ami and precious little Clive.

To you, A M, because we walked through fire.

And to Geraint, for being special, being there when I was truly burnt, and showing me the lights. x

Index

Adams, Nikki 142, 143
Adriatic Sea 96–97
Adriatic Straits 37–38
Africa 145–147, 148 *see also entries for individual countries*
African care workers 192
African immigrants to Europe 115, 116
African prostitutes 100–101, 102, 105–106, 108, 109 *see also* African trafficked women; Nigerian trafficked women
African sex workers in London 132
African trafficked women 145–147, 148, 150 *see also* African prostitutes; Nigerian trafficked women
AFRUCA (Africans Unite Against Child Abuse) 149–150
AIDS 62, 63, 66, 67
Al-Hussein, Prince Zeid Ra'ad Zeid 225, 226–227, 229
Albania 37–38, 69, 70–83, 84–93, 94–97
  and British press 69
  crossing to Italy from 95, 96–98
  Devoll region 78, 79, 80–81, 82
  human trafficking from 71–72, 73, 74, 75, 79–83
  increase in sex industry recruitment 236
  International Organisation for Migration (IOM) branch 82

IOM funds reintegration centre for women 75
migration from 79
reduction in foreign women being trafficked 235
Save the Children report on child trafficking in 74
on UK government 'safe country list' 239
Albanian authorities, Chinese migrants apprehended by 82–83
Albanian boys 233
Albanian Communist Party 70
Albanian criminals 69, 71, 72
Albanian Mafia 71, 81, 228
Albanians 36–37, 38, 69, 71, 175, 183
  going to England 89
  jobs and income 78–79
Albina (Natasha's daughter in Burrell) 85, 86, 87–88, 89, 92, 94, 95
Aldon (Albanian boy) 88, 91–92, 94
  mother 91, 92, 93, 221
Alessia (Italian friend) 104, 105–110, 111
Alexandru (Anna's husband) 30–31
Alma (Albanian in Burrell) 88, 89, 90–91
  brother 88–90
Alma (Albanian in Scotland) 70
Amnesty International 44, 69–70, 213, 214, 227

'Does That Mean I Have Rights'
    report 204–205, 210, 213, 217, 224
Anderson, Bridget 190–193
Andrews, Bronagh 138
Angela (sex worker) 109, 110
Anna (Moldovan woman) 30–38,
    39–40, 63, 69, 84, 217, 234
    sold 32–34
    works in bars 33–35
    escapes then returns to Uri 35, 36
    abducted and sold to Albanian 36–37
    tries to cross Adriatic Straits to Italy
        37–38
    forced to work in brothel 38
Annan, Kofi 211, 225, 226
Annette (Crossroads volunteer) 144,
    145–147, 150–152, 153, 174, 225
    arrested 151–152
Anti-Slavery International 4, 8, 122,
    242
Arbana, Sevim 72–75, 82, 84, 85, 88,
    96
Ariyo, Debbie 149–150
Arjan (Albanian youth) 85–86, 87, 91
Article 18: 101–102
Ashford, Bronzefield Women's Prison
    152, 153
Asylum and Immigration (Treatment
    of Claimants, etc.) Act (2004) 151,
    192
Augustina (Romanian girl) 157–159,
    160–161, 162–163, 165, 172
Australian back-packers 132
Axhami, Tasim 181
Ayers, Jane 131, 132–134, 135–136,
    137, 138

Balkans 2, 3, 4, 183, 198, 228, 231 see
    also entries for individual countries
    reports on human trafficking in 42
Bangladesh 230
Banja Luka Prison 57
Barjami, Ilir 180
Bassano del Grappa, Italy 104

BBC 139, 154, 213
BBC TV 202
Belgrade 53, 57
Bell, Bethany 27
Benin City, Nigeria 119–120
    Women's Health and Action
        Research Centre 120
Beqirat, Emiljan 181
Bermond, Major Valerie-Claire 214,
    223
Bevan, Detective Inspector Jay 163,
    164, 165, 166, 168
Bijeljina, Bosnia 51, 52–61, 63, 235
    Lara refuge 56, 60, 61, 235
    Motel Neno 60–61
Birmingham, 'Cuddles' massage
    parlour 212–213
Blake, William 127
Bolkovac, Kathy 45–46, 47
Booth, Darren 180
Bosnia and Herzegovina (BiH) 33, 47,
    215, 228
    Arizona Market 48
    EU Force in (EUFOR) 234
    European Union Police Mission 57,
        215–216
    increase in sex industry recruitment
        234
    International Police Task Force
        (IPTF) in 44–46, 49
    mass rape in camps 231
    Prosecutor's Office 235
    reduction in foreign women being
        trafficked 234
    since the civil war 63
    trafficking of women through 52–53,
        58–59
    trafficking of women to 42, 43, 44,
        48
    troops still in 234
    United Nations Mission in
        (UNMIBH) 43, 44, 45, 46
Bosnian Bar Owners' Association 55
Bosnian TV 56, 67

boys, trafficking in 233
Brazilian sex workers in London 132
Brazzaville, Congo-Brazzaville
    145–146
Bright (Sicilian sex worker) 118–121,
    122–125
Brighton 69–70, 78
Britain *see also* United Kingdom
  agricultural industry 90
  children, unaccompanied, arriving in
      147–150
  Chinese residents 188–189
  construction industry 192
  harm-reduction programmes 141
  human trafficking into 155–156,
      157–159, 161–162, 172–174, 175
  campaign against 179–185 *see also*
      Charing Cross Clubs and Vice;
      Holmes, Paul
  human trafficking offence 126
  migrant workers in 90, 189–190,
      193–194, 241–242
  migrants coming to 89, 90
  sex industry in *see* British sex industry
  South-East Asians smuggled into
      198
  'temporary admission' to 174, 175
  trafficked women in 128, 129–130,
      133–135
British American Security Information
    Council (BASIC) 224
British Army lieutenant 213
British Government, immigration
    position 238, 241
British Nationality Act (1981) 166–167
British sex industry 126–143, 144–153,
    156–157 *see also* Charing Cross
    Clubs and Vice; Crossroads
    Women's Centre; Glasgow, sex
    industry; London, sex industry
  anal sex 133
  exit-strategy 141
  research on men paying for sex
      138–139

women killed 140
workers, number of 139–140
Bromley, Kent 170
Bromley Magistrates' Court 152
Bronzefield Women's Prison, Ashford
    152, 153
brothel timesheets 178
Brown, Neil 182
Bruce, Robert Gordon 223–224
Bucharest 12–13
Burrell, Albania 84, 85–93, 94, 95,
    221
  children's centre 85, 86, 88, 94
  grandfather in 87

Cangonj, Albania 78–80, 82, 84, 86
cards, sex workers' 132–133, 141
Carl (UN civilian police officer) 5
Catania, Sicily 124, 125
Catholic Sisters of the Good Shepherd
    116–119
Celje, Slovenia 66
Centre for Strategic and International
    Studies 227–228
Charing Cross Clubs and Vice (CO14)
    128, 168–172, 183
  China Unit 198
  Financial Investigation Unit 168,
      177, 178
  Operation Kontiki 169–171
  Street Offences and Juvenile
      Protection Unit 170
  Vice Unit 169, 171, 172, 240
    officer 171–172
    reception centre 240
children, unaccompanied, arriving in
    Britain 147–150
China, Fujian province 186, 187, 188,
    189, 190, 194, 195, 198, 200, 202
China, human trafficking and
    smuggling from 186–188, 189,
    190, 194–197, 198–199
China, 'one child' policy 187–188
Chinese factory workers 192

Chinese migrants
  apprehended by Albanian authorities
    82–83
  found dead in lorry at Dover 187,
    188, 189, 190, 202
  travelling through Italy 198
Chinese nurses 192
Chinese residents in Britain 188–189
Chinese teenagers and disappearance
  197
Chinese triads 128, 135, 183, 198
Chisinau, Moldova 11–17, 18, 25,
  26–30, 32, 64, 233, 234
  airport incident 29
  apartment 25, 28
  'Beverley Hills' suburb 27–28
  Central Market 16
  Green Hills Café 11, 26, 28
  International Organisation for
    Migration shelter 14, 25, 26, 28,
    38
  Russian restaurant 28–30
Christian (Alessia's friend) 104
Ciorescu, Moldova 30, 39
Clark, PC Peter 198
Climbié, Victoria 149
Cockburn, Andrew 56
cockle pickers 187, 189, 190, 192
Colnbrook Removal Centre 171
Comitato per i Diritti Civili delle
  Prostitute (Committee for the Civil
  Rights of Prostitutes) 95, 99–101,
  102–103
  Stella Polare ('Northern Star')
    project 102, 103
Congo, Democratic Republic of
  (DRC) 146, 224, 225, 231
Congo-Brazzaville 145–146
construction industry, British 192
Convention on Action Against
  Trafficking in Human Beings
  175–176
Corbajram, Artur see Plakici, Luan
Cornwall, daffodil farm 90

Corso, Carla 99–101, 102–103, 104,
  107, 119
Cosa Nostra 71
Council of Europe 175
  trafficking convention (2004) 238
Court of Appeal 163
Criminal Justice Protection Unit 160
Cristel (Crossroads volunteer)
  144–145, 151, 152, 153
Croatia 97
Crossroads Women's Centre 143, 144,
  151, 152 see also English Collective
  of Prostitutes
Crown Prosecution Service 151, 163,
  164, 182, 238
Croydon, Lunar House Immigration
  and Nationality Directorate 151,
  154, 155, 156, 175
Customs and Excise, HM 90
Cyprus, fax from businessman in
  40–41

daffodil farms, Cornish 90
Danube, River 19
Dawkins, Natalia 129, 130
Day, Lawrie 178
Dayton Peace Agreement 44
Dehin (Maggie's friend) 218, 219–220,
  221, 222, 223
Devoll region, Albania 78, 79, 80–81,
  82
di Lecce, Signora Franca 111
Dickson, Sandra 131
Dimitri (Anna's son) 31–32
Doboj Hospital 56
'Does That Mean I Have Rights'
  report 204–205, 210, 213, 217,
  224
Doru (IOM employee) 11–12, 13, 14,
  15, 25, 30
Dover, Chinese migrants found dead
  in lorry 187, 188, 189, 190, 202
Dragona (Romanian girl) 160, 162
Durakovic, Ferida 231

Durres, Albania 95, 96, 97, 220
  ferry to Trieste 95, 96–98
DVDs, counterfeit 198
Dyncorp 45–46

East European factory workers 192
Eaves (women's housing association)
  129–131
ECPAT (End Child Trafficking,
  Pornography and Prostitution) 149
Edinburgh 40, 63, 69, 104, 106
  working as mental health outreach
  worker in 42
Eide, Kai 229
'Elena' (Lithuanian girl) 180–181
Elswick Lodge 197
'End Child Exploitation' report 150
English Collective of Prostitutes
  142–143 see also Crossroads
  Women's Centre
Erika (Izabela's friend) 157, 159–160
EU Force in Bosnia (EUFOR) 234
European Union, May 2004 expansion
  192
European Union Police Mission 57,
  215–216
Eurostar train 199
'Evaluation of the Victims of
  Trafficking Pilot Project' 175

Fabiola ('Useful Women' worker) 95,
  96
facilitators 3–4
Ferizye, Kosovo 23
Fier, Albania 81
'Forced Labour and Migration to the
  UK' report 190–193
Foreign and Commonwealth Office
  (FCO) 206
Franco (Papa Giovanni volunteer)
  105–110, 114
French KFOR soldiers 223
French UN liaison member 214–215,
  216

French UNPROFOR soldier 231

'Galahad' (online pseudonym) 139
Galic, Milan 215
Galloway, Shaun 178
Gatwick Airport, Costa Coffee outlet
  181
George (Cypriot businessman) 40–41
German KFOR troops 217
girls as spoils of war 231
Glasgow
  Base 75 healthcare service 138, 141,
  142
  sex industry 137–138, 141, 142
  sexual health clinic 138
Glasgow City Council policy on sex
  industry 137–138
GMB Union 241
Goldsmith, Lord 163
Golic, Djenan 215–216
Gorceag, Liliana 15, 16, 22, 23, 24, 25,
  63–64
Gorceag, Viorel 234
Gostivar, Macedonia 33–34, 36, 217
Greece 75, 78, 90
Greek migrants to England 90
Gregu, Elidon 180
Guardian 132, 148, 191, 240–241
Guehenno, Jean-Marie 229

Hadzic, Fadila 65–67, 68
Hague Tribunal 231
harm-reduction programmes in
  Britain 141
Harmondsworth Holding Centre
  171
Harrison, David 217
He, Ming 188, 202
He, Mr 186–187, 188, 189, 190, 195,
  202–203
He Yun Jin 197
Hermine (translator) 99, 103
Holmes, Paul 172–174, 175, 176–177,
  178–179, 182, 198, 232, 240

Home Office 129, 147, 151, 153, 166, 174, 239, 241
  Worker Registration Scheme 134–135
Hong Kong 189
'Hopes Betrayed' report 44, 47, 55
Hounslow, Middlesex 170
Hoxha, Enver 70
Hsaio-Hung Pai 191
Human Rights Act (1951) 239
Human Rights Act (1998) 202
Human Rights Watch 44, 45
  'Hopes Betrayed' report 44, 47, 55
human trafficking *see also* trafficked girls/women; traffickers
  into Britain 155–156, 157–159, 161–162, 172–174, 175
  campaign against 179–185 *see also* Charing Cross Clubs and Vice; Holmes, Paul
  from China 186–188, 189, 190, 194–197, 198–199
  as fastest growing form of organised crime 177, 178
  global scale of 232–233
  into Kosovo 216
  offence in Britain 126
  as police performance indicator 179, 242
  research into 76
  in Scotland 138
  and smuggling, difference between 190
  to Turkey 29
Humberside police 183–184

IFOR (Implementation Force) 43
Ilir (Albanian in Burrell) 87
Immigration Act (1971) 174
Immigration and Nationality Directorate, Lunar House, Croydon 151, 154, 155, 156, 175
Immigration Law Practitioners Association (ILPA) 193

Imotski, Croatia 66
Independent 90
India 230
Ingram, Paul 224
Institute of War and Peace Reporting (IWPR) 231
Interception of Communications Act (1985) 182
interim security facility (ISF) 212
International Labour Office (ILO) 232, 233
International Labour Organisation (ILO) 190–191
International Organisation for Migration (IOM) 9, 11, 24, 29, 31, 38, 39, 42, 81, 211, 233, 234, 235
  Albania 82
  Chisinau shelter 14, 25, 26, 28, 38
  funds Albanian reintegration centre for women 75
  London 239
  Moldova 14–15, 69, 234
  research on trafficking, South-eastern Europe 236–237
  Tirana 75–76, 82, 198–199
  'Trafficking of Women for Sexual Exploitation' report 13, 228–229
  Voluntary Assisted Return and Reintegration Programme 136
International Peace Research Institute 123
International Police Task Force (IPTF) 44–46, 49, 55, 234
Interpol 38, 84
Iris (translator) 188, 195, 199
IS91 papers 171
Islami, Mrs 154
Italian Carabinieri 38
Italian Mafia 71, 228
Italy 17, 27, 32, 37, 38, 39, 73, 84, 89, 98–103, 104–110, 111, 120–121, 158, 174, 206

Chinese migrants travelling through 198
Church in 102
crossing from Albania to 95, 96–98
immigration law, Article 18: 101–102
Interior Ministry 124
Moldovan Embassy 27
Nigerian traffickers in 236
organisations supporting exploited male migrants 233
prostitution in 99–103, 104, 105–110
sex industry in 126
Izabela (Moldovan girl) 155, 156–157, 158–160, 161

Jabez Lam 188–189, 190, 194, 197, 198, 201
Jeal, Simon 182
John Paul II, Pope 111
Jones, Sian 69–70

Kalayan organisation 193, 194
Kanun, law of 71
Kelly, Liz 128
Kelmendi, Mabbule (Maggie) 1, 2, 4–5, 8, 164, 172, 206–207
father 1
visit to Prizren 217–221, 222, 223
Kenar (rapist) 155
Kenya 146–147
Keung (Chinese migrant) 194, 195–196, 197, 199–200, 201–202
KFOR (Kosovo Force) 6, 8, 9, 20, 204, 205, 213, 214
immunity from prosecution 213
personnel 217, 223
troops 223–224
Khan, Rashidoon 230–231
kidneys, sale of 27, 118
Kiev 25
Kinnell, Hilary 139–140
Kizlaite, Vilma 181
Koluder, Monja 215–216
Kolya (Olga's son) 16, 22, 23, 25

Korca, Albania 77, 82, 84
Kosova Women's Network 8
Kosovo 1–2, 5–10, 20, 21–23, 43, 76, 86, 92, 118, 204, 205, 206–212, 213, 214–222, 223–224
bars and nightclubs off limits to UN personnel 6–7
human trafficking into 216
Power Station A/B 1
prostitution in 208–210, 211
trafficking of women 6, 7–8, 9, 53–54
United Nations Mission in see UNMIK
Kosovo Police Service 24
Kotesti, Moldova 27
Kreso, Edin 215
Kuala Lumpur 186
Kucevic, Tasim 234–235
Kukes, Albania 221
Kurbiel, Lisa 230

La Strada (international women's organisation) 65, 68
Laducer, Dennis 46
Lake Ohrid 77
Lam, Jabez 188–189, 190, 194, 197, 198, 201
Lampedusa 115
Lan (Chinese migrant) 194–195, 196–197, 199–202
arrives in Britain 199–200
Lara (Bosnian women's organisation) 50–51, 52, 58, 60
refuge 56, 60, 61, 235
Lasha Valley, Bosnia: Kiss bar 49
Latham, Lord Justice 163
Lawrence, Felicity 191
Lazaros, Antos 40–41
Leeds 187
Leko, Tihana 211–212, 213
Li, Mr 202
Libya 115
Limanowska, Barbara 237, 238
Lin Xiu King 197

Lina (Maka's girlfriend) 180, 181
Lithuania 180, 181
Lithuanian women 180, 181
Liuba (IOM employee) 14, 15
Liverpool 27, 187
Loconte, Angelo 71
Lonci (Romanian man) 157–158
London 150, 164, 187
    African sex workers in 132
    Berwick Street and Market 127
    Brazilian sex workers in 132
    Central London Law Centre 188,
        194, 202
    Charing Cross Clubs and Vice Unit
        (CO14) see Charing Cross Clubs
        and Vice Unit
    Charing Cross Police Station
        167–168
    Charing Cross Road area 196
    Chinatown 200
    Dean Street 127
    Eaves women's refuge 129
    Golders Green, Middleton Road
        155, 158–159, 160
    Greek Embassy representative 90
    Hackney 194, 196, 200, 201
    Heathrow Airport 90, 147, 148, 149,
        150, 171, 180, 186
    Homerton Hospital 196, 199
    human trafficking training course 2,
        3, 4, 172–173
    'Demand for Trafficked Women by
        Peacekeepers in the Balkans' paper
        4
    Imperial College 139
    International Organisation for
        Migration in 239
    Kennington, Eaves Housing HQ 129
    Kentish Town 144
        Crossroads Women's Centre see
            Crossroads Women's Centre
    Lambeth sex workers project 141
    Metropolitan Police, proposed
        human-trafficking unit 184–185

North Finchley Road 159
    Palmer's Green 155, 158
    sex industry 126–128, 131–136, 141,
        147, 165
    Soho 126–128, 133, 183
        flats, walk-up 127–128
    South Bank 164
    Thai sex workers in 132, 135–136,
        236
    Waterloo International Station
        149–150, 199
London Metropolitan University 128
Lubizhde, Kosovo 20
    Palm Tree bar 20–22, 24
Lunar House Immigration and
    Nationality Directorate, Croydon
    151, 154, 155, 156, 175
Lydia (Moldovan) 18, 19, 21

Macedonia 33–35, 75, 217
Mafia
    Albanian 71, 81, 228
    Italian 71, 228
    Moldovan 28
    Sicilian 116
Maggie see Kelmendi, Mabbule
maids 127, 169, 170
Maka, Shaban 180
Makler 12, 13–14, 16, 32
Malaysians 198
Manchester, sex industry 136
Manchester Action on Street Health
    (MASH) 136, 141
Manchester City Council policy on sex
    industry 137
Mandela, Chrisovalandou 90
Manuel (Albanian boy) 85–86, 87, 91
Mara (Moldovan girl) 155, 156–157,
    158, 160
Maria Rita, Sister 116–117, 118
Marjolein (Dutch woman in Sicily)
    112
Marshall, Denise 129, 130
Marx, Karl 127

massage parlours, women offered for work in 137
Max (pimp) 156
Maxwell, Grahame 240–241
MC* (artist) 207
meetings, Rule of Law 50
men, trafficking in 233
Mendelson, Sarah 227–228, 229–230, 231
Merdinaj, Taulant 180
Metropolitan Police, proposed human-trafficking unit 184–185
Middlesbrough prison 166
migrant workers in Britain 90, 189–190, 193–194, 241–242
migration, reasons for 90
Mila (THBS coordinator) 209, 210
Milakovic, Milka 55, 56, 57–58
Milakovic, Milorad 49, 54–56, 235
  trial 57, 58
  video tapes 58
Milakovic, Sasa 55, 56, 57–58
Milakovic, Slavisa 55, 56, 57–58
Millennium bar, near Tuzla (formerly Mlin bar) 58, 62, 234, 235
Milosevic, Slobodan 71
Min Quan organisation 188–189
Ming He 188, 202
Ministry of Defence 238
Minjir, Moldova 27
Mirage Travel Agency 12
Mitrovica, Kosovo 223
Mlin bar, near Tuzla (later Millennium bar) 58, 62, 234, 235
Moldova 9, 10, 11–17, 19, 26–27, 228, 233–234
  human trafficking as one of biggest national industries 12–16, 18
  Interior Ministry 29
  International Organisation for Migration in 14–15, 69, 234
  'Moral Police Squad' 14
  orphanages 28
  prostitution 28

recruiters, female 236
on UK government 'safe country list' 239
Moldovan Embassy in Italy 27
Moldovan Embassy in Tel Aviv 157
Moldovan Institute for the Blind 25
Moldovan Mafia 28
Moldovan women 53, 209, 211, 233
Monk, Richard 46
Montenegro 19, 237–238
Moravia Foundation 82
Morecambe Bay 187, 189, 190, 192
Mostar, Bosnia 62, 64–68, 215
  Buybook bookshop 64–65
  La Strada organisation office 65, 68
  Stari Most Bridge 64, 65

Nadia (Moldovan) 24
Nairobi 147
Namibia 224
Natalia (IOM employee) 14–15, 28–29, 38–39
Natasha (Albanian in Burrell) 84, 85, 86, 87–88, 91–93, 94, 221
Natasha (translator) 15, 23, 25, 26–27, 30, 39–40
National Criminal Intelligence Service (NCIS) 137, 184
  Threat Assessment 182–183, 184
National Geographic 56
National Register of Unaccompanied Children 149
NATO (North Atlantic Treaty Organisation) 213, 224, 229 see also KFOR
  IFOR (Implementation Force) 43
  peacekeepers 231
  Resolution 323 on Trafficking in Human Beings 213–214
  SFOR (Stabilisation Force) 43, 56, 57, 58, 234
  zero-tolerance policy for personnel engaged in human trafficking 214

Neretva river 64, 65
Newcastle airport 197
Nezavisne Novine 235
Nicoletta (Romanian woman) 160, 162
Nicoll (Moldovan) 40–41
Nigeria 119–120, 121
 Edo State 120
Nigerian trafficked girls/women 112,
 113–114, 118–124, 148 *see also*
 Annette
 life of 120–124
Nigerian traffickers 114, 116,
 119–120, 124, 236
Norway 240
Norwood, Jill 207–209, 210, 211, 223
nuns, Italian 116, 119
nurses entering UK 192

Obasanjo regime 115
Obilic, Kosovo 1–2, 206, 223
Olga (Moldovan woman) 40, 47,
 63–64, 69, 205, 234
 appearance 15
 arrives in Kosovo 20
 escapes from bar 24–25
 eyesight problems 25
 first meeting with 15–17
 parents 15–16
 sold 17, 18–20
 works in Kosovan bars 20–24
Operation Kontiki 169–171
Operation Maxim 164
Operation Newbridge 148
Operation Pentameter 240–241, 242
Operation Return 180

Pai, Hsaio-Hung 191
Pakistan 230
Paladin Team 149
Palermo, Sicily 111–121, 122
 Buon Pastore (Good Shepherd)
 convent 116–119, 124
 Noce district 112
 Pellegrino del Terra café 113–114
Pellegrino del Terra office 114–115,
 116, 125
 Santa Chiara all'Albergheria church
 113
Palermo Agreement: international
 definition of human trafficking 3
Papa Giovanni organisation 104–105,
 107, 109
Parliamentary Joint Committee for
 human rights 242
Pec, Kosovo 23
Pellegrino del Terra (Pilgrims of the
 Earth) 112–115, 116, 125
Pentecostal churches 121
Penzance, Orthodox priest in 90
Peycke, Alice 161–162
pimp, relationship with 36
Pisha, Xhevahir 180–181
Pjeter (Albanian in Burrell) 88, 89,
 90–91
Pjeter (Albanian on ferry) 97, 98
Pjevic, Meliha 235
Plakici, Luan 154–155, 156–157, 158,
 159, 160, 164, 165–167, 172, 177
 accomplice 155, 158, 159, 160, 162
 appearance 154
 charged 158
 lifestyle 155
 trial and appeal 160–161, 162–163,
 164–165, 166, 168, 179
Podgorica, Montenegro 237–238
police 'performance indicator', human
 trafficking as 179, 242
'Pope' (Serbian Orthodox priest)
 59–60
Popik, Olena 62–63, 64, 65–68, 215,
 216
 photograph 67–68
Poppy Project 129–131, 132, 141,
 159–160, 161–162, 172, 174, 180,
 181, 182, 185, 213, 238–239
 'Sex in the City' report 131
 UKIS evaluation 174–175
Praed Street Project 131–133, 141

Prague 158
priests, traditional (*ohen*) 121–122
Prijedor, Bosnia 55, 56, 57, 58
  Crazy Horse 1 and 2 nightclubs 55
  mayor 56
  Sherwood Castle nightclub 49, 55,
    56, 57, 58
Pristina, Kosovo 2, 5–9, 24, 204, 205,
    206–212, 214–218, 223–224
  airport 206
  the Depot bar 223
  Grand Hotel 206, 207
  Kukri (expat pub – later Phoenix)
    5–6, 207
  Mother Theresa Boulevard 5
  Sunny Hill suburb 216–217
  United Nations Mission in Kosovo
    see UNMIK
Prizren, Kosovo 20–24, 47, 217–222,
    223
  De Rada Street bus station 219, 221
  Shpati bar 24
  Sylvia bar 21–23, 24, 25
  Te Nazja bar 219–222
Proceeds of Crime Act (2002) 177–178
Punternet 139, 142

Radovanovic, Mara (Lara organisation
    leader) 50–51, 52–56, 58–61, 62,
    69, 92, 235
  appearance 52, 60
  and Milakovic 54-56
  at Motel Neno 60–61
Rague, Danijel 215
Raisa (sex worker) 108
Raluca (Romanian girl) 157–159, 160,
    172
Rama, Edi 72
rape, mass 231
Ratel, Jonathan 57
recruiters 13, 18, 236
Rees, Madeleine 4, 46–51, 54, 212
  appearance 47
  and Olena Popik 62–63

Reflex 180, 181, 182, 183, 184, 240,
    242
Refugee Convention (1951) 239
Refugee Women's Resource Project
    238–239
Regan, Linda 128
Renton, Daniel 74
Richmond, Surrey 170
Roberts, Julia 169–171
Rogaly, Ben 190–193
Rogova, Igballe (Igo) 8–9, 216–217,
    220
Roma (bear owner) 77
Romania 12–13, 18–19, 33, 75,
    157–158, 160
Romanian women 53
Romany migrants 90
Rome 111, 120–121, 124
  refugee organisation 111
Rosa (Sicilian sex worker) 117–118
Rosenberg, Ruth 75–76, 77, 82,
    198–199
Royal Marine commandos 213
Rule of Law meetings 50
Rwanda 231
Ryanair 111

Sainsburys 90
Salisbury 45
Sarajevo 47–51, 55, 56–57, 60, 62, 63,
    66, 69, 231
  Office of the High Commissioner for
    Human Rights in Bosnia and
    Herzegovina 47–51
saunas, British, women offered for
    work in 137
Save the Children report on child
    trafficking in Albania 74
Schengen visa 12, 75, 79
Scotland, human trafficking into
    138
security facility, interim (ISF) 212
Serbia 19, 33, 42, 53
Serbian driver 18, 19, 21

Serbs 216
Serious Organised Crime Agency
   (SOCA) 182, 184, 242
'Sex in the City' report 131
Sexual Offences Act (2003) 167, 238
SFOR (Stabilisation Force) 43, 56, 57,
   58, 234
Sheffield 180, 181, 184
shelters, need for 237, 238
Shultz, Major Christian 223
Sicilian Mafia 116
Sicily 111–121, 122, 124–125
Sierra Leone 231
Silvana (Albanian IOM employee) 75,
   76
Simeon (recruiter) 17, 18
Skopje 199
slave trade, seventh-century Muslim
   232
Slave Trade Act (1807) 232
smuggling and human trafficking,
   difference between 190
'snakeheads' (Ren She) 186, 187, 190,
   194, 195–197, 198, 199, 200, 201,
   202, 203
Sofia 12–13
South-East Asian women, trafficking
   in 183
South-East Asians smuggled into
   Britain 198
South Yorkshire police 180, 183–184
South Yorkshire refuge for trafficked
   women 239
Spain 109
Stella (Olga's school friend) 16, 17, 18,
   19, 20, 21, 25
Stockholm Syndrome 236
'Stopping traffic' report 128
Sudanese refugee 115
Sunday Telegraph 217
Sussex, University of 70, 78
Sweden 239–240
Swing, William Lacy 225
Syracusa, Bruno 115

Taylor, Diana 132
Taylor, Gina 175
Taylor, Detective Inspector Guy
   163–166, 167, 168
Tel Aviv, Moldovan Embassy 157
Thai sex workers in London 132,
   135–136, 236
Thailand, women trafficked from 198
Threadgold, Tina 136–137, 138, 141
Times, The 46
Timisoara, Romania 12–13, 19
Tirana, Albania 38, 70, 72–77, 78, 84,
   86
   International Organisation for
      Migration office 75–76, 82,
      198–199
   Rinas Airport 72, 75
   Sky Tower 73–74
   Useful Women's building 72, 84
Titterton, Detective Sergeant Steve
   184
Tomara (IOM press officer) 9–10, 11
Tonin (Albanian in Burrell) 85
Trade Union Congress 190
trafficked girls/women see also human
   trafficking
   African 145–147, 148, 150
   in Britain 128, 129–130, 133–135
   demand for, by peacekeepers 4, 44,
      45, 46–47, 49, 50, 55, 58, 204–205,
      213, 217, 227, 228, 229
   in Kosovo 6, 7–8, 9, 53–54
   Nigerian 148 see also Annette
   South-East Asian women 183
traffickers 229 see also human
   trafficking
   female 236
   Nigerian 114, 116, 119–120, 124,
      236
'Trafficking in Human Beings in
   South-Eastern Europe' report 39,
   74, 80, 237
'Trafficking of Women for Sexual
   Exploitation' report 13, 228–229

Transparency International 71
Triads 128, 135, 183, 198
Trieste 95, 96, 98–103
    Androna degli Orti 99
    ferry from Durres 95, 96-99
Turkey, human trafficking to 29
Tuzla, Bosnia 49–50, 51, 58–59, 234
    Eagle base 58, 59
Tyneside 192
    Elswick Lodge 197

Uganda 145
'UK Action Plan on Trafficking in
    Human Beings' 238
Ukraine 66
Ukrainian women 53
Ungureanu, Gheorghi 27
UNICEF (United Nations Children's
    Fund) 28, 74, 80, 228, 233, 234,
    235
    'End Child Exploitation' report 150
    'Trafficking in Human Beings in
    South-Eastern Europe' report 39,
    74, 80, 237
United Kingdom see also Britain
    Census (2002) 189
    forced labour and migration to
    190–193
    Government, immigration position
    238, 241
    Government 'safe country list' 239
    Immigration Service 174–175, 199
    migrant workers, recruitment of 79
    migrant workers in 90, 189–190,
    193–194, 241–242
    migrants forced to work in industries
    4
    nationwide anti-trafficking campaign
    240–241
    nurses entering 192
    sex industry reforms 239
United Nations 2, 43, 57, 204, 205,
    206, 216 see also UNICEF;
    UNMIK

CIVPOL (civilian police) 5–6, 8
Convention on the Privileges and
    Immunities of the UN (1946) 43,
    226
Department of Peacekeeping
    Operations (UNDPKO) 224–225,
    226, 227, 229, 230
    French liaison member 214–215,
    216
General Assembly 226
High Commission for Refugees 230,
    234
international definition of human
    trafficking (Palermo Agreement) 3
International Police Task Force
    (IPTF) 44–46, 49, 55, 234
Mine Action Coordination Centre
    225
Mission in Bosnia (UNMIBH) 43,
    44, 45, 46
Office on Drugs and Crime
    (UNDOC) 228
Organised Crime Bureau 7
peacekeepers 224, 225, 226, 229, 231
    see also trafficked girls/women:
    demand for, by peacekeepers
    immunity 43–44, 227, 230
peacekeeping operations 225, 227
personnel, Zeid report on standards
    for 225, 226–227, 229
Preventive Deployment Force (UN
    PREDEP, later UN SKOPJE) 35
Programme on HIV/AIDS 227
Protection Force (UNPROFOR) 43,
    231
Protocol Against the Smuggling of
    Migrants 190
Security Council 229
Special Committee on Peacekeeping
    Operations 227
'Special Measures for Protection
    from Sexual Exploitation and
    Abuse' 211
Team 6: 7

Transition Assistance Group
   (UNTAG) 224
Truce Supervision Organisation
   (UNTSO) 225
Victim Advocacy and Assistance
   Unit 211–212
University of North London 128
University of Sussex 70, 78
UNMIK (United Nations Mission in
   Kosovo) 5, 6, 8, 204, 206, 231
and Amnesty International report
   204–205
off-limits list 210, 214, 218, 219
Office of Registration of Foreigners
   208
officers 210
police 223
Regulation 2001/4 211
Trafficking and Prostitution
   Investigation Unit (TPIU – later
   Trafficking in Human Beings
   Section – THBS) 6, 7, 204, 207,
   208, 209
   registration of foreign women
      210–211
Trafficking in Human Beings
   Department 223–224
Uri (Macedonian bar owner) 34, 35
US State Department: Human Rights
   Practices in Albania report 81–82
'Useful Women of Albania' (NGO)
   70, 72, 73, 74–75

Valentino (ferry crew member) 98,
   99
Vera (Maggie's mother) 1
Verona, Italy 104
Vicenza, Italy 104–110, 111
   Church of St Josephina 105

Police Station 106
   prostitution in 104, 105–110
Vidovic, Zdravko 215
Vilnius, Lithuania 180
visa, Schengen 12, 75, 79
Vlore, Albania 37–38, 84–85, 86, 89
voodoo rituals 121–122
Vullnetari, Julie 69–70, 76–77, 78–80,
   81, 82, 84
   family 78

Wacker, Perry 188
Walker, Judge 180
Ward, Helen 139, 140
Welcome to Britain (TV programme)
   154
Weng Miu Fang 197
West Sussex police 148
West Sussex social services 148
West Yorkshire police 183–184
Wilson, Brian 6–8, 207
Windsor 187
Wiwoloku, Vivian 112–115, 116–117,
   118, 124
Wole (Nigerian man) 115, 116
women, breaking down of 54
women as spoils of war 231
World Bank 79
World Trade Organisation 79

Xhudo, Gus 72

Ying Zhang 138
Yvetta (Sicilian sex worker) 117, 118

Zeid Al-Hussein, Prince Zeid Ra'ad
   225, 226–227, 229
Zenica, Bosnia 66, 215
Zhang, Ying 138